The interpretation of Hegel has been a focal point of philosophical controversy ever since the beginning of this century, both among Marxists and in the major European philosophical schools. Yet despite wide differences of emphasis most interpretations of Hegel share important similarities. They link his idea of Reason to the revolutionary and rationalist tradition which led to the French Revolution, and they interpret his dialectic as implying a latently atheist and even materialist world outlook.

Lucio Colletti directly challenges this picture of Hegel. He argues that Hegel was an essentially Christian philosopher, and that his dialectic was explicitly anti-materialist both in intention and effect. In contrast to earlier views, Colletti maintains that there is no contradiction between Hegel's method and his system, once it is accepted that his thought is an exercise in Absolute Idealism stemming from a long Christian humanist tradition. He claims, on the contrary, that intellectual inconsistency is rather to be found in the works of Engels, Lenin, Lukacs, Kojève and others, who have attempted to adapt Hegel to their own philosophical priorities.

Colletti places his argument in the context of a broad re-examination of the whole relationship between Marxism and the Enlightenment, giving novel emphasis to the relationship between Marxism and Kant. He concludes by re-asserting the importance in Marxism of empirical science against the claim of 'infinite reason', while at the same time showing how Marx did transform key ideas in Hegelian thought to construct a consistently materialist dialectic.

Lucio Colletti

Verso

Marxism and Hegel

Translated from the Italian by Lawrence Garner

First published as Part II of
Il Marxismo e Hegel
by Editori Laterza, Bari, 1969

This translation first published by NLB, 1973

Verso Edition 1979
Verso Editions, 7 Carlisle Street, London W1

Printed in Great Britain by
Lowe & Brydone Printers Limited, Thetford, Norfolk

ISBN: 978-0-90260-873-2

I. Hegel and the 'Dialectic of Matter'

The central theme of Hegel's thought is his thesis of the identity of idealism and philosophy. As stated in the *Logic*: 'Every philosophy is essentially an idealism or at least has idealism for its principle, and the question then is only how far this principle is actually carried out.'[1] Just exactly what one is to understand by *idealism* is explained by Hegel with great clarity. Idealism is the point of view which denies that things and the finite world have true reality. 'The idealism of philosophy consists in nothing else than in recognizing that the finite has no veritable being.'[2] Idealism ascribes being to the infinite, the Spirit, God. The subsequent elucidation, in which Hegel extends the identity of philosophy and idealism to the identity of idealism and religion, *idealism and Christianity*, follows logically and does not come as a surprise. 'This is as true of philosophy as of religion; for religion equally does not recognize finitude as a veritable being, as something ultimate and absolute or as something underived, uncreated, eternal. Consequently the opposition of idealistic and realistic philosophy has no significance. A philosophy which ascribed veritable, ultimate, absolute being to finite existence as such, would not deserve the name of philosophy.'[3]

The intuitive world-view that lies at the basis of these propositions is the same as that of Christianity. The finite is the limited, the

1. G. W. F. Hegel, *Science of Logic*, translated by A. V. Miller (London, 1969), pp. 154–5 [hereafter referred to as *L*]. I have attempted to furnish the reader with the reference to the standard English translation of the works cited by Colletti. Where this has not been possible, a translation of the original text – unless otherwise indicated – has been made. It has been necessary to modify some of the standard translations, particularly the Wallace translation of the first volume of the *Encyclopedia*, the *Logic*. I have indicated at the end of each note whenever modifications have been made.

2. ibid., p. 154.

3. ibid., p. 155.

perishable, the ephemeral. The finite 'seems' to be, and *is not*. The finite is that which is fated to come to an end: that which is evanescent and devoid of value. 'When we say of things that *they are finite*, we understand thereby that . . . non-being constitutes their nature and being. Finite things *are*, . . . but the truth of this being is their *end*. The finite not only alters, like something in general, but it *ceases to be*; and its ceasing to be is not merely a possibility, so that it could be without ceasing to be, but the being as such of finite things is to have the germ of decease as their being-within-self: the hour of their birth is the hour of their death.'[4]

Given these premisses, the problem which presents itself to philosophy is to conceive coherently, in all its aspects, the 'principle of idealism', the idea of Christianity. All 'true' philosophies have the same principle; there remains, however, the question of seeing 'how far this principle is actually carried out'. 'In a previous Remark the principle of idealism was indicated and it was said that in any philosophy the precise question was, how far has the principle been carried through. As to the manner in which it is carried through, a further observation may be made. . . . This carrying through of the principle depends primarily on whether the finite reality still retains an independent self-subsistence alongside the being-for-self.'[5]

Thus the problem is to conceive idealism in a logically coherent fashion. But note that this task is not to be carried out simply as a logically coherent development, but rather as a development that implies at the same time the *actualization* of the principle, in other words, the translation of idealism into *reality*. If in fact the principle of philosophy is that the finite is *non-being* and only the infinite *is*, philosophy can lay claim to logical consistency in its operations only under one condition: that it puts an end to the finite and validates only the infinite, thereby annihilating the world and replacing it with 'true' reality.

Hegel's thesis, in this regard, is that no philosophy has succeeded until now in solving this problem, in realizing the idea of Christianity. The principle of idealism has hitherto been contradicted and

4. ibid., p. 129. 5. ibid., pp. 160–1.

negated everywhere in its practical execution: philosophy has always been inconsistent with itself. The responsibility for this is traced back by Hegel essentially to a question of *method*. Philosophy has adopted, Hegel states, the point of view of the 'intellect', the principle of non-contradiction or of the mutual exclusion of opposites.* Thinking that the problem of its 'actualization' could be simply reduced to one of 'logical' coherence, philosophy has embraced the 'perspective' which presumes 'that the finite is irreconcilable with the infinite and cannot be united with it, that the finite is utterly opposed to the infinite'.[6] This perspective seems, at first sight, the most natural. It allows one to 'keep the infinite pure and aloof from the finite'.[7] It seems therefore the method best suited for an affirmation of the principle of idealism in all its purity. In reality, this very *non-contradiction* which passes for the principle of absolute logical coherence is, in the case of philosophy, the source of the most deep-rooted inconsistency.

The 'intellect' separates and divides, keeps opposites apart from one another, posits on one side the finite, on the other, the infinite. It makes their separation a rigid one, as if to underline that the former is only dross and nothingness, and that 'being, absolute

* *Translator's note:* The conventional translation of the German term *Verstand* by the English 'understanding' has in most places been changed to 'intellect' in this text. This agrees better with both the Italian rendering of *Verstand* as 'intelletto', and with Colletti's general polemical position, which tends towards a revaluation of *Verstand* as against *Vernunft*, or 'Reason'. Colletti tends to reverse the traditional valuation conveyed (e.g.) in this passage from a standard commentary on Hegel: 'By the understanding (*Verstand*) Hegel means that stage of the development of mind at which it regards opposites as mutually exclusive and absolutely cut off from each other. The Aristotelian laws of identity, contradiction, and excluded middle are the canons of its procedure. Distinguished from understanding is reason (*Vernunft*) which is that stage of the development of mind which rises to the principle of the identity of opposites. For understanding each category remains an insulated self-existent being . . . static, fixed, and lifeless. To the eye of reason, however, the categories are seen to be alive with movement, to be fluid, to . . . flow into each other, as we have seen that being flows into nothing' (W. T. Stace, *The Philosophy of Hegel*, London, 1955, p. 101.) Here, reason is depicted as what is superior to 'mere understanding', the world of common sense and natural science, etc. Colletti's defence of the latter category is best conveyed by changing from the neutral philosophical term 'understanding' (itself an expression of the very tradition he attacks) to the more meaningful 'intellect'.

6. ibid., p. 130. 7. ibid., p. 137.

being' is reserved only for the infinite. However, Hegel goes on, with 'the express assertion that the finite . . . cannot be united with (the infinite), . . . it (the finite) remains absolute on its own side'. The possibility of 'passing over' into the 'other' is excluded. There is no escape from its evanescence. Since the *non-being* of the finite is understood here as a negation '*fixed in itself*', that 'stands in abrupt contrast to its affirmative', the intellect does not realize that it regards the finite as '*imperishable* and *absolute*'. Since the transience of things cannot cease to exist, it becomes 'their unalterable quality, that is, their quality which does not pass over into its other, that is, into its affirmative'. Finitude, never ceasing in its ceasing, '*is thus eternal*'.[8]

The consequence is just the opposite of the philosophical project. The finite, which ought to have disappeared, lives on. The infinite, which ought to have been the absolute or the totality, finds itself, on the contrary, to be just '*one of the two*'. 'As *only* one of the two it is itself finite, it is not the whole but only *one* side; it has its limit in what stands over against it; it is thus the *finite infinite*. There are present only *two finites*.'[9]

The method of the 'intellect', which, by safeguarding the principle of non-contradiction, seemed thereby to assure itself a perfect coherence, proves in fact to be incapable of expressing 'the fundamental concept of philosophy, the true infinite', the Christian *Logos*. The intellect reifies everything that it touches. It transforms that which is not a thing into the *finite*. It is not the principle of philosophy or idealism, but of *Unphilosophie*. It is the point of view of materialism.

Having started from the premiss that the finite is that which is ephemeral and devoid of value, philosophy is forced by the 'intellect' to enunciate the opposite of what it had in mind. Its logical inconsistency could not be clearer. 'On the one hand, it is admitted that the finite *is not in and for itself*, that neither independent reality nor absolute being can be ascribed to it; that it is something transitory. The next moment, all of this is quickly forgotten, and the finite is represented as independent and persisting on its own *vis-à-vis* the

8. ibid., p. 130.

9. ibid., p. 144.

infinite, completely separated from the latter and delivered from annihilation. While thought thus believes that it has elevated itself to the infinite, just the opposite happens; i.e. it attains to an infinite that is only a finite, and it retains the finite, which was to have been left behind, making it thus into an absolute.'[10]

The intellect, in short, 'is embarrassed by the difficulty of passing from the finite to the infinite'.[11] It engenders a dualistic opposition in which the infinite itself declines to the level of the finite. Moreover, since the intellect regards the passage from one pole to the other as a process in the course of which the finite is abstracted or left out of account – although allowed to subsist – the infinite manages to take shape only as 'the negative . . . of determinateness in general, as the empty beyond'. This becomes possible in so far as its opposition to the finite is understood to mean that the latter is equivalent to the *real*, and the infinite, on the other hand, to the *ideal*, 'that is, . . . a *mere* "ideal" '.[12] The finite belongs to the *here and now*, the infinite to the *beyond*, the one down below, the other up above. Both of them, Hegel states, are '*assigned* a *distinct* place – the finite as determinate being, here on *this* side, and the infinite . . . as a beyond in the dim, inaccessible distance, outside of which the finite is and remains'.[13] The consequence is that the finite, which ought to have been the ephemeral and the perishable, *remains*, i.e. becomes a solid reality which cannot be dissolved; whereas the infinite, which ought to have turned out the 'absolute being', appears merely as something abstract or mentally conceived. The finite, which was declared '*not* a true being', becomes the real or *positive*; the infinite, which ought to have been the 'absolutely necessary', i.e. the positive *par excellence*, becomes instead the *non*-finite, the *negative*, a mere ideal.

Thus there are two errors at one and the same time: the infinite as the finite, i.e. God as *object*; and, in addition, God separated from the world, confined to the 'beyond', segregated apart at an unattainable

10. G. W. F. Hegel, *The Logic*, translated from *The Encyclopaedia of the Philosophical Sciences*, by William Wallace (London, 1892), Second Revised Edition, p. 177 (translation modified). Hereafter referred to as *En.L.*

11. ibid., p. 72. 12. *L.*, p. 146, p. 150. 13. ibid., p. 140.

distance. The terms of the problem to be solved by idealism are all here. Its actualization implies the elimination of these errors. In order to comprehend the infinite in a coherent fashion, the finite must be destroyed, the world annihilated: the infinite, in fact, cannot have alongside itself another reality which limits it. On the other hand, once the finite is expunged and that which thrust the infinite into the *beyond* – making it an 'empty ideal', devoid of real existence – is suppressed, the infinite can pass over from the beyond to the *here and now*, that is, become flesh and take on earthly attire. The difference between the old and the new philosophy is the difference between commonplace theology and speculative theology, between theism and philosophy, and between pre-critical metaphysics and absolute idealism.

This is what Feuerbach saw clearly. At the beginning of the *Vorläufige Thesen zur Reform der Philosophie* he says: 'Speculative philosophy distinguishes itself from ordinary theology by the fact that that divine being which the latter . . . has sent far off into the beyond, the former transposes into the here and now, making it present, determinate, and actual.'[14] In the *Principles of the Philosophy of the Future* he adds: 'It (philosophy) made God – who in theism is only a being of fantasy, a far-removed, indeterminate, and cloudy being – into a present and determinate being.'[15]

The difference between these two theologies is the key, according to Feuerbach, to understanding the difference between the two metaphysics, that is, between Hegel's metaphysics and pre-Kantian metaphysics (above all Cartesian and Leibnizian). 'The theist conceives God as an existing and personal being external to reason and in general apart from man; he, as subject, thinks about God as an object. He conceives God as . . . a spiritual and unsensuous being'; but in so far as 'the essential characteristic of an objective being, of a being outside thoughts or the imagination, is sensation', the theist 'distinguishes God from himself in the same way in which he

14. Ludwig A. Feuerbach, *Vorläufige Thesen zur Reform der Philosophie*, in *Kleine Schriften* (Frankfurt, 1966), p. 124.

15. Ludwig A. Feuerbach, *Principles of the Philosophy of the Future*, translated by M. Vogel (Indianapolis, 1966), pp. 11–12.

distinguishes sensuous objects and beings as existing apart from him; in short, he conceives God from the point of view of sensation. The speculative theologian or philosopher, on the other hand, conceives God from the point of view of thought. He therefore does not interject the disturbing notion of a sensuous being midway between himself and God. He thus identifies, without any hindrance, the objective, conceived being with the subjective, thinking being.'[16]

This way of viewing things which characterizes theism and 'commonplace theology', and which is appreciably less noticeable in Spinoza – 'the actual founder of modern speculative philosophy', that philosophy which has in Schelling 'its redeemer', and in Hegel 'the thinker who perfected it'[17] – comes out with distinctive clarity in the case of Descartes and Leibniz. 'The beginning of Descartes's philosophy (represents) the abstraction from sensation and matter.' 'However, Descartes and Leibniz considered this abstraction merely as a subjective condition in order to know the immaterial, divine being; they conceived the immateriality of God as an objective attribute independent of abstraction and thought; they still shared the viewpoint of theism in conceiving the immaterial being only as an object, but not as a subject, as the active principle. . . . To be sure, God is also in Descartes and Leibniz the principle of philosophy, but only in general and in the imagination, not in actuality and truth. God is only the prime and general cause of matter, motion, and activity; but particular motions and activities and specific, real, and material objects are considered and known as independent of God. Leibniz and Descartes are idealists only as concerns the universal, but mere materialists as concerns the particular.'[18]

This is precisely the logical inconsistency which we have seen pointed out by Hegel. The old philosophy is half idealism, half materialism. It is idealism in its substance or *content* – the infinite, the Spirit, God. It is materialism in its *form* or method. The principle of identity and non-contradiction, which is the principle of 'common sense' and of 'everyday human understanding' prevents

16. ibid., pp. 8–9. 17. Ludwig A. Feuerbach, op. cit., p. 124.
18. Ludwig A. Feuerbach, op. cit., p. 13 (translation modified).

it from putting an end to the finite and destroying the world; whence its inability to comprehend in a coherent fashion the infinite as the 'whole' or the 'totality'; whence its powerlessness to realize itself, i.e., to have God prevail as the one and only true reality.

Once the problem has been seen, it then becomes a question of examining a solution. The solution has a precise name: the means by which Hegel makes 'philosophy' coherent and *realizes* absolute idealism, is *the dialectic of matter* – the dialectic of matter precisely as accepted, later, by the dialectical materialism of Engels, Plekhanov and Lenin.

Let us resume the problem from the beginning: the finite does not have true reality. 'The idealism of philosophy consists in nothing else but the recognition that the finite has no veritable being.'[19] Hegel belongs to the Platonic-Christian tradition. He is within this tradition, but develops it further. He does not stop at the mere negation of the finite: he combines this negation with an affirmative proposition; in other words, he completes the proposition that 'the finite is not a true being' with the proposition that 'the finite is *ideal*'. The definition of idealism given us by the *Logic* begins like this: 'The proposition that *the finite is ideal* (*ideell*) constitutes *idealism*.'[20] The definition is repeated again in the *Encyclopedia*: '. . . The truth of the finite is . . . its ideality. . . . This ideality of the finite is the chief maxim of philosophy.'[21]

In practical terms, the innovation means this: one no longer says only that the finite does not have true reality, does not have independent being; but one adds that the finite has as 'its' essence and foundation that which is 'other' than itself, i.e. the infinite, the immaterial, thought. The consequence that derives from this is crucial. If, in fact, the finite has as its *essence* the 'other' than itself, it is clear that, in order to be itself as it truly, or 'essentially', is, it can no longer be itself – i.e. the self that it is 'in appearance': *finite* – but must be the 'other'. The finite 'is not' when it *is* really finite; vice versa, it 'is', when it 'is not', it is 'itself' when it is the 'other', it comes to birth when it dies. The finite is dialectical.

19. *L.*, p. 155. 20. ibid., p. 154. 21. *En.L.*, p. 178.

Once again: 'When we say of things that *they are finite*, we understand thereby that . . . non-being constitutes their nature and being.' The meaning of this proposition is also now clear. It means that, in order to relate to themselves, finite things have to do so through the 'other'; or, as Hegel explains, 'Their relation to themselves is that they are *negatively* self-related and in this very self-relation send themselves away beyond themselves, beyond their being'[22] – send themselves away *into thought*.

The mechanism could of course be simpler. Hegel could say that he does *not* take into consideration the finite, that he puts it aside, that he transcends it. In actual fact he does just this, but by designating the procedure in another way. Instead of stating overtly that he does *not* take into consideration the finite, he states that he does so in relation to that which the finite *is not*, or, better put, states that the finite has as its 'essence' its *opposite*. The advantage that derives therefrom is evident: the act by which *he* abstracts from or discounts the finite, can now be represented by Hegel as an *objective* movement carried out by the finite itself in order to go beyond itself and thus *pass over* into its essence. 'It is the very nature of the finite to transcend itself, to negate its negation (i.e. its actual finitude or "illusory being") and to become infinite. Thus the infinite does not stand as something finished and complete above or superior to the finite, as if the finite had an enduring being *apart from or subordinate to* the infinite. Neither do *we* only, as subjective reason, pass beyond the finite into the infinite; as when we say that the infinite is the Notion of reason and that through reason we rise superior to temporal things, though we let this happen without prejudice to the finite which is in no way affected by this exaltation, an exaltation which remains external to it. But the finite itself, in being raised into the infinite, is in no sense acted on by an alien force; on the contrary, it is its nature to be related to itself as limitation, . . . and to transcend the same, or rather, to have negated the limitation and to be beyond it.'[23] If therefore the finite shows itself to be 'dialectical', such that it

22. *L.*, p. 129.

23. ibid., p. 138 (Colletti's parentheses). For the sake of uniformity, Miller's term, the *Notion*, has been used throughout whenever the reference is to Hegel's *Begriff* – although

'collapses (from) within', such that it is 'inwardly self-contradictory' and therefore 'sublates itself, ceases to be',[24] all of that does not occur through the work of an extraneous power (such as a subjective abstraction of ours), but because the finite has as its essence and foundation the 'other', and its being 'in itself' is therefore, without the need for any mediation, a *passing over* into that other. The finite, in short, is simply that which must become infinite by itself as a consequence of its very nature. 'The infinite is its *affirmative* determination, that which it truly is in itself. Thus the finite has vanished in the infinite and what *is*, is only the *infinite*.'[25]

The 'true' finite, then, is not the finite which is *outside* the infinite, but the finite within the latter, the finite as it is in the Idea. 'Real' are not those things external to thought, but those things penetrated by thought ('pensate'): i.e. those things which *are no longer things* but simple 'logical objects' or ideal moments. The negation, the 'annihilation' of matter is precisely in this passage from 'outside' to 'within'. Just as it is admitted that the finite 'once identified with the infinite, certainly cannot remain what it was out of such unity, and will at least suffer some change in its determinations',[26] so it is 'also commonly admitted that when thinking appropriates a given object, this thereby suffers an alteration and is changed from something sensuous to something thought'; but the important thing is to understand that 'not only is the essential nature of the object not affected by this alteration but that it is only in its Notion that it is in its *truth*, whereas in the immediacy in which it is given it is only *appearance* and a contingency'.[27] And Hegel continues thus: 'The *comprehension* of an object consists in nothing else than that the ego makes it *its own*, pervades it and brings it into *its own form*, that is, into the *universality*. . . . As intuited or even in ordinary conception, the object is still something *external* and *alien*. When it is comprehended, the being-in-and-for-self which it possesses in intuition and

---

Walter Kaufmann's rendering of it as *Concept* would appear more felicitous (see his translation of the Preface to the *Phenomenology* [New York, 1966] and his comment on p. 7 and p. 9). (Trans.)

24. ibid., p. 136.

25. ibid., p. 138.

26. *En.L.*, p. 178 (translation modified).

27. *L.*, p. 590.

pictorial thought is transformed into a *positedness*; the *I* in *thinking* it, pervades it. But it is *only* as it is in thought that the object is truly *in and for itself*; in intuition or ordinary conception it is only an Appearance.'[28]

The proposition, in short, is that 'this material as it appears *apart from* and *prior* to the Notion has no *truth*; this it has solely in its ideality or its identity with the Notion'. Thus, just as in the old metaphysics and, if anything, to a greater degree, the finite is excluded and negated here also; but with the difference that – since it has been established that 'only in its Notion does something possess actuality and to the extent that it is distinct from its Notion it ceases to be actual and is a non-entity'[29] – Hegel can now give to the *exclusion* of matter which he carries out the form of an *inclusion* or of a positive statement. Matter is not negated: it is affirmed by virtue of that which it is not. Hegel, then, does not exclude it, but includes it. But, since 'in spirit . . . the content is not present as a so-called *real existence*': rather, 'in the simplicity of the ego such external being is present only as sublated, it is *for me*, it is *ideally* in me';[30] it is also clear that this affirmation is in effect a negation; that is, by declaring matter 'essential' only as it is in thought, it is *ipso facto* excluded that the former has any reality as it is outside and antecedent to the Notion. The element of continuity in relation to the Platonic-Christian tradition is in this *negative* conception of the sensible world. On the other hand, the element of further development – and we will see this better below – is represented by the transcending of Christian Eleaticism, i.e. the fact that the infinite or the Spirit is no longer conceived as a 'being' and, therefore, as a one-sided *substance* that has the negative outside itself, but is conceived as *reason*, i.e. as the logical unity or coexistence of opposites ('sameness' and 'otherness', infinite and finite *in* the infinite), and, thus, as a tautoheterology or dialectic.

The finite has as its essence and foundation what is 'other' than itself. The finite, then, is itself and the negative (the opposite) of itself at one and the same time, it is internally self-contradictory, it sublates itself and ceases to be; which means that – in order to be

28. ibid., p. 585. 29. ibid., p. 591 30. ibid., p. 50.

'truly' itself – the finite must not be itself, but the other, that it has to negate itself as the finite external to the infinite and *pass over* into its opposite, i.e. become the 'ideal finite', a moment within the Idea. On the other hand, once the finite's 'illusory' independence has been negated, once it has been recognized that the finite does not have being in and of itself, that it is only 'illusory being (*Schein*)', and that 'its' essence lies beyond itself, the finite becomes exactly the illusory being or *appearance* of that essence, the *beyond* of that beyond; it becomes, in other words, the positive, through which it becomes flesh and takes on earthly attire.

The real becomes ideal, and the ideal real. The concrete makes itself abstract, and the abstract concrete. And just as 'individual, sensuous things (are) *ideal* in principle, or in their Notion, (and) still more (so) in spirit, that is, as sublated',[31] i.e. not as real determinations but as determinations of the Idea; so this self-negation of the world, this self-idealization on its part counts, vice versa, as a self-realization of the Idea or the infinite, about which Hegel states explicitly that 'it is . . . *determinate* being', that 'it *is* and *is there*, present before us', and that it 'is *reality* in a higher sense than the former reality which was *simply* determinate'.[32]

In so far as it is dialectical, the finite negates itself, sublates itself, and disappears; i.e. if one wants to consider the finite, one must not consider the finite, but rather the infinite; in order to grasp being, one must grasp thought, the Idea; there are no things, there is only *reason*; there is no *exclusive* determinacy, a 'this right here', that excludes its opposite, but a rational inclusion, a 'this together with that' – i.e. the unity of 'sameness' and 'otherness', of 'being' and 'non-being', of finite and infinite, *in* the infinite. On the other hand, just as being is *thought* without need of any mediation, so *thought* in its turn *is*, without any mediation; just as things are *reason*, so reason is *things*; just as the finite is an illusory being that has its essence beyond itself, so that essence, which is the absolute, has in the positive or finite its manifestation. To cite Hegel: 'The illusory being is not *nothing*, but is a reflection, a *relation* to the absolute; or, it *is* illusory being in so far as *in it the absolute is reflected*. This positive

31. ibid., p. 155. 32. ibid., pp. 148–9.

exposition thus arrests the finite before it vanishes and contemplates it as an expression and image of the absolute. But the transparency of the finite, which only lets the absolute be glimpsed through it, ends by completely vanishing; for there is nothing in the finite which could preserve for it a distinction against the absolute; it is a medium which is absorbed by that which is reflected through it.' And Hegel concludes thus: 'This positive exposition of the absolute is therefore itself only an illusory activity, a reflective movement (*ein Scheinen*); for what is truly positive in the exposition and the expounded content, is the absolute itself.'[33]

The world has disappeared. That which *seemed* finite, in reality is infinite. An independent material world no longer exists. On the other hand, in so far as the finite lingers on in its process of disappearing, it is restored as 'other' than itself. It is not the finite, but the positive manifestation of the Absolute. It is not, does not *signify*, 'this' determinate object – bread and wine, for example – but signifies the Spirit. '*Hier werden Wein und Brot mystische Objekte* (Here ... bread and wine ... become mystical objects ...).'[34] 'The spirit of Jesus, in which his disciples are one, has become a present object, a reality, for external feeling.'[35] But this reality is only '*die objektiv gemachte Liebe*, *dies zur Sache gewordene Subjektive* (the love made objective, this subjective element become a *thing*)'. 'In the love-feast . . . the corporeal vanishes and only the feeling of life is present.'[36]

In a certain sense, as Marx says, everything 'is left, just as it is; but now it has received the meaning of a determination of the Idea'.[37] A world was there before, a world is there afterwards. . . . Only now the 'wafer' is no longer water and flour. The 'principle' of idealism has been actualized. In place of the world now annihilated, one has substituted the 'true' reality. It is not, however, the Revolution that has taken place, but only the Transubstantiation. 'Empirical reality is therefore taken up just as it is. It is also declared

33. ibid., p. 532.

34. G. W. F. Hegel, *Early Theological Writings*, translated by T. M. Knox (Chicago, 1948), p. 250.

35. ibid., pp. 250–1.

36. ibid., p. 251 (translation modified).

37. Karl Marx, *Werke* (Berlin, 1964), Vol. 1, p. 206.

to be rational, although not on account of its own intrinsic rationality, but because the empirical fact has in its empirical existence another significance other than itself. The fact which is one's point of departure is not apprehended as such, but only as mystical effect.'[38]

The dialectic of matter is all here. The finite is infinite, the Real is *Rational*. In other words, the determinate or real object, the exclusive 'this right here', no longer exists; what exists is *Reason*, the Idea, the logical *inclusion* of opposites, the 'this together with that'. On the other hand, once being is reduced to thought, thought, in its turn, *is*; i.e., the logical unity of opposites comes to exist and becomes incarnate in a real object. Everything is itself and its opposite, 'it is' and 'it is not'. This contradiction puts it in motion, in other words, causes it to die as thing so that it may be reborn as thought or infinity. As Hegel says: 'Everything finite has this characteristic: that it sublates itself.'[39] On the other hand, 'if', as Marx says, 'one finds in logical categories the substance of all things, one imagines one has found in the logical formula of movement the *absolute method*, which not only explains all things, but also implies the movement of things'. In other words, the real object is resolved into its *logical* contradiction – this is the first movement; in the second movement the logical contradiction becomes, in its turn, *objective and real*. The philosopher is by now a perfect Christian. What distinguishes one from the other, as Marx says, is only this: that 'the Christian, in spite of logic, has only one incarnation of the *Logos*', whereas 'the philosopher has never finished with incarnations'.[40]

If we open Book 2 of Hegel's *Science of Logic*, we will find the 'dialectic of matter' stated in plain terms. Concluding his critique of the principle of identity and non-contradiction, Hegel emphasizes that, contrary to this principle, one must affirm that '*everything is inherently contradictory*, and in the sense that this law in contrast to the others expresses rather the truth and the essential nature of things'. It is 'one of the fundamental prejudices of logic as hither-

38. ibid., pp. 207–8. 39. *En.L.*, p. 147 (translation modified).
40. Karl Marx, *The Poverty of Philosophy* (New York, 1963), pp. 106–7.

to understood and of ordinary thinking, that contradiction is not so characteristically essential and immanent a determination as identity'. Nevertheless, 'if it were a question of grading the two determinations and they had to be kept separate, then contradiction would have to be taken as the profounder determination and more characteristic of essence. For as against contradiction, identity is merely the determination of the simple immediate, of dead being; but contradiction is the root of all movement and vitality; it is only in so far as something has a contradiction within it that it moves, has an urge and activity'.

On the other hand, just as every thing is contradictory, so *logical* contradiction, in its turn, exists and is real. Hegel continues: '. . . Contradiction is usually kept aloof from things, from the sphere of being and of truth generally; it is asserted that *there is nothing that is contradictory*', as if contradictions were just 'a contingency, a kind of abnormality and a passing paroxysm of sickness'. But, 'now as regards the assertion that *there is* no contradiction, that it does not exist, this statement need not cause us any concern; an absolute determination of essence must be present in every experience, in everything actual, as in every notion. . . . Further, (the contradiction) is not to be taken merely as an abnormality which only occurs here and there, but is rather the negative as determined in the sphere of essence, the principle of all self-movement, which consists solely in an exhibition of it. External, sensuous motion itself is contradiction's immediate existence. Something moves, not because at one moment it is here and at another there, but because in this "here", it at once is and is not. The ancient dialecticians must be granted the contradictions that they pointed out in motion; but it does not follow that therefore there is no motion, but on the contrary, that motion is *existent* contradiction itself.'

And Hegel concludes: 'Similarly, internal self-movement proper, *instinctive urge* in general, . . . is nothing else but the fact that something is, in one and the same respect, *self-contained and* deficient, *the negative of itself*. Abstract self-identity is not as yet a livingness, but the positive, being in its own self a negativity, goes outside itself and undergoes alteration. Something is therefore alive only in so far as it contains contradiction within it, and moreover is this power to hold and endure the contradiction within it.'[41]

One finds all of this in the *Science of Logic*. However one may choose to evaluate the two pages cited above, it is a fact that the birthplace of *dialectical materialism* is to be found here. Even if one chooses to leave open the question of what a 'dialectic of matter' could possibly mean, it remains an incontrovertible fact that the first 'dialectician of matter' was Hegel; the first and – let us add – also the only one, since after him there has been mere mechanical transcription.

Identity is only the determination of the mere immediate, of *dead being*; whereas contradiction is the root of movement and vitality. This is Hegel and, at the same time, it is also *Anti-Dühring*. 'So long as we consider things as static and lifeless, each one by itself, alongside of and after each other,' Engels tell us, 'it is true that we do not run up against any contradictions in them. . . . But the position is quite different as soon as we consider things in their motion, their change, their life, their reciprocal influence on one another. Then we immediately become involved in contradictions. Motion itself is a contradiction: even simple mechanical change of place can only come about through a body at one and the same moment of time being both in one place and in another place, being in one and the same place and also not in it. And the continuous assertion and simultaneous solution of this contradiction is precisely what motion is.'[42]

For the *Science of Logic*, something is alive only in so far as it contains within itself contradictions, or only in so far as it is itself and the negative of itself at one and the same time. In *Anti-Dühring*, similarly, 'life consists just precisely in this – that a living thing is at each moment itself and yet something else. Life is therefore also a contradiction which is present in things and processes themselves, and which constantly asserts and solves itself; and as soon as the contradiction ceases, life too comes to an end, and death steps in.'[43]

41. *L.*, pp. 439–40.

42. Frederick Engels, *Herr Eugen Dühring's Revolution in Science* (*Anti-Dühring*), translated by Emile Burns (London, 1939), p. 132.

43. ibid., p. 133.

Two conceptions that ought to be, it seems, totally different from one another, two authors that we would expect to find the very antithesis of one another – Hegel, the idealist, and Engels, the materialist – define in the same way both reality and that which seems to them abstract or devoid of reality.

I hope the reader will permit me the citation of another text: 'Everything that surrounds us may be viewed as an instance of Dialectic. We are aware that everything finite, instead of being stable and ultimate, is rather changeable and transient; and this is exactly what we mean by that Dialectic of the finite, by which the finite, as that which in itself is other than itself, is forced beyond its own immediate or natural being to turn suddenly into its opposite. . . . All things, we say – that is, the finite world as such – are doomed (*zu Gericht gehen*); and in saying so, we have a vision of Dialectic as the universal and irresistible power before which nothing can stay however secure and stable it may deem itself. Power, as one of God's determinations, does not, it is true, exhaust the depth of the divine nature or the Notion of God; but it certainly represents an essential moment in all religious consciousness. . . . We find traces of its (the Dialectic's) presence in each of the particular provinces and phases of the natural and the spiritual world. Take as an illustration the motion of the heavenly bodies. At this moment the planet stands in this spot, but implicitly it is the possibility of being in another spot; and that possibility of being otherwise the planet brings into existence by moving. Similarly the "physical" elements prove to be Dialectical. The process of meteorological action is the exhibition of their Dialectic. It is the same dynamic that lies at the root of every other natural process, and, as it were, forces nature beyond itself.'[44]

This is subheading 81 of the *Encyclopedia*, or rather, its *Zusatz* (additional remark) ¶1. In fact, when Plekhanov, in his *Essays in the History of Materialism*, arrives finally at the place where he has to indicate what the 'dialectic' is for Marx, he cannot find anything better to do than, first, to quote and transcribe extensively from this paragraph (with the exception, of course, of the reference to God and

44. *En.L.*, p. 150 (translation modified).

religion), and, then, to summarize its most important conclusion as follows: 'The essence of everything finite lies in the fact that it cancels itself and passes into its opposite.'[45] In other words, every thing is, once again, self-contradictory, every thing is itself and the negative of itself, in one and the same respect.

We will conclude the presentation of texts by returning to the page of the *Logic* cited above: '. . . Identity is merely the determination of the simple immediate, of dead being; but contradiction is the root of all movement and vitality; it is only in so far as something has a contradiction within it that it moves, has an urge and activity.' When Lenin arrived at this page during the course of his reading of the *Logic*, he feverishly noted down, as if overcome by irresistible sympathy for the argument: 'movement and "*self*-movement" . . . , "change", "movement and vitality", "the principle of all self-movement", "impulse (*Trieb*)" to "movement" and "activity" – the opposite to "*dead Being*" – who would believe that this is the core of "Hegelianism", of abstract and abstruse . . . Hegelianism?? This core had to be discovered, understood, *hinüberretten* (rescued), laid bare, refined, which is precisely what Marx and Engels did.'[46]

We shall leave Marx aside. It is a fact that Lenin, as well as Engels, sees in this page of the *Logic* the 'kernel' worth saving from Hegel's philosophy, the breaking through of a genuine realism in contradiction to the system's 'shell' and to the 'mystique of the Idea'. The firm belief that dominates him at this point is what he elevated into a criterion for all of his readings of Hegel: 'I am in general trying to read Hegel materialistically: Hegel is materialism which has been stood on its head (according to Engels) – that is to say, I cast aside for the most part God, the Absolute, the Pure Idea, etc.'[47]

The page from Hegel that we are presently considering is at the beginning of Remark 3 to Chapter 2,C of Book 2, in the *Science of*

45. George V. Plekhanov, *Essays in the History of Materialism*, translated by Ralph Fox (London, 1934), p. 174.

46. V. I. Lenin, *Collected Works*, translated by Clemens Dutt (Moscow, 1961), Vol. 38 (*Philosophical Notebooks*), p. 141.

47. ibid., p. 104.

Logic. Before taking leave of this passage, I should like to reproduce the remarks with which Hegel concludes this *Zusatz* and which Lenin, in accordance with his 'criterion', neglected to transcribe and comment upon: 'Finite things, therefore, in their indifferent multiplicity are simply this, to be contradictory and *disrupted within themselves and to return into their ground*. As will be demonstrated later, the true inference from a finite and contingent being to an absolutely necessary being does not consist in inferring the latter from the former as from a being that *is and remains the ground*; on the contrary, the inference is from a being that, as is also directly implied in *contingency*, is only in a state of collapse and is *inherently self-contradictory*; or rather, the true inference consists in showing that contingent being in its own self withdraws into its ground in which it is sublated, and further, that by this withdrawal it posits the ground only in such a manner that it rather makes itself into a positedness. In ordinary inference, the *being* of the finite appears as ground of the absolute; because the finite is, therefore the absolute is. But the truth is that the absolute is, because the finite is the inherently self-contradictory opposition, because it is *not*. In the former meaning, the inference runs thus: the being of the finite is the being of the absolute; but in the latter, thus: the non-being of the finite is the being of the absolute.'[48]

The 'reading' given by Lenin of these pages rests, as one can see, on a basic misinterpretation. He 'tried' to read Hegel 'materialistically' precisely at the place where the latter was . . . negating matter. Haunted by the famous propositions of *Anti-Dühring* and led astray by the very method that he had laid down for himself – which meant a lapse of attention wherever Hegel talks about God – Lenin did not realize that Remark 3 to Chapter 2, which opens with the statement that 'everything is inherently contradictory' and proceeds in the way shown above, bears upon one precise topic: the problem of proving the existence of God.

The question which Hegel is discussing here is the same one which we take as our starting-point: the logical inconsistency introduced into philosophy by the principle of non-contradiction; the

48. *L.*, p. 443.

impossibility of realizing the 'principle' of idealism while employing the method of the 'intellect' or, as stated in this case, 'ordinary inference'. The understanding or intellect, which separates the finite from the infinite, does not succeed, as Hegel says, in putting an end to the finite. The consequence is the contradiction into which the so-called cosmological proofs for the existence of God fall. The latter, in fact, naturally take as 'their point of departure a *Weltanschauung* which views the world as an aggregate of contingent facts', and therefore as a mass of worthless things; except that they take this point of departure as a 'solid foundation' that has to 'remain and be left in the purely empirical form' that it had before. 'The relation between the beginning and the conclusion to which it leads has a purely affirmative aspect, as if we were only reasoning from one thing which *is* and continues to *be*, to another thing which also is;'[49] with the consequence that the world, which is what is created, becomes, in their syllogism, the 'major premiss', whereas God, who is the creator and therefore foremost, becomes instead the minor premiss. The effect becomes the cause, and the cause effect. Thus, as Hegel states, Jacobi was able to make the 'justified criticism that thereby one sought to establish conditions (i.e. the world) for the unconditional (*das Unbedingte*); that the infinite (God) was in this way represented as the dependant and derivative'.[50]

In other words, the 'understanding' shores up the finite. Keeping it from *passing over* into its opposite – if the finite, as Hegel says, were 'touched . . . by the infinite, it would be annihilated'[51] – the understanding turns the finite into a 'fixed being' that is and remains solidly grounded. The *dialectic of matter*, however – i.e., the dialectical conception of the finite, the conception of the finite as 'ideal', and therefore *idealism* (in so far as it leads the finite to destroy itself and thus eradicates any materialistic grounding) – this dialectic of matter realizes for the first time the 'principle' of philosophy, i.e. God, enabling Him to prevail in a coherent fashion as the unconditional and the absolute. In 'ordinary inference' and reasoning, the being of the finite is made 'absolute'; i.e., the finite is regarded as a

49. *En.L.*, p. 104 (translation modified). 50. ibid., p. 105 (translation modified).
51. ibid., p. 177.

reality that subsists independently or for itself. With the mode of reasoning followed by philosophy or idealism, however, the dialectical conception of matter enables one to state that, precisely 'because the finite is the inherently self-contradictory opposition, because it is *not*, . . . the absolute is'. The first case, in which the finite 'remains' and is a 'fixed being', is the kingdom of death: 'fixed being', says Hegel, is '*dead being*'; it is matter that has not been transvalued into and as Spirit. The second case, the 'passage' or 'movement' by which the finite negates 'itself' passing over into the 'other', is termed *living being* (*vitalità*), precisely in the same sense that for the Christian death is the beginning of the true life, which commences when one passes from the here and now over to the beyond.

The meaning and function of the 'dialectic of matter' in Hegel's thought is that (in his own words): 'It certainly constitutes an essential moment of all religious consciousness.' However, the meaning that the dialectic of matter has in Engels and Lenin is, as is well known, quite different: it represents for them the most advanced and developed form of *materialism*. One might presume at this point that, under the common name, there must lie *two* different conceptions. In reality, this hypothesis must be dismissed. The lengthy comparison of texts which we have indulged in, and the others that we will present below, prove, it seems to us, two things: (a) that all the basic propositions of the 'dialectic of matter' were originally formulated by Hegel; (b) that dialectical materialism has confined itself to transcribing those propositions from his texts. Since the authors of dialectical materialism, in the process of recopying them, have made clear that they understood these statements to imply a materialist stance *already in Hegel's text*, the conclusion must be drawn (I believe) that they simply committed an error of interpretation. An error which by now lies at the basis of almost a century of theoretical Marxism.

II. Hegel and Spinoza

For Hegel, the problem of the *realization* of idealism and, therefore, of overcoming the logical inconsistency that has marked philosophy until now, coincides in essence with the development and the reformulation of Spinoza's thought. Spinoza is, for him the very essence of philosophy. '. . . The fact is that Spinoza is made a testing-pointing in modern philosophy, so that it may really be said: You are either a Spinozist or not a philosopher at all';[1] because 'to be a follower of Spinoza is the essential commencement of all Philosophy. . . . When man begins to philosophize, the soul must commence by bathing in this ether of the One Substance, in which all that man has held as true has disappeared; this negation of all that is particular, to which every philosopher must have come, is the liberation of the mind and its absolute foundation.' Hence, 'what constitutes the grandeur of Spinoza's manner of thought is that he is able to renounce all that is determinate and particular, and restrict himself to the One, giving heed to this alone'.[2]

But there is more. 'The substance of this system is *one* substance', Hegel writes. 'There is no determinateness that is not contained and dissolved in this absolute; and it is sufficiently important that in this necessary notion, everything which to natural picture thinking or to the understanding with its fixed distinctions, appears and is vaguely present as something self-subsistent, is completely reduced to a mere *positedness*.'[3] 'Spinoza,' Hegel adds, 'makes the sublime demand of thought that it consider everything under the form of eternity, *sub specie aeterni*, that is, as it is in the absolute',[4] i.e., not as it is in empirical or *de facto* reality, but as it is *in* the Spirit or in the Idea.

1. G. W. F. Hegel, *Lectures on the History of Philosophy*, translated by E. S. Haldane and Frances H. Simson (New York, 1955), vol. III, p. 283. Hereafter this work shall be referred to as *H.P.* 2. ibid., pp. 257–8. 3. *L.*, p. 536. 4. ibid., p. 538.

But although Spinoza saw that *omnis determinatio est negatio*, and, therefore, that the finite, the determinate does not have an autonomous existence, the fundamentally 'dualistic' (i.e., that makes distinctions and separations) nature of the *intellect* has caused it to posit the finite *outside* the absolute – without seeing that while it was restoring to the finite that substantiality which had been denied it, the absolute, in its turn, becomes circumscribed and limited. Thus, although Spinoza understood that the real is a negative, something non-existent and which therefore must return to the ground of its being, he always represented the movement from the world to God, from nothingness to the absolute, from modes and attributes to Substance, as merely a 'drop' (*caduta*) into unity – i.e. as merely a subjective movement or movement of 'external reflection' that traces back and submerges everything in absolute identity, rather than as a movement of that identity itself. The point of arrival for this drop, that into which the real or the finite is to be dissolved, is evident: it is Substance. But just exactly where this movement begins and where the drop comes from are not known; for, just as the absolute is conceived as merely a motionless identity or as something that stands beyond the finite, so the latter nonetheless always remains as an external premiss from which the movement takes its beginning and by which, therefore, the absolute itself remains limited. The result is that the circle is broken: the way in which *we* come to *know* the absolute remains external to that which the absolute *is*, with the consequence that thought and being, thought and extension remain separated like two 'attributes adopted *empirically*', and that, 'profound and correct as they are', the Notions remain definitions, i.e. *Verstandesbegriffe* (Notions of the intellect) and not *Vernunftbegriffe* (Notions of Reason).[5]

'The attribute,' Spinoza says, 'is that which the understanding thinks of God.' But 'here the question is: How does it come that besides the Deity there now appears the intellect, which applies to absolute substance the two forms of thought and extension? and whence come these two forms themselves?' These, Hegel says, are applied to Substance from the outside, they do not come forth from

5. ibid., p. 537.

within it. But 'thus everything proceeds inwards, and not outwards; the determinations are not developed from substance, it does not resolve itself into these attributes'.[6] In short, the finite still remains, despite everything, outside; and the infinite, having the other opposite itself, always remains a one-sided infinite, 'de-fined', a motionless identity akin to the Eleatic model, a Substance that is unable to become self-conscious subjectivity.

Furthermore, even that which proceeds from the absolute comes forth only in an external and mechanical way. In Hegel's words: 'Consequently, the Spinozistic exposition of the absolute is *complete* in so far as it starts from the absolute, then follows with the attribute, and ends with the mode; but these three are only enumerated *one after the other*, without any inner sequence of development, and the third is not negation *as* negation, not the negatively self-related negation which would be *in its own self* the return into the first identity, so that this identity would then be veritable identity,'[7] that is, dialectical identity, the 'identity of identity and non-identity'. Rather, there is repeated more or less what happens 'in the oriental conception of *emanation*', where the emanations of the absolute 'are *distancings* (*Entfernungen*) from its undimmed clarity', and 'the successive productions are less perfect than the preceding ones from which they arise'. 'The process of emanation is taken only as a *happening*, the becoming only as a progressive loss. Thus being increasingly obscures itself, and night, the negative, is the final term of the series, which does not first return into the primal light.'[8]

Of course, Spinozism is a form of idealism, of absolute *immaterialism*. 'Spinoza maintains that there is no such thing as what is known as the world; it is merely a form of God, and in and for itself it is nothing. The world has no true reality, and all this that we know as the world has been cast into the abyss of the one identity. There is therefore no such thing as finite reality, it has no truth whatever; according to Spinoza what is, is God, and God alone.' Those, therefore, who have accused Spinoza of atheism do not know what they are talking about. Those 'who defame him in such a way as this are therefore not aiming at maintaining God, but at main-

6. *H.P.*, III, p. 264. 7. *L.*, p. 538. 8. ibid., pp. 538–9.

taining the finite and the worldly; they do not fancy their own extinction and that of the world'.[9]

Nonetheless an objection, if not of atheism, is directed at Spinoza. It is 'objected that God is conceived only as Substance, and not as Spirit'.[10] '. . . In the system of Spinoza all things are merely cast down into this abyss of annihilation. But from this abyss nothing comes out; and the particular of which Spinoza speaks is only assumed and presupposed from the ordinary conception, without being justified. Were it to be justified, Spinoza would have to deduce it from his Substance; but that does not open itself out, and therefore comes to no vitality, spirituality or activity. His philosophy has only a rigid and unyielding substance, and not yet spirit . . .'. In it, 'God is not spirit (because) He is not the Three in One. Substance remains rigid and petrified, without Böhme's sources or springs'.[11]

In this summary, the interpretation that Hegel gives of Spinoza, the philosopher with whom he has the closest ties, brings out again all the basic themes already identified in the course of our analysis: the annihilation of the world ('there is no such thing as what is known as the world'); the twofold movement by which the appearance of the Idea in the concrete, the *positive exposition of the absolute*, is counterbalanced by the dissolution of the finite in the Idea (whereas in Spinoza 'everything proceeds inwards, and not outwards'); the transformation of Substance into a Subject; and finally the problem of the principle of non-contradiction.

As the *Science of Logic* says: '. . . The Eleatic Being or Spinoza's substance is only the abstract negation of all determinateness, without ideality being posited in substance itself.'[12] And the *History of Philosophy*: 'Taken as a whole, . . . the Idea of Spinoza . . . is just what ὄν was to the Eleatics. This Idea of Spinoza's we must allow to be in the main true and well-grounded; absolute substance is the truth, but it is not the whole truth; in order to be this it must also be thought of as in itself active and living, and by that very means it must determine itself as mind.'[13]

9. *H.P.*, III, pp. 281–2. 10. ibid., p. 280. 11. ibid., p. 288.
12. *L.*, p. 161. 13. *H.P.*, III, p. 257.

The crucial point, as one can see, is always the same: the proposition that *the finite is ideal.* This amounts to carrying over the finite into the infinite, being into thought. On the one hand, this enables one to truly 'annihilate' the finite, and on the other to transform Substance into Subject. Eleatic being, which as such is only the abstract negation of every determination, the universal that *excludes* the particular (whence its one-sided and inflexible nature as an object), becomes thereby a unity of opposites, 'being' and 'non-being' together, a tautoheterology or dialectic. This unity is what Hegel properly calls self-consciousness or reason. Properly so, because what else could reason be if not an epistemological *principle*, the simultaneous presence in the mind of both the alternatives from which one has to choose in action as in thought? Hegel's limitation does not lie here. Rather, it consists in the notion that 'it is *only* as it is in thought that the object is truly *in and for itself*'; that is to say, it consists in taking reason, not as an attribute and property of the natural being that is man, but as God, *Logos*, Christian Spirit, substance itself – since reason must serve man not just as reason but *also* as reality.

Here is the really decisive point: the substantification of reason as a consequence of the Christian posture, i.e. as a consequence of the equation of reason with Spirit and therefore with God. That things as they are in thought are reduced, from the *sensate* objects that they were, to objects of thought – this is clear. No one doubts that. As Marx himself says, '. . . The concrete made up of thought, is in fact a product of thinking. . . .'[14] What is not clear however – or at least is not so until one adopts the premiss that thought is spirit and spirit, God – is why the 'object of thought' (*il pensato*) must be immediately equated with reality, and why, vice versa, all true existence must be denied to the real object as it is, in itself outside and prior to the Notion.

'The idealism of the noble Malebranche is in itself more explicit' than that of Spinoza, Hegel states. 'It contains the following funda-

14. Karl Marx, *Introduction to the Critique of Political Economy*, in *A Contribution to the Critiques of Political Economy*, translated by N. I. Stone (Chicago, 1904), p. 294 (translation modified).

mental thoughts: because God includes within himself all eternal truths, the ideas and perfections of all things, so that they are *his* and his alone, we see them only in him. . . . As then the eternal truths and Ideas (essentialities) of things are in God, are ideal, so also is their existence in God ideal, not an actual existence.'[15]

This Christian posture is the real pivotal point of all Hegel's thought. This enables him to open up Eleaticism, in other words, to break out of the framework of all 'institutionalized' conceptions of thought and to knock down the schemata of scholastic 'intellectualism' (that 'intellectualism' which, as we have seen, persists even in Spinoza). This is the source of his conception of the infinite, and of his distinction between 'reason's' infinite and that of the 'understanding' or intellect ('the main point' of philosophy, Hegel says, 'is to distinguish the genuine Notion of infinity from spurious infinity, the infinite of reason from the infinite of the intellect'[16]).

From this assumption too comes the recognition that real 'unity' is *totality*, i.e. not merely 'being', but 'being' and 'non-being' together, not merely identity, but the 'identity of identity and non-identity'. Except that, along with this transformation of Substance into Subjectivity, there is in Hegel a simultaneous, concomitant conversion of the latter into the former (the positive exposition of the absolute), precisely because reason, being for him Spirit or God must also count as the *sole* reality.

Marx states: 'Hegel's positive achievement in his speculative logic' is that 'the universal *fixed thought-forms*' have been 'depicted . . . as a whole, as moments in the process of abstraction'. Hegel, that is, has no longer given us simply fixed abstractions but 'the whole process of abstraction' or 'the self-encompassing abstraction'. 'In his *Logic* Hegel has imprisoned all these spirits together', i.e. he substituted 'the fact of abstraction revolving within itself, for these fixed abstractions'.[17] But in so far as this negativity that is reason is not established for him *on the basis* of a real object, but rather stays clear of it

15. *L.*, p. 161.

16. ibid., p. 137.

17. Karl Marx, *Economic and Philosophical Manuscripts*, in *Karl Marx: Early Writings*, translated and edited by T. B. Bottomore (London and New York, 1964), pp. 215–16 (translation modified).

by positing itself as *existing for itself*, it becomes, Marx says, '*an abstraction which is then crystallized as such* and is conceived as an independent activity, as activity itself'.[18]

It is commonly said that the Hegelian totality excludes nothing. It represents the unity of subject and object, of thought and world. It encompasses everything and leaves nothing outside itself. That the Hegelian concept of totality also includes the Eleatic identity and moreover expands it into the 'identity of identity and non-identity' by incorporating the finite into itself as *ideal* – all this is true and is precisely what we have attempted to point out up till now. But although the Hegelian 'totality' is a further *development* of the original Eleatic principle (identity as 'fixed abstraction' or identity of a 'logical essence' with itself, which has dominated the entire scholastic tradition), it remains nonetheless true that this development occurs within the framework of a well-defined *continuity* with that *negative* conception of the sensate or finite peculiar to the Platonic-Christian tradition. Which means that the Hegelian 'totality' is itself so *one-sided* and incomplete as to *exclude* and leave out the *principle of matter*, i.e. that other feature of identity which found expression, not in Parmenides, but in the Aristotelian principle of determination. The meaning of the latter is precisely that the finite is a real finite only when it it lies *outside* the infinite; that being is real being only when it is *independent* of thought; that objects acquire their distinctive determinations only through the exclusion of the negative, of its opposite, i.e. of that logical universal which encompasses *everything* that the particular object itself *is not*.

Hegel includes everything – the principle of dialectical totality excludes nothing. In actual fact, since Hegel transforms the logical *inclusion* of opposites that is reason into the very principle of *idealism* (reason is the sole reality, there is nothing outside of it), he *excludes* precisely that exclusion of opposites (the *externality* of being in relation to thought) that is the very principle of *materialism*. It is true enough, therefore, that Hegel incorporates being into thought, the finite into the infinite. But since the finite as it is

18. ibid., p. 217 (Colletti's emphasis).

'within' is very different from the finite as it is 'outside' – the object in reality (*Gegenstand*) is one thing and the logical object (*Objekt*) is another – the Hegelian totality, in order to be truly such, would have to be able to fuse the two principles together: dialectical *contradiction* and *non-contradictory* identity, the unity of opposites and their mutual exclusion.

Reason is a totality. This is what Hegel saw clearly. But since this 'totality' is also nothing but reason, it is clear that, in addition to being itself, this totality must also be 'intellect'; in addition to 'totality', it must also be only *'one of the two'*; and that, in short, thought – in addition to being the unity of thought and being *in* thought – must also be a *function* of a reality external to itself.

Now this is precisely what Hegel fails to see. With him, unity dominates and cancels out all distinctions; the 'rational' totality obliterates the 'intellect'; the principle of reason excludes that of matter. The consequence is that reason, having to serve simultaneously and in one and the same respect as thought and reality, becomes crystallized into a thing, i.e. becomes a *simple*, positive unity, incapable of opening itself up and of taking into account what is different from itself; it acquires thereby the *exclusory* character that is a property of matter.

All 'true' philosophies are a form of idealism. Materialism is *Unphilosophie*, anti-philosophy, and since discussion is possible only where there is unity of principles, the history of philosophy is only the history of idealism, the history of the progressive realization of the Idea or Christian *Logos*, the history of the *realization* of God. In his early work devoted to the *Relationship of Scepticism to Philosophy*, Hegel quotes Leibniz: 'I have found that most sects are right in a good part of what they propound, but less so with regard to what they reject.'[19] Hegel adds: 'The superficial view of philosophical disputes takes account only of the differences of the systems, whereas the ancient rule: *contra negantes principia non est disputandum* (no argument is possible where basic principles are opposed),

19. G. W. F. Hegel, *Verhältniss der Skepticismus zur Philosophie*, in *Sämtliche Werke* (Glockner), I, p. 218 (from the French).

enables one to realize that whenever philosophical systems argue with one another . . . there exists already agreement as to principles.'[20] The differences between philosophies that have existed until now are therefore traced back solely to 'the higher or lower degree of abstraction with which Reason has presented itself in the various principles and systems'. And the method by which these differences between the philosophies are to be overcome is the very same one by which Hegel enlarged on Eleaticism. It is a matter of expanding the idea that 'they propound' so that it also includes the other ideas that 'they reject'; i.e. it is a question of replacing the 'fixed abstractions' with the 'self-encompassing abstraction' and therefore of integrating idea with idea. But note this: one is integrating idea with idea, not idea with matter, for '*anders ist es freilich, wenn Philosophie mit Unphilosophie streitet* (it is another matter when philosophy argues with anti-philosophy).[21]

The shortcoming of pre-critical metaphysics, even in its most illustrious representative, Spinoza, has not therefore been that it was a metaphysics, i.e. that it removed from its objects the supersensible and the absolute; the content of that philosophy (God, the soul, etc.) was indeed 'genuinely . . . speculative'. The shortcoming is rather to be traced to the *method* or intellectual form which it made use of – i.e., to the fact that it was a 'mere view on the part of the intellect of Reason's objects (*Vernunftgegenstände*)'.[22] 'This system of metaphysics became a dogmatism,' states the *Encyclopedia*, 'because, in accordance with the nature of finite determinations, it had to assume that given two mutually contrasting statements, one had to be true and the other false'.[23]

In other words, dogmatism did not come to that philosophy through its apriorism, i.e. from the fact that it took as its starting-point a prefixed *idea*, an external 'given' (the very principle of idealism), which, while denying all reality to anything that was outside or *external* to the idea, arrogated directly to itself the status of reality. On the contrary, dogmatism came to it through the adoption of the principle of non-contradiction, the method of the

20. loc. cit. 21. loc. cit. 22. *En.L.*, p. 60.
23. ibid., p. 61 (translation modified).

'understanding', which, in so far as it makes the finite 'dead being', i.e. a 'fixed', motionless reality (motionless precisely in the sense that it is not obliterated by 'passing over' into the infinite or the Idea), makes it also a solid foundation which is and remains. This, according to Hegel, is the source of that philosophy's dogmatism; not the fact that it presupposes as 'given' *ideas* and knowledge that are purely aprioristic ('knowledge which we possess without knowing whence it came, and entrust to principles the origin of which is unknown', Kant would say[24]); not in taking its starting-point from an *innate* or apriorist mode of knowing; but rather in taking up 'facts', the finite, the 'a posteriori' as 'given', or in other words, in presupposing that an object which must be known is *given* us. This is the contradiction or logical inconsistency which, according to Hegel, has befallen that philosophy. Although it knew perfectly well that 'the world has no true reality', that 'there is no such thing as finite reality' and that 'there is no such thing as . . . the world; it is only a form of God', it was not able to develop this knowledge in a coherent way; for it remained snarled in the knots of 'ordinary human understanding' – i.e. in that point of view which is common to the materialism of 'common sense' and to science. Thus, while being *philosophic* (or idealist) in substance, those metaphysics turned out to be *scientific* (or materialist)[25] in form; claiming, like Spinoza, that absolute substance could be an *ordine geometrico demonstrata*, or following, as with Leibniz, 'the same general plan in his philosophy as the physicists adopt when they advance a hypothesis to explain existing data'.[26] The result has been, as Hegel states in relation to Spinoza, that his 'notions, profound and correct as they are, are *definitions*, which are

24. Immanuel Kant, *Critique of Pure Reason*, translated by F. Max Müller (New York, 1966), p. 5.

25. G. W. F. Hegel, *Science of Logic*, vol. I, p. 53: 'I have said what is essential in the preface to the *Phenomenology of Spirit* about this method (of science) and, in general, the subordinate form of scientific method which can be employed in mathematics; but it will also be considered in more detail in the logic itself. Spinoza, Wolff, and others have let themselves be misled in applying it also to philosophy and in making the external course followed by Notion-less quantity, the course of the Notion, a procedure which is absolutely contradictory. Hitherto philosophy had not found its method.'

26. *H.P.*, III, p. 329.

immediately assumed at the outset of the science', just as happens with 'mathematics and other subordinate sciences'.[27]

Note that this argument does not mean at all that Hegel falls into the error, so wide-spread today,[28] of thinking that pre-critical metaphysics is materialism and therefore that materialism (which, in epistemology, is then reduced to the Kantian *critical* thesis that existence is not a predicate or the appendage of a concept) is of religious origin and therefore equivalent to either Thomist 'realism' or to the Cartesian dualism of *res extensa* and *res cogitans*. Of course Hegel does not fall into this error. He has a profound knowledge of the history of philosophy and is well aware that just as the two Cartesian *res* are both 'substances' (i.e. universals), so 'Descartes's sublimest thought' is 'that God is that *whose notion includes within itself its being*'.[29] The meaning of Hegel's argument is just the opposite: pre-Kantian metaphysics is true philosophy, it is a form of idealism; materialism exists in it only in the scientific *form*, i.e. in the way in which the principle is elucidated and developed. In a word, it exists only *formally*, and precisely because the error is only one of form, so the correction must also be only one of form, on this crucial point Hegel could not be clearer. It was Jacobi, rather than Kant, who pointed out the error of the old metaphysics! 'If Kant attacked previous metaphysics rather in respect of its matter' or of its contents (God, the soul, etc.), 'Jacobi has attacked it chiefly on the side of its method of demonstration, and signalized most clearly and most profoundly the essential point, namely, that a method of demonstration such as this is fast bound within the circle of the rigid necessity of the finite, and that *freedom*, that is the *Notion*, and with it *everything that is true*, lies beyond it and is unattainable by it. According to the Kantian result, it is the peculiar matter of metaphysics that leads it into contradictions, and the inadequacy of cognition consists in its *subjectivity*; according to Jacobi's result, the fault lies with the method and the entire nature of cognition

27. *L.*, p. 537.
28. As is well-known, this rather wide-spread error is found in Antonio Gramsci as well, cf. *Il materialismo storico e la filosofia di Benedetto Croce*, Turin, 1948, p. 138.
29. ibid., p. 705.

itself, which only apprehends a connection of *conditioned-ness* and *dependence* and therefore proves itself inadequate to what is in and for itself, to what is absolutely true. In point of fact, as the principle of philosophy is the *infinite free Notion*, and all its content rests on that alone, the method proper to Notion-less finitude is inappropriate to it.'[30]

The conclusion is unequivocal. The principle and the contents of the old metaphysics must be preserved and developed further. It becomes merely a matter of giving it another form, of changing the method, i.e. of freeing metaphysics from the impediments that have been engendered up till now by the 'intellect'. Dogmatism is not to be found in metaphysics. *Dogmatism* is to be found in *materialism*, in *science* and in common sense.

30. ibid., pp. 816–17.

III. Dialectical Materialism and Hegel

Hegel's argument, as so far reconstructed, takes us right to the core of 'dialectical materialism'. The only point of divergence lies in Engels's interpretation of Hegel's text. In it the meaning of the argument is unwittingly overturned: it is no longer the old metaphysics which is dogmatic because it remains a captive of the finite and the scientific understanding; rather, the intellect is dogmatic because it is metaphysical. In other words, Engels takes as an element intrinsically related to metaphysical thinking the very principle of non-contradiction which Hegel considered an obstacle to the full elaboration of a metaphysics *per se*. For Hegel the principle of non-contradiction was represented by science, the logic of the finite, to which he counterposed a purely metaphysical logic of the infinite (the idealist dialectic). For Engels, however, scientific non-contradiction is a form of metaphysics, and the idealist or metaphysical logic is instead the logic of the new 'science'.

Engels writes: 'the old method of investigation and thought which Hegel calls 'metaphysical', which preferred to investigate *things* as given, as fixed and stable, . . . had a good deal of historical justification in its day. It was necessary first to examine things before it was possible to examine processes. One had first to know what a particular thing was before one could observe the changes going on in connection with it. And such was the case with *natural science.* The old metaphysics which accepted things as finished objects arose from a *natural science* which investigated dead and living things as finished objects.'[1]

Obviously, this critique is basically the same as Hegel's; but with an unconscious confusion that alters its entire hue and orientation.

1. Frederick Engels, *Ludwig Feuerbach and the Outcome of Classical German Philosophy* (New York, 1941), p. 45 (Colletti's emphasis).

For Hegel, the old metaphysics derived its dogmatism from the 'intellect', i.e. from its use of the method characteristic of science and common sense (the principle of non-contradiction); which means that in the process of opposing that particular metaphysics, Hegel was not attempting to oppose metaphysics *per se*, but only the manifestations of what he regarded as dogmatism: *materialism* and *science*. For Engels, however – for whom the term, 'dogmatism', was instinctively (and, moreover, rightly) associated with 'metaphysics' – the argument takes on this distorted meaning: the cause of metaphysics is none other than *science*, and therefore in order to stamp out metaphysical dogmatism, it is necessary above all to oppose the non-contradictory thinking of science. The result of this rather naïve switch (the consequences of which, as we shall see, are very serious) is that, in the process of repeating Hegel's argument, Engels and 'dialectical materialism' *think* that they are opposing idealism and metaphysics, whereas they end up struggling against materialism and science.

'The analysis of Nature into its individual parts, the grouping of the different natural processes and natural objects in definite classes, the study of the internal anatomy of organic bodies in their manifold forms – these were the fundamental conditions of the gigantic strides in our knowledge of Nature which have been made during the last four hundred years. . . . But this method of investigation has also left us as a legacy the habit of observing natural objects and natural processes in their isolation, detached from the whole vast interconnection of things; and therefore not in their motion, but in their repose: not as essentially changing, but as fixed constants; not in their life, but in their death. And when, as was the case with Bacon and Locke, this way of looking at things was transferred from natural science to philosophy, it produced the specific narrow-mindedness of the last centuries, the metaphysical mode of thought.'[2]

Metaphysics has its origin, accordingly, in modern science – that science which, despite all of its partial achievements, has grafted onto philosophy the 'narrowness' of its own method and of its metaphysical mental habit. In comparison with this science, Engels

2. F. Engels, *Anti-Dühring*, op. cit., p. 27.

extols the grandeur of Greek philosophy where 'dialectical thought still appears in its pristine simplicity'. 'Among the Greeks – just because they were not yet advanced enough to dissect, analyse nature – nature is still viewed as a whole, in general. The universal connection of natural phenomena is not proved in regard to particulars; for the Greeks it is the result of unmediated, intuitive perception.' This is what accounts for 'the inadequacy of Greek philosophy'; but it also accounts for 'its superiority over all its subsequent metaphysical opponents' – since, 'if metaphysics' (i.e., in this case the science of nature), 'in regard to the Greeks . . . was right in particulars, in regard to metaphysics the Greeks were right as concerns the whole'.[3] Consequently, if science is to change over today from a simple 'empirical science' into a theoretical 'natural science', it 'is . . . forced to go back to the Greeks'.[4] In fact, with dialectical materialism we have 'once again returned to the point of view of the great founders of Greek philosophy, the view that the whole of nature, from the smallest element to the greatest, from grains of sand to suns, from protista to men, has its existence in eternal coming into being and passing away, in ceaseless flux, in unresting motion and change'.[5]

The entire argument is grounded in a Hegelian *philosophy of history* based on three stages, but in a very popularized version. The first stage gives us a picture of the world 'in which nothing remains what, where and as it was, but everything moves, changes, comes into being and passes out of existence. This primitive, naïve, yet intrinsically correct conception of the world was that of ancient Greek philosophy, and was first clearly formulated by Heraclitus: everything is and also is not, for everything is in *flux*, is constantly changing, constantly coming into being and passing away.'[6] This is the first phase, represented by Ionian philosophy, which grasps 'correctly' the overall picture of phenomena, but which lays more emphasis on 'the movements, transitions, connections, rather than

3. F. Engels, Old preface *to Anti-Dühring*, in *Anti-Dühring* (Moscow, 1947), p. 395 (translation modified).

4. op. cit.

5. F. Engels, *Dialectics of Nature* (New York, 1940), p. 13.

6. F. Engels, *Anti-Dühring*, op. cit., pp. 26–7.

the things that move, combine, and are connected',[7] more on the Totality than on individual details. Engels proceeds to a second phase, which is the exact antithesis of the first one, and which he identifies with the modern *science of nature* as it has developed 'from the second half of the fifteenth century'. The task to be confronted by this second phase was to rectify the shortcomings of the first; that is, to examine more closely those details which Ionian philosophy had overlooked to the exclusive benefit of the 'overall picture' and the total vision. But since 'in order to understand these details, we must detach them from their natural or historical connections, and examine each one separately, as to its nature, its special causes and effects, etc.',[8] thereby setting aside the question of the whole, the result was that in the process of avoiding the shortcoming of Greek philosophy, modern science fell into the opposite and even more serious error of limiting itself to 'arrangement in classes, orders and species',[9] without grasping the Totality. This, as we saw, accounts for the metaphysical character of modern science. Finally in the third phase, represented by Hegel's dialectical philosophy and by the 'materialist revolution' which Engels presumes to have carried out, the arguments of the Greeks are vindicated and revived. The period of 'dissection' and analysis, opened up by modern science and which represented the negation of the original Totality conceived by Ionian philosophy, is, in its turn, negated by the third epoch. This phase, being the 'negation of the negation', signals the restoration of the Totality (the 'return to the Greeks'!), although this time not in its 'primitive naïveté', but rather enriched by all the individual determinations. In the first phase, the vision of the Whole obscured that of the part; in the second, the vision of the part, that of the Whole; in the third, the individual part is finally apprehended within the Totality.

One might object that what Engels says about science concerns only the 'old style' of science, non-dialectical science, in opposition

7. F. Engels, *Socialism: Utopian and Scientific*, translated by Edward Aveling (New York, 1935), p. 45.
8. F. Engels, *Anti-Dühring*, op. cit., p. 27.
9. F. Engels, *Socialism: Utopian and Scientific*, op. cit., p. 46.

to which he posits a 'new' science permeated and revitalized by the dialectic. And one might also recall that in *Feuerbach*, as well as in many other places, Engels observes that 'while natural science up to the end of the last century was predominantly a *collecting* science, a science of finished things (and, therefore, metaphysical), in our century it is essentially a *classifying science*, a science of the processes, of the origin and development of these things and of the interconnection which binds all these natural processes into one great whole'.[10]

Nonetheless there are serious and well-grounded reasons for doubting that there ever really existed any science (apart, of course, from 'dialectical materialism' itself . . .) other than the one criticized by Engels. The 'old' science, merely 'accumulative' and metaphysical, which he is discussing here, is – let us not forget it – also the science of Kepler, Galileo, and Newton. However, the 'new' science which ought to be contrasted with this old one seems for the most part, and notably for Engels, only a science that . . . is yet to come. It is certainly true that he continually repeats that 'old style' science has had its day, and that it loses more ground every day to the 'new' science, which by its very nature is philosophical and dialectical. But Engels also observes with some impatience that, 'although on the whole it (abstract identity) has now been abolished in practice, theoretically it still dominates people's minds, . . . the bulk of natural scientists are still held fast in the old metaphysical categories and helpless when these modern facts, which so to say prove the dialectics in nature, have to be rationally explained and brought into relation with one another'.[11]

The truth is that what Engels was asking for so insistently could only be obtained, not from science, but from an acritical restoration of Hegel's old 'philosophy of nature'; and that what he wanted was not, in the final analysis, an ever greater emancipation of science (i.e., the only form of knowledge available to us) from any remaining *speculative* bonds on it, but just the opposite: a grafting of the old metaphysics onto science or – as one of his more ominous expressions

10. F. Engels, *Ludwig Feuerbach*, op. cit., pp. 45–6.
11. F. Engels, *Dialectics of Nature*, op. cit., p. 183 and p. 154.

goes – the advent of the moment in which 'philosophy takes its revenge posthumously on natural science'.[12]

Science is a form of metaphysics because it is founded on the principle of identity and non-contradiction. Identity, in its turn, is a form of metaphysics because it is *abstract*; and it is abstract because it gives us the finite outside the infinite, the *individual object* outside the 'totality', the 'this right here' to the exclusion of *everything* that it *is not*. Note that metaphysical abstractions are not those cognitions which have as their object supersensible universals (God, the soul, etc.) or, as Kant would say, 'knowledge which transcends the world of the senses, and where experience can neither guide nor correct us'.[13] Nor are they the abstractions which separate the logical *universal* from the world of experience, making it an a priori that exists for itself. Rather, the metaphysical abstraction is that which separates and differentiates the *individual object* from the universal. Metaphysics – or, as Hegel would say, *dogmatism* – is, in short, the 'ordinary human intellect', common sense; i.e. it is precisely that point of view to which were traced back, even traditionally speaking, all materialistic approaches to reality.[14]

Engels writes: '. . . Sound common sense, respectable fellow as he is within the homely precincts of his own four walls, has most wonderful adventures as soon as he ventures out into the wide world of scientific research.' Here, in fact, 'the metaphysical mode of outlook, justifiable and even necessary as it is in domains whose extent varies according to the nature of the object under investigation, . . . reaches a limit beyond which it becomes one-sided, limited, abstract, and loses its way in insoluble contradictions. And this is so because in considering individual things it loses sight of their connections; in contemplating their existence it forgets their

12. ibid., p. 154 (Colletti's emphasis).

13. Immanuel Kant, op. cit., p. 5.

14. G. W. F. Hegel, *Science of Logic*, p. 45: 'In general it (*reflective* understanding) stands for the understanding as abstracting, and hence as separating and remaining fixed in its separations. Directed against reason, it behaves as ordinary common sense and imposes its view that truth rests on sensuous reality, that thoughts are *only* thoughts, meaning that it is sense perception which first gives them filling and reality and that reason left to its own resources engenders only figments of the brain.'

coming into being and passing away; in looking at them at rest it leaves their motion out of account; because it cannot see the wood for the trees'.[15] The part is *abstract*, the whole is *concrete*. As usual, Engels restates Hegel, but without even suspecting the twofold movement – the world's *self-idealization* and self-negation and the Idea's *self-realization* – that is implicit in these two statements. When Hegel says that the finite – taken by itself or separately from the other – is abstract, he can say that in complete congruence with the principle of his philosophy, i.e. with the notion that the finite *is ideal*, a moment within the Idea. As the *Phenomenology* says, 'Being which is *per se* straightway non-being we call a show, a semblance (*Schein*)'.[16] And if the finite, the particular, does not have being in itself, but has as its 'essence' or foundation the 'other', it is clear not only that, in order to be itself, the finite has to 'pass over' into the infinite, cancel itself out; but it is also clear that, taken outside this relationship of it *within* the Idea and therefore as *real*, the finite must appear to Hegel as something 'abstract', separated from its 'true' essence. In fact, it is not a matter of chance that from Hegel's viewpoint materialism is only a delusion, the deceitfulness of common sense that mistakes 'illusory being' for true reality.

But once again, whereas this argument in Hegel is clear and self-consistent, in Engels it becomes pure nonsense. Engels, who wants to be a *materialist*, regards as 'abstract' the finite outside the infinite (the object external to thought) and as 'concrete' the totality. He does not see: (a) that the Hegelian 'totality' is the infinite. Reason, the Christian Logos (as the *Phenomenology* says, 'Beyond the sensuous world which is the world of appearance', there opens up 'a super-sensible world . . . as the true world. . . .) Away remote from the changing vanishing present (*Diesseits*) lies the permanent beyond (*Jenseits*)'[17]; (b) that when Hegel says that the infinite 'is . . . *determinate* being', that 'it *is* and *is there*, present before us' or that *the totality is the concrete*, he has in mind the passing over of the beyond

15. F. Engels, *Anti-Dühring*, p. 28.
16. G. W. F. Hegel, *The Phenomenology of Mind*, translated by J. B. Baillie (New York, 1967), p. 190. Hereafter referred to as *Phen.*
17. ibid., p. 191.

into the here and now, i.e. the incarnation or positive exposition of the absolute.

With reference to this exposition of the absolute Hegel writes in the *Phenomenology*, 'the supersensible is the established truth of the sensible and perceptual. The truth of the sensible and the perceptual lies, however, in being appearance. The supersensible is then *appearance qua appearance*'. And immediately afterwards, almost as a presage of the misunderstandings of dialectical materialism, Hegel becomes more specific: 'We distort the proper meaning of this, if we take it to mean that the supersensible is therefore the sensible world, or the world as it is for immediate sense-certainty and perception. For, on the contrary, appearance is just not the world of sense-knowledge and perception as positively *being*, but this world as superseded or established in truth as an inner world.'[18]

This incarnation of the supersensible marks (as shown with great clarity in the *Phenomenology*) a radical overturning of the world of common sense and materialism. What is real for materialism, here becomes 'illusory being'; what for it is unreal or non-thing (the infinite), here is the supreme reality. Hegel particularly emphasizes how the world of philosophy – i.e., idealism 'realized', the *realization* of the Idea – is the world of common sense *stood on its head*, the inverted world, *die verkehrte Welt*.[19] Reality is not the world, but 'immanence', the transubstantiation, the beyond that has come to the here and now, the soul that has made itself the *anima mundi*. 'This bare and simple infinity, or the absolute notion, may be called the ultimate nature of life, the souls of the world, the universal life-blood, which courses everywhere and whose flow is neither disturbed nor checked by any obstructing distinction, but is itself every distinction, that arises, as well as that into which all distinctions are dissolved; pulsating within itself, but ever motionless, shaken to its depths, but still at rest. It is self-identical, for the distinctions are tautological; they are distinctions that are none.'[20]

Now precisely this *verkehrte Welt*, this world 'stood on its head' – which represents the substantification of reason or the 'positive exposition of the absolute' – is what Engels also takes up as the truly

18. ibid., p. 193. 19. ibid., p. 203. 20. ibid., p. 208.

real and objective. The individual object is the abstract, the totality the concrete. The finite is ideal, the infinite real. Once these two essential cornerstones of Hegel's reasoning have been taken up, more or less unconsciously, it is not surprising that Engels should find himself unable to overturn Hegel's dialectic and therefore to put it back 'on its feet'. The dialectic in Hegel, Marx says, stands on its head, *auf dem Kopf*. 'It must be turned right side up again, if you would discover the rational kernel (*den rationellen Kern*) within the mystical shell (*in der mystischen Hülle*).'[21] The interpretation of this text is essential for us. The 'rational kernel' is precisely the Hegelian theory of reason itself; i.e. the discovery, arrived at by passing through the broadening of Eleaticism, etc., that reason is 'being' and 'non-being' together, finite and infinite *within* the infinite, a tautoheterology and dialectic. The 'mystical shell', on the other hand, is the immediate translation of reason into a positive moment, its substantification; a substantification that follows from the proposition that reason must be, at one and the same time and without making any distinctions, reason *and* reality, i.e. Christian *Logos*. If this interpretation of ours is correct, the breaking of the 'mystical shell' and thus the 'overturning' of the dialectic (to make use once again of these abused metaphors) can only consist in the recovery of the principle of identity and non-contradiction or, what is the same thing, the recovery of the materialist point of view. Reason is a *totality*; this is what Hegel saw clearly. But since this totality is only *reason*, i.e. thought, it must also be only 'one of the two', i.e. a totality and, at the same time, a *function* or predicate of an individual object *external* to it.

We have seen what the interpretative line of Engels is, on the other hand. He does not understand the real meaning of the 'dialectic of the finite' – the world's self-idealization and self-negation; and not having understood the actual nature of this first movement, he does not understand either, consequently, the meaning of the second 'passage' that is complementary to it and integrates it: the self-realization of the Idea (which is precisely what Hegel appro-

21. Karl Marx, *Capital*, translated by Samuel Moore and Edward Aveling (London and New York, 1967), vol. I, p. 20.

priately calles *Wirklichkeit* as opposed to *Realität*). The consequence is that what Engels and all of 'dialectical materialism' after him present as the highest and most developed form of *materialism* is none other than *absolute idealism.* The 'positive exposition of the absolute' is mistaken for a form of materialist objectivity. The 'dialectic of matter', by which the finite becomes *ideal* and cancels itself out, is confused with the observation and 'scientific verification' of processes and changes that take place under their own force and at the level of simple matter of fact.

There is no need to describe the extent to which this 'mistake' has affected and weighed upon the development of theoretical Marxism. Here, we are only concerned to point out its profound repercussions within the field of the interpretation of Hegel's thought, and how it engendered a series of problems that – with all due respect for the individual interpreters – we can only regard as either imaginary or misconceived.

One can read in the *Encyclopedia*: 'As far as concerns the immediate consciousness of the existence of external things, this means no more than to have sense-consciousness. Such a consciousness is the most elementary form of knowledge. All one needs to know about it is that this immediate knowledge of the *being* of external things is illusion and error; that in the sense-world as such there is no truth; and that the *being* of these external things is rather something accidental and ephemeral, illusory being. . . .'[22]

This is one of the many professions of idealism that we have come to know, from a direct study of Hegel's texts. Its meaning does not appear to be in doubt. It implies the negation of any extralogical existence. It implies that 'this material as it appears *apart from* and *prior* to the notion has no *truth*; this it has solely in its ideality or its identity with the Notion'. It implies that *identity* of thought and being, or the 'inseparability' of the latter from the former, which – as Hegel always saw with great lucidity – is the principle common to both Descartes and Spinoza, on the one hand, and to his own philosophy and post-Kantian idealism in general, on the other. The fundamental proposition of Descartes's philosophy, he reiterates, is

22. *En.L.*, p. 140 (translation modified).

'the inseparability of the representation of *God* from his *existence*, such that the latter is contained in the very representation of God and the former cannot exist without the attribute of existence, which is thus necessary and eternal'. With Spinoza, he adds, 'we come upon the same statement that the essence or abstract conception of God implies existence. The first of Spinoza's definitions, that of the *Causa Sui* (or Self-Cause), explains it to be *cujus essentia involvit existentiam*. . . . The inseparability of the notion from being is the main point and fundamental hypothesis. . . .'[23]

On the one hand, then, we have *idealism*. On the other, however, we also have in Hegel the dialectic of matter. The *Science of Logic*, for example, tells us that 'qualitative nodes and leaps occur in chemical combinations when the mixture proportions are progressively altered; at certain points in the scale of mixtures, two substances form products exhibiting particular qualities'. 'For example, different oxides of nitrogen and nitric acids having essentially different qualities are formed only when oxygen and nitrogen are combined in certain specific proportions, and no such specific compounds are formed by the intermediate proportions.'[24] Now let us open the *Dialectics of Nature*. Discussing the passage from quantity into quality and vice versa, Engels calls to our attention that 'the sphere, however, in which the law of nature (!) discovered by Hegel (!) celebrates its most important triumphs is that of chemistry. Chemistry can be termed the science of the qualitative changes of bodies as a result of quantitative composition. That was already known to Hegel himself (*Logic*, pp. 356–7). As in the case of oxygen: if three atoms unite into a molecule, instead of the usual two, we get ozone, a body which is very considerably different from ordinary oxygen in its odour and reactions. Again, one can take the various proportions in which oxygen combines with nitrogen or sulphur, each of which produces a substance qualitatively different from any of the others!'[25]

The 'law', as one can see, is absolutely the same; even the examples are the same. It is a fact not only that the dialectic of matter of

23. ibid., p. 139 (translation modified).

24. *L.*, p. 369.

25. F. Engels, *Dialectics of Nature*, op. cit., pp. 30–1.

'dialectical materialism' is the same one that we find in Hegel's work; but also that the 'leap' from quantity into quality is here esteemed a *law of nature* not unlike, and in fact of much more general application than the law of falling bodies or of universal gravitation – a law of nature 'discovered' by Hegel, just as Galileo and Newton discovered theirs.

Let the reader now adopt the point of view of 'dialectical materialism', and let him make the experiment of thinking through together the two aspects of Hegel's thought just cited. The conclusion can only be that in the philosophy of Hegel – a thinker with extraordinary *internal* coherence – there exists a profound contradiction. His idealist side is clearly visible and undeniable. On the other hand, the dialectic of matter is in all respects identical to that of 'dialectical materialism'. The necessary conclusion can only be that Hegel is *half idealist, and half materialist*; that his entire philosophy is divided and disconnected by a deep contradiction; and that its 'method' and its 'system' are permanently in conflict with one another. In short, the 'reading' of Hegel made by Engels, Plekhanov, and Lenin (the second and third, it should be noted, already on the authority of Engels) is taken up as a self-evident standard of evaluation which is beyond debate; while all the time the 'contradiction' that lies within the standard itself is being quietly projected into the object under evaluation. This is the source of the series of 'unreal' problems mentioned above: the question of Hegel's *materialism*; the question of the contradictoriness of his philosophy – problems, it may be said, that do not remain confined to the area of 'dialectical materialism', but which (as we shall see) reverberate also among the non-Marxist or 'Western Marxist' interpreters of Hegel's thought. And finally the relationship between the 'young Marx' and the 'old Marx' – a problem which is, I readily admit, altogether unresolvable wherever Marx's thought in his full maturity is regarded as identical with that of Engels and the entire tradition of 'dialectical materialism'.

IV. Hegel and the 'Theory of Reflection'

In the 1812 Preface to the first edition of the *Science of Logic* where he undertakes to examine the 'complete transformation' that 'in the last twenty-five years' had taken place in philosophic thought, Hegel gives emphasis to the discredit and desuetude into which metaphysics had fallen in the meanwhile. 'That which, prior to this period, was called metaphysics has been, so to speak, extirpated root and branch and has vanished from the ranks of the sciences. The ontology, rational psychology, cosmology, yes even natural theology, of former times – where is now to be heard any mention of them or who would venture to mention them? Inquiries, for instance, into the immateriality of the soul, into efficient and final causes, where should these still arouse any interest? Even the former proofs of the existence of God are cited only for their historical interest or for purposes of edification and uplifting the emotions. The fact is that there no longer exists any interest either in the form or the content of metaphysics or in both together.'[1]

In calling attention to these forms and contents of the 'old metaphysics', Hegel knows full well that they represent precisely what had been the object of the analysis and 'theoretical destruction' carried out in the *Critique of Pure Reason*. (It is, moreover, likely that the twenty-five years from which he dates the 'complete transformation' are calculated beginning exactly with 1787, the year of the second edition of the *Critique* and of its expanded version that included the famous 'Refutation of Idealism'.) In any case, the reference to Kant is explicit. 'The exoteric teaching of the Kantian philosophy – that the understanding cannot go beyond experience,' without thereby producing anything but fantasies, 'was a justification from a philosophical quarter for the renunciation of speculative

1. *L.*, p. 25.

thought'. The consequence is that 'philosophy (*Wissenschaft*) and ordinary common sense thus cooperating to bring about the downfall of metaphysics, there was seen the strange spectacle of a cultured nation without metaphysics – like a temple richly ornamented in other respects but without a holy of holies'.[2]

The success of critical philosophy was aided and abetted by 'the cry of modern educationists', the vulgar pragmatism of the times that 'demanded attention to immediate requirements', and, in general, by the belief that 'just as experience was the primary factor for knowledge, so for skill in public and private life, theoretical insight may even be harmful'. The result has been that 'theology, which in former times was the guardian of the speculative mysteries and of metaphysics (even though the latter was subordinate to it), [has] given up this science in exchange for feelings, for what was popularly matter-of-fact, and for historical erudition'. And so 'there vanished from the world those solitary souls who were sacrificed by their people and exiled from the world to the end that the eternal should be contemplated and served by lives devoted solely thereto – not for any practical gain but for the sake of blessedness', leaving their place to the fatuity of ordinary human understanding and the philosophy of the luminaries, i.e. of that age – previously disdainfully termed *der Dogmatismus der Aufklärerei* (the dogmatism of Enlightenment lucubrations) in the early writing on *Belief and Knowledge*,[3] – in which, with the 'shadows' of metaphysics chased away, Hegel sarcastically remarks that 'Outer existence seemed to be transformed into the bright world of flowers – and there are no *black* flowers, as we know'.[4]

The void opened up by 'critical philosophy' – the temple richly ornamented but without the holy of holies that Hegel now prepares to reconsecrate by presenting the *Science of Logic* to the public – will be filled precisely by 'the science of logic which constitutes metaphysics proper or purely speculative philosophy'.[5]

These pages of Hegel are important and meaningful, of course,

2. ibid., pp. 25–6.
3. G. W. F. Hegel, *Glauben und Wissen*, in *Sämtliche Werke*, op. cit., Vol. I, p. 284.
4. *L.*, p. 26.
5. ibid., p. 27.

and should not therefore be judged too hastily. One finds in them – as in all his work, incidentally – the stamp of a vigorous and hardy mode of thought, full of that fascination which, at times, the great conservatives know how to generate. There re-echoes through them the note of an imposing 'organicism', and a concern for the division and internal diaspora of modern 'civil society' and for the devastating utilitarianism which the incipient capitalist mode of life bears with it. Nevertheless, these are pages to be judged also with sobriety and dispassionately.

The main object of their polemic is the *Reflexionsphilosophie*, which arose with the Enlightenment, and – against this historical background – from Kant. An Italian Marxist scholar, who was the first to draw our attention to these pages, has rightly observed that, whereas Kant 'is here called upon to represent the *pars destruens*' in the divergence of modern thought from the old metaphysics (corresponding, moreover, 'to what was the direct and clear-cut impact of Kantianism on the culture of the times'), it is 'significant that Hegel does not give him a sympathetic judgment'. 'Hegel,' he concludes, 'thus openly presents himself as the most self-conscious restorer of metaphysics' (although 'on the crest of the latest movement of thought' and therefore 'naturally up to the level of the transformation that had taken place in those years'[6]).

This assessment is, in our view, important. It is further backed up, in Luporini's argument, by a reference to that famous passage of the *Holy Family* in which Marx discusses the Enlightenment, its battle against metaphysics, and the role which Hegel's philosophy assigned to itself *vis-à-vis* the latter: 'Seventeenth-century metaphysics, beaten off the field by the French Enlightenment, to be precise, by French materialism of the eighteenth century, was given a *victorious and solid restoration* in German philosophy, particularly in *German speculative philosophy* of the nineteenth century. After Hegel linked it in so masterly a fashion with all subsequent metaphysics and with German idealism and founded a metaphysical universal kingdom, the attack on *speculative metaphysics* and metaphysics in general again corresponded, as in the eighteenth century, to the attack on

6. Cesare Luporini, *Spazio e materia in Kant* (Florence, 1961), pp. 13–15.

theology. It will be defeated forever by materialism which has now been perfected by the work of *speculation* itself and coincides with humanism.'[7]

The importance of this assessment lies, on our view, in the fact that it is one of the exceedingly rare acknowledgments of the metaphysical character of Hegel's thought that one can find today in the camp of 'dialectical materialism'. It even seems to break, in some places, with Engels's theory (elaborated later by Lukács, in particular), according to which 'dialectic' and 'metaphysics' are always alternative and antithetical terms. Furthermore, in the process of underlining the great importance of the Kantian critique of the ontological argument ('that critique is founded, as is known, on the irresolvability of existence into a mere concept, a central point in Kant's thought'), Luporini rightly observes that it is precisely 'on the question of the rejection of this anti-idealist position of Kant's (that) the Hegelian restoration of metaphysics, in the final analysis, is based, (a restoration) which is thus, as has been observed many times, a reconstruction of theology in speculative form, even though it is no longer a theology with a transcendental and personal God'.[8]

Nevertheless, despite the perceptiveness of his observations, this author as well ends up recognizing as Hegel's principal merit his conception of '*objectivity*' – which is here directly understood in terms akin to the materialist meaning of objectivity. The superiority of Hegel over Kant lies in the discovery of the '*essential* and *necessary* character of contradiction'. This recognition of the *objectivity* of contradiction – which, it should be noted, 'will remain basically valid from the point of view of *dialectical materialism* as well'[9] – is what, according to the author, represents the reason for that 'intellectual continuity which, despite all their differences, the founders of dialectical materialism established between themselves and Hegel'.[10]

Luporini continues thus: 'Vehicle for that continuity is the "dialectical method", passed over from idealism to materialism, and the dynamic nucleus at work is none other than the objectivity of

7. K. Marx and F. Engels, *The Holy Family or Critique of Critical Critique*, translated by R. Dixon (Moscow, 1956), p. 168.

8. Luporini, op. cit., pp. 71–2.

9. ibid., p. 18.

10. loc. cit.

contradiction (implying the positivity of the negative). Contradiction as a property of the "contents of categories", as a property of things and of the "essence of the world", and therefore such that "intellectual determinations", in so far as they reflect [NB] or take in that reality, posit it in the "rational" – this is the perspective, on the basis of which an immense wealth of real contents and positive determinations could be drawn into Hegel's system. Thus Engels will come to write that "the idealist systems also filled themselves more and more with a materialist content" and that "ultimately, the Hegelian system represents merely a materialism idealistically turned upside down in method and content".'[11]

Thus, on the one hand, intellectual categories and determinations '*reflect*' reality. On the other, however, Hegel rejects the Kantian critique of the ontological argument – rejects, in other words, the thesis that existence is not an attribute of thought, not a concept, but something external to or *different* from thought itself. On the one side, then, the Hegelian statement on the 'objectivity of contradiction', was understood to mean that reason is then the *reflection* of this objectivity. On the other, there is the opposing Hegelian affirmation of idealism, i.e. his negation of the existence of any empirical reality external to thought that has to be 'reflected' by the latter – and his consequent 'restoration of metaphysics'. In short, materialism on the one side, idealism on the other, and both of them in the same author. As Luporini writes: 'That idealism-materialism, or materialism inverted into an idealist form, which contained the "revolutionary method" of the dialectic, had at the same time been a *restoration* of metaphysics, precisely as a consequence of its systematic form and the premisses and implications that followed therefrom. It undoubtedly contained . . . explicitly in the entirety of its development and in the wealth of its contents that revolutionary element, even if mystified in its idealist-systematic form. And nonetheless, for all that, it was a restoration.'[12]

It is a fact that the problems raised here cannot be resolved by simply turning one's back on Hegel. Nor is the meaning of our

11. F. Engels, *Ludwig Feuerbach. . .*, op. cit., p. 24.
12. Luporini, op. cit., pp. 19–20.

argument intended to be that of a mere rejection. If what we have said until now concerning the importance and meaning of the Hegelian theory of *reason* makes any sense (and we will attempt to expand on this below), it is clear that a contribution on Hegel's part to the concept of *objectivity* must exist. As a matter of fact, objectivity must, after all, be capable of being established and recognized by someone – and the latter can be none other than reason. Reality cannot be something that is apprehended without any thought at all. Materialism is not a theory of faith or 'immediate knowledge' either. Feuerbach himself, in spite of being one of those who erred most in the direction of sensism, stated that being 'is thinkable only through mediation; it is thinkable only through the predicates on which the essence of an object is based'.[13] Clearly, this means that objectivity cannot be what is immediately apprehended by sensation, but something which, in order to be established and recognized, must make use (as we shall see) of rational criteria – i.e., of mediation and therefore, beyond any doubt, of deduction itself.

But it is one thing to recognize this, i.e. the contribution of Hegel's theory of reason as an indispensable moment in the determination of objectivity; it is another to think that objectivity, just as we find it in Hegel (i.e. the 'positive exposition of the absolute') is the same objectivity as that of materialist 'reflection'. Moreover, that there is a contradiction here is clear from the case of Lukács. In the camp of 'dialectical materialism', Lukács is the major defender of an *immediate* continuity between Hegel and Marxism. While neglecting to note even once Marx's thesis concerning the Hegelian restoration of metaphysics, he explicitly states what Luporini seems to say only in a veiled form: that Hegel made *de facto* use of the 'theory of reflection', the *Widerspiegelungstheorie*, or, what amounts to the same thing, that he was a follower of the materialist epistemology! After having noted – in terms we need not recall here – what he takes to be Kant's mode of conceiving the 'criterion of truth', Lukács proceeds thus: 'Objective idealism had to look about for other criteria. Schelling finds them in the revival of the Platonic

13. L. Feuerbach, *Principles of the Philosophy of the Future*, op. cit., p. 42.

theory of Ideas: agreement with the Ideas is to be the criterion of truth, since philosophical statements, artistic creations, etc., are indeed nothing other than reflections of these Ideas in human consciousness. Here we are dealing with a mystical materialism, a materialism stood on its head, with a mystification of the nature of objective reality into Platonic Ideas.' 'The Hegelian dialectic (however) goes much farther in this regard than its predecessors.' It 'shows, on the one hand, that apparently motionless things are in reality processes, and on the other hand, it grasps the objectivity of objects (*Gegenständlichkeit der Objekte*) as products of the "alienation (*Entäusserung*)" of the subject. . . . *The view of objects as "alienations" of the spirit now gives to Hegel the possibility of simply making use of the theory of reflection with regard to the gnoseological analysis of reality, without acknowledging it.* He can compare each and every thought with the objective reality corresponding to it – and the exactness of the criterion of truth as correspondence with objective reality is not lacking in individual instances – although this reality is not viewed as actually independent of consciousness, but rather as the product of the "alienation" of a subject higher than the individual consciousness. And since the process of "alienation" is a dialectical one, Hegel goes at times farther than the old materialists themselves in this undesired and unconscious use of materialist criteria of right knowledge.'[14]

The argument is a monument of logical consistency! Schelling's philosophy is 'mystical materialism stood on its head'. The title, as one can see, is taken away this time from Hegel and awarded instead to Schelling and Platonism in general (which is 'upside-down materialism' in the same sense, one might say, that materialism is 'upside-down Platonism'). Hegel, on the other hand, who conceives objects as products of the alienation of the subject, i.e. as *dependent* objects created by thought, embraces the materialist theory of 'reflection', precisely *by virtue of* this conception of his. In other words, he embraces just that theory according to which it is thought that *depends* on objects and it is judgment that strains to correspond

14. Georg Lukács, *Der junge Hegel* (Neuwied and Berlin, 1967), 3rd edition, pp. 653–4 (Colletti's emphasis).

to things. Finally, in individual instances, i.e. in the elaboration of the details internal to the system, 'the Hegelian dialectic has therefore an immense advantage over the other forms of gnoseology in classical German idealism' because 'it can operate in areas of human knowledge with an epistemology – even if it is not legitimately arrived at – based on the reflection of reality'. On the other hand, when it leaves behind the details in order to draw a conclusion, i.e. to embrace the system or 'the totality of knowledge', Hegel can resolve the qurstion of the epistemological criteria – the question: *with what* the object of knowledge must correspond in order to be recognized as true – in a way no less mystical and mystifying than his predecessors;[15] i.e. only by a recourse to the 'Platonism' of Schelling.[16]

15. ibid., p. 655.

16. This interpretation of Hegel's thought in terms of a materialist theory of 'reflection' reappears also in G. Lukács's work entitled *Prolegomena to a Marxist Aesthetics* (the translation is from the Italian translation, Rome, 1957; the quotations also refer to that text – translator's note). On pp. 70–1, for example, referring to the Hegelian theory of syllogism, Lukács writes: 'This is a matter of real links in reality, in nature, and in society that in logic acquire their most abstract reflection, which nonetheless tends to correspond to reality. Nor is it crucial that Hegel's theory of knowledge is not based on the point of view of the theory of reflection. His logic, nevertheless, aims objectively at such a reflection of objective reality.' On p. 67, the author states that 'the great advance in logic brought about by Hegel's method' results from the 'priority of content with respect to form'. On the other hand, Lukács continues, one can find in Hegel 'at the same time an inordinate idealist tendency in the question of objectivity'. 'In the process of polemizing with the logic of the metaphysical and subjective understanding, Hegel says, "It is not *we* who frame the notions. The notion is not something which is originated at all." The materialist dialectic', Lukács continues, 'in which objectivity is guaranteed by the reflection of reality, which moves and exists independently, this dialectic can naturally consider problems of objectivity in a much more flexible and dialectical way than Hegel himself. The latter was often inclined to a certain rigidity, (propping himself up in one way or another with Platonism in order to avoid a relapse into subjective idealism, since objectivity for him is present only in the sphere of thought or the "spirit" ' (pp. 67–8). This confusion (barely disguised by the involuted form) between objectivity, as the objectivity of 'intelligible essences' (in terms of the Kantian ontology), and objectivity as the empirical-material manifold is the note that distinguishes Lukács's entire interpretative argument. On the other hand, just what he understands by *metaphysics* can be gleaned from the above quotations. Metaphysics for Lukács is 'the logic of the metaphysical understanding' and above all Kant's Analytic! In this sense the reference to subheading 163 of the *Encyclopedia* is extremely interesting. There, Hegel is polemizing against the central problem of the *Critique*: the problem of

This is basically the same point of view that we have also found in Lenin. Both celebrate Hegel's 'dialectic of matter', convinced that it is a genuine materialism. They discard, however, 'God, the Absolute, the Pure Idea, etc.', as if all of that were just a 'façade'

---

the origin and formation of our knowledge. As is known, this is an instance of the *critical* problem par excellence. It presupposes, on the one hand, the rejection of knowledge (concepts) 'already given', *innatism*. On the other hand, it presupposes the distinction between being and thought, existence and concept (since, if one were to assume instead the identity of thought and being, the problem as to how they come together and how, from this conjuncture, knowledge is born, obviously could not even be posed). Now, even on this point, it is significant that, one minor reservation apart, Lukács aligns himself with Hegel against Kant. And to think that, as is evident from the text, Hegel is polemizing in this passage of the *Encyclopedia* precisely with the element of materialism still present, albeit embryonically, in the framework of the *Critique*! Hegel writes: 'It is a mistake to imagine that the objects which form the content of our mental ideas come first and that our subjective agency then supervenes, and by the aforesaid operation of abstraction, and by correlating the points possessed in common by the objects, frames notions of them. Rather the notion is the genuine first; and things are what they are through the action of the notion, immanent in them, and revealing itself in them (*des ihnen innewohnenden und in ihnen sich offenbarenden Begriffs*). In religious language we express this by saying that God created the world out of nothing. In other words, the world and finite things have issued from the fullness of the divine thoughts and the divine decrees. Thus religion recognizes thought and (more exactly) the notion to be the infinite form, or the free creative activity, which can realize itself without the help of a matter that exists outside it.' It is evidently in reference to these texts of Hegel's that Lukács can talk about Hegel's 'propping himself up with Platonism'. How he can at the same time, however, state that Hegel gives 'priority to content with respect to form', is, at least for me, a total mystery. Another thing to be pointed out is that in the *Prolegomena* (p. 85) Lukács refers to the processes of hypostatization, i.e. the substantification of reason or the 'positive exposition of the absolute', but only in a parenthetical way and without drawing any conclusions therefrom. He cites a brief notation of Lenin's with reference to Aristotle's *Metaphysics*, cf. V. I. Lenin, *Collected Works*, Vol. 38 (*Philosophical Notebooks*), p. 372: 'Primitive idealism: the universal (concept, idea) is a *particular* being.' The problem is that whereas Lenin is here adopting Aristotle's critique of the Platonic theory of the forms and extending it to Hegel, Lukács thinks (and this shows the offhanded character of his readings) that Lenin's critique is addressed to Aristotle! The extent to which Lukács's entire text is interlaced with contradictions, the reader can judge from the following example as well. On p. 68, Lukács ascribes to Hegel a conception of the 'particular' as the 'foundation' and substratum of judgment. On p. 100, however, while discussing the dialectic of 'sense-certainty' in the first chapter of the *Phenomenology*, Lukács takes up Feuerbach's critique of this chapter, pointing out that for Hegel 'the particular is "the non-true, the non-rational, that which is purely a matter of belief"', and that 'in his *Zur Kritik der Hegelschen Philosophie* Feuerbach protests with good reason against this degradation of particularity'!

without any relationship to the former and as if theology and idealism represented little more than passing moments in Hegel's philosophical career. When one thinks about it, the mechanism is very simple. They hail in Hegelian idealism that which they had previously learned from 'dialectical materialism', surprised to discover in Hegel exactly what they already learned from Engels (and without ever giving due weight to the fact that Engels had only transcribed it from Hegel in the first place). Once they have verified this identity of views, they draw the conclusion that Hegel's philosophy contains certain materialist germinations that stand in contradiction with the system's principles. They thereby impute to Hegel the radical inconsistency of having produced a philosophy of 'idealism-materialism'. What, on the contrary, they never consider – although, in general terms, this possibility is just as reasonable as the first one – is the opposing hypothesis; i.e., the hypothesis that Hegel is an absolutely coherent idealist, and that 'dialectical materialism' is simply an idealism unaware of its own nature.

One might object that this criticism is rendered in part superfluous by the much more effective criticism that time and events have themselves carried out in the interim. 'Dialectical materialism', after surviving for many decades only as a 'state philosophy', is by now so far gone in decline that every day it becomes more difficult to recognize its adherents. Nevertheless, since nothing is ever simple, it must be recognized that certain of its theses still hold the field, albeit with another name and in different clothes. Philosophies that have nothing in common with 'dialectical materialism', share nonetheless the essentials of its judgment of Hegel. Indeed, if one wanted to engage in a discussion of cultural politics, it could even be held that in new hands these theses can at last carry out their true appointed function with full effectiveness – the function, that is, of replacing and passing itself off as Marx's thought, in whatever way possible.

Typical in this sense are the cases of Kojève and Marcuse. Of course for them the 'dialectic of matter' has no importance whatever. Nonetheless, whether because they are influenced by the authority that always emanates from 'official' philosophies or because (as is more likely) they are carried away by an irresistible taste for intellectual 'coquetry', not only do they at times interpret the dialectic of things or of the finite which they find in Hegel as a form of true and proper materialism, they even discover in it the 'theory of reflection'! Kojève writes that for Hegel 'Each philosophy correctly reveals or describes a turning point or a stopping place . . . of the real dialectic, of the *Bewegung* of existing Being. And that is why each philosophy is "true" in a certain sense. But it is true only relatively or temporarily: it remains "true" as long as a new philosophy, also "true", does not come along to demonstrate its "error". However, a philosophy does not by itself transform itself into another philosophy or engender that other philosophy in and by an autonomous dialectical movement. The Real corresponding to a given philosophy itself becomes really other . . . , and this other Real is what engenders another adequate philosophy, which, as "true", replaces the first philosophy which has become "false". Thus, the dialectical movement of the history of philosophy . . . is but a reflection, a "superstructure", of the dialectical movement of the *real* history of the Real.'[17] 'In Hegel there is a real Dialectic'; 'the philosophical method is that of a pure and simple description, which is dialectical only in the sense that it describes a dialectic of reality.'[18]

And now we come to Marcuse. His entire argument seems to be pervaded with a fundamental indecisiveness. Marcuse cannot make up his mind if Hegel is to be depicted as an idealist or as a materialist. Incapable of choosing between these alternatives, he calmly states on the even pages the very opposite of what he tells us on the odd ones.

Hegel tends (e.g.) towards materialism. 'His "pan-logism",' Marcuse claims, 'comes close to being its opposite: one could say that he takes the principles and forms of thought from the principles and forms of reality, so that the logical laws reproduce those governing the movement of reality'.[19] In this sense, 'the movement of thought reproduces the movement of being'; 'the interplay and

17. Alexandre Kojève, *Introduction to the Reading of Hegel*, edited by A. Bloom and translated by J. H. Nichols, Jr. (New York, 1969), pp. 184–5.

18. ibid., p. 186.

19. Herbert Marcuse, *Reason and Revolution* (Boston, 1960), p. 25.

motility of the notions reproduces the concrete process of reality'.[20] The enormous difference between Hegelian Logic and traditional logic has often been brought out, Marcuse continues, with the statement that Hegel 'replaced the formal by a material logic': 'the categories and modes of thought derive from the process of reality to which they pertain. Their form is determined by the structure of this process'.[21] 'The philosophical method he elaborated was intended to reflect the actual process of reality and to construe it in an adequate form.'[22] '. . . The movement of categories in Hegel's logic is but a reflection of the movement of being.'[23]

On the other hand, as we also know, Hegel is *not* a materialist, he represents rather its most resolute antithesis. For him, as Marcuse states, 'Everything . . . exists more or less as a "subject".'[24] For this reason, 'thought is more "real" than its objects.'[25] '. . . The object gets its objectivity from the subject. "The real" . . . is a universal that cannot be reduced to objective elements free of the subject (for example, *quality, thing, force, laws*). In other words, the real object is constituted by the (intellectual) activity of the subject; somehow, it essentially "pertains" to the subject. The latter discovers that it itself stands "behind" the objects, that the world becomes real only by force of the comprehending power of consciousness.'[26] 'The object is not *per se*; it is "because I know it".'[27] '. . . The *subject* itself constitutes the objectivity of the thing.'[28] '. . . Behind the appearance of things is the subject itself, who constitutes their very essence.'[29] 'Common sense and traditional scientific thought take the world as a totality of things, more or less existing *per se*, and seek the truth in objects that are taken to be independent of the knowing subject.'[30] For Hegel, however, 'thinking consists in knowing that the objective world is in reality a subjective world, that it is the objectification of the subject.'[31] For him, 'Notion is the "essence" and "nature" of things . . .'.[32]

The reason for these oscillations – which lead our author to state,

20. ibid., p. 64.
21. ibid., p. 121.
22. ibid., p. 122.
23. ibid., p. 131.
24. ibid., p. 63.
25. ibid., p. 73.
26. ibid., p. 94.
27. ibid., p. 104.
28. ibid., p. 107.
29. ibid., p. 110.
30. ibid., p. 112.
31. ibid., p. 118.
32. ibid., p. 128.

for example on p. 143, that 'objective being, if comprehended in its true form, is to be understood as . . . subjective being', and then on p. 144 to write that 'thought is true only in so far as it remains adapted to the concrete movement of things and closely follows its various turns' – is doubtless to be sought in the boredom and annoyance suffered by temperaments like Marcuse's when confronted with the need for coherent logical argument. However, a further motive for his vagaries must certainly be sought in the spell exercised by 'dialectical materialism' on him. When Marcuse comes across that page of the *Science of Logic* cited above, where Hegel states that 'non-being constitutes the being of things' and that 'the hour of their birth is the hour of their death', it is clear that his reading is in this instance heavily influenced by the interpretative tradition inaugurated by *Anti-Dühring*. Marcuse's remark is that 'these sentences are a preliminary enunciation of the decisive passages in which Marx later revolutionized Western thought. Hegel's concept of finitude freed philosophic approaches to reality from the powerful religious and theological influences that were operative even upon secular forms of eighteenth-century thought. The current idealistic interpretation of reality in that day still held the view that the world was a finite one because it was a created world and that its negativity referred to its sinfulness. The struggle against this interpretation of "negative" was therefore in large measure a conflict with religion and the church. Hegel's idea of negativity was not moral or religious, but purely philosophical, and the concept of finitude that expressed it became a critical and almost materialistic principle with him. The world, he said, is finite not because it is created by God but because finitude is its inherent quality.'[33]

It is unnecessary to dwell on the point that, in order to hold up this interpretation of his, Marcuse has to abridge (just two pages later) the famous Hegelian definition of idealism he himself cites: 'The proposition that the finite is ideal constitutes idealism. The idealism of philosophy consists in nothing else than in recognizing that the finite has no veritable being.'[34] He leaves out just that part which directly disproves his fanciful reconstruction of the struggle

33. ibid., pp. 136–7.

34. *L.*, p. 154.

engaged in by the atheist Hegel against the superstitious and fanatical Enlightenment: 'This is as true of philosophy as of religion; for religion equally does not recognize finitude as a veritable being, as something ultimate and absolute or as something underived, uncreated, eternal.'[35] What concerns us here is only to point out, as a

35. ibid., p. 155. It may be pointed out that an almost equally grievous distortion of Hegel's attitude towards religion is to be found in Lukács's *Der junge Hegel.* The line of argumentation followed by Lukács can, in this instance, give an idea of the kind of forced interpretations with which the entire work is laden. Lukács makes a point of adopting, in various places, Feuerbach's thesis concerning the relationship theology-philosophy in Hegel (a thesis that corresponds perfectly to the relationship Hegel himself establishes between religion and philosophy: cf., in this regard, the essay on Hegel, full of textual references, by K. Löwith, 'La onto-teo-logica di Hegel e il problema della totalità del mondo', in *De Homine*, no. 2–3, Sept., 1962, pp. 18–66). On p. 636, for example, Lukács writes: 'The focal point of Feuerbach's critique, i.e. that Hegel's philosophy dissolves Christian theology and then re-establishes it, concerns the third part of the *Phenomenology*. . . .' On p. 637, this assessment is emphasized in the following terms: 'Philosophy has a critical stance towards religion also in Hegel; for him too it is a critique of religion. This critique is not, however – as with the materialist Feuerbach – designed to unmask the inner falsehood of the entire world of religious representations and to trace back the contents of religion from their distorted form to what they really are. Hegel's critique of religion is rather a way of preserving and making eternal all of religion's contents, through a mere critique of the form in which it manifests itself, of the way in which it is *represented* (*Vorstellungscharakter*). Obviously, as we shall see, this critique also runs over into the content and thus contains a certain repudiation of religious contents as well. Its basic orientation is, however, as rightly stressed by Feuerbach, a restoration of religion and theology.' Previously, on p. 633, and still on this line, Lukács had observed, while examining the *Phenomenology*, that 'here the significance of the Enlightenment is diminished and the function of religion in the development of mankind's consciousness is forcefully given a central position'. Nevertheless, all of these admissions appear to be made by Lukács with the intention of 'digesting' them and re-establishing, *malgré eux*, the antithetical point of view. On p. 646, for example, Lukács points that 'the Hegelian form of the revival of religion and the way in which he blends idealist philosophy into religion and theology' – the latter being 'objectivist' – 'do not stand opposed to the knowledge of objective reality. On the contrary, for Hegel the value of religion consists precisely in the fact that the highest objective categories of the dialectic find expression, to be sure in an unsatisfactory form, in it, and that it represents the penultimate stage in arriving at the proper knowledge of objective reality.' One need hardly point out how the confusion, analysed above, between material objectivity and the objectivity of 'ideal essences' enables Lukács to view the entire matter in a most positive light. On p. 648, 'the conflicting and ambivalent nature of Hegel's philosophy of religion' – which of course is not at all ambivalent *per se* but only in Lukács's version – is imputed to . . . the Enlightenment, and, in particular, to the German Enlightenment, as well as (one suspects) Kant. On p. 649, the

distance between Kant and Hegel appears, in this respect, to be re-established ('These differences mean that in this area Hegel is more ambiguous than Kant. Kant's philosophy of religion is, despite all reservations one might have, the philosophy of an Enlightenment deism'). But, as one can see right away, the position is quickly reversed. In point of fact, having brought out the influence of Spinozist pantheism (parenthetically, Hegel does not regard Spinoza's philosophy as a pantheism but rather as an *acosmism*), Lukács writes: 'This pantheism gave to German idealists the possibility of depicting objective reality, nature and society in a scientific fashion, i.e. as ruled by their own immanent laws, and to flatly reject any notion of a beyond . . . The undeniable ambiguity of classical German idealism and in particular that of Hegel consists in the fact that they attempt to reconcile what is irreconcilable, that they deny that the world was created and set in motion by God at the same time that they would philosophically redeem the religious notions connected with Him' (pp. 649–50). Let the reader count the number of times that the word *ambiguity* appears in the lines of Lukács cited in this note; we would ask him to consider whether it is permissible to write intellectual history while using and abusing this category – in a way which, once introduced, renders every operation legitimate. Whoever maintains that precisely the historico-materialist interpretation should be the one to make use of these 'ruthless' procedures which call into question the 'particular consciousness' of the philosopher (or, more accurately, his good faith), should read the passage from Marx's notes to his dissertation in which he discusses Hegel and the left-Hegelians. (cf. *Marx-Engels Gesamtausgabe*, Moscow, vol. I, 1/1, p. 64: 'It is a matter of pure ignorance when Hegel's students interpret this or that characteristic of his system as the result of compromises or the like – in a word, they interpret them in *moral* (*moralisch*) terms . . . That a philosopher is guilty of this or that apparent logical inconsistency as a result of this or that compromise, is conceivable. He himself may be conscious of this. But what he is not conscious of is that the possibility of this apparent compromise has its innermost roots in some shortcoming or inadequate grasp of his very own principle. If a philosopher has actually compromised himself, then it is up to his students to explain that which *for the philosopher himself has the form of an exoteric consciousness, in terms of his inward, essential consciousness.* In this way, what appears as an advance in moral consciousness [*Gewissen*] is at the same time an advance in knowledge [*Wissen*]. The private [*partikulär*] moral consciousness of the philosopher is not brought under suspicion, but rather the essential form of his consciousness is reconstructed, raised to a determinate shape and meaning, and thereby at the same time superseded.') Finally as far as concerns the thesis that 'German classical idealism and Hegel in particular' have always denied 'that the world was created and set in motion by God', it may be pointed out that the texts which can disprove Lukács and Marcuse are available to all those who wish to read them. Leaving aside the *Lectures on Religion*, one need only open the *Science of Logic* in order to read there: 'This realm is truth as it is without veil and in its own absolute nature. It can therefore be said that this content is the exposition of God as he is in his eternal essence before the creation of nature and a finite mind' (p. 50). Furthermore, it is characteristic, as Löwith has recalled (art. cit., p. 20), 'that Hegel should recommend the study of his Berlin lecture of 1829 on the proofs for the existence of God in order to complement his contemporaneous lecture on logic, and that his last course should have had as its subject the ontological proof'.

conclusion to this chapter, how the belief that Hegel's 'dialectic of matter' is actually a form of materialism is so strong as to win over even those interpreters who like Marcuse, are neither materialists nor have any leaning towards materialism. Let us now go on from this observation and reinforce the argument with some additional material.

V. Hegel and Scepticism

The Hegelian dialectic of matter is, in its *critical-negative* part, the same dialectic as that of ancient scepticism. Hegel states in the *Lectures on the History of Philosophy* that if there exists a mutually exclusive opposition between the principles of Stoicism and Epicureanism, 'the negative mean to these one-sided principles is the Notion, which, abrogating fixed extremes of determination such as these, moves them and sets them free from a mere state of opposition'.[1] Precisely 'this movement of the Notion, the revival of dialectic – directed as it is against these one-sided principles of abstract thinking and sensation (which are respectively the principles of the Stoa and Epicurus) – we now see in its negative aspect, both in the New Academy and in the Sceptics'.[2]

The meaning of Hegel's argument is already entirely contained in these initial statements. The virtue of scepticism or Pyrrhonism lies in having revived the dialectic. The importance of the dialectic resides in the fact that, by establishing an interrelation between those material or finite determinations which the 'intellect' separates and distinguishes from one another, it renders them *mobile, fluid, unstable*; thus it destroys sense-certainty in the existence of *external* things. Common sense and 'dogmatic' philosophy believe, according to Hegel, in the existence of that which is. For example, they venture to say things like, 'This is yellow'. Now scepticism, with its 'tropes' (i.e., with its 'determinate modes of opposition'), shows that one can ascribe equally well to any given thing two opposing qualities. And since these tropes 'proceed against what we call common belief in

1. Concerning the equation that Hegel, in polemic with Schulze, makes between the positions of the so-called 'New Academy' (Carneades in particular) and the Pyrrhonism of Sextus, cf. G. Della Volpe, *Logica come scienza positiva* (Messina-Florence, 1956), pp. 107–8. In this regard, see also the excellent treatment of the entire problem in N. Merker, *Le origini della logica hegeliana* (Milan, 1961), pp. 185 ff.

2. *H.P.*, p. 310.

the immediate truth of things, and refute it',[3] one can say that even the least polished among them, such as the tropes of antiquity, are 'quite valid . . . against the dogmatism of the common human understanding. . . . This last says directly, "This is so because it is so" ', satisfied with the fact that it 'takes experience as authority'.[4]

The importance, therefore, of ancient scepticism is that it *annihilates matter* by making it dialectical. In the process of dissolving things and the entire finite world, it annihilates, by that very act, the determinations of the 'intellect', or in other words, all those determinate propositions and statements founded on the principle of non-contradiction, to which thought remains bound as long as it considers itself tied to and constricted by the existence of real factual data. Of course, 'older Scepticism is indeed the subjectivity of knowledge only, but this is founded on an elaborately thought out annihilation of everything which is held to be true and existent, so that everything is made transient'.[5]

Thus, 'the essential nature of Scepticism consists in this': that by means of 'the disappearance of all that is objective, all that is held to be true, . . . all that is definite, all that is affirmative',[6] it carries out a liberation of self-consciousness from the enslavement of materialism, i.e. from the enslavement of admitting that consciousness is not everything, but that there exist things outside it. When 'this security disappears', when self-consciousness 'loses its equilibrium', which consists in sticking closely to the things themselves, it 'becomes driven . . . in unrest' and experiences 'fear and anguish'. But 'sceptical self-consciousness is just this subjective liberation from all the truth of objective Being, and from the placing of its existence in anything of the kind; Scepticism thus makes its end the doing away with the unconscious servitude in which the natural self-consciousness is confined, the returning into its simplicity, and, in so far as thought establishes itself in a content, the curing it' and the freeing it from this fixation.[7]

The meaning and weight that this relationship with scepticism has within the framework of Hegel's work is extremely significant

3. ibid., p. 346. 4. ibid., pp. 356–7.
5. ibid., p. 332. 6. ibid., p. 341. 7. loc. cit.

– even if it has not always been noted. Lukács, for example, in *Der junge Hegel* states, with the tone of one saying something self-evident, that although 'Schelling establishes a close relationship between the dialectic and scepticism', 'with Hegel there is certainly no scepticism to be found'.[8] From these remarks it would appear that the question of any relationship between Hegel's dialectic and scepticism could not even arise. In point of fact, the texts say just the opposite. In addition to the fundamental early writing on the *Relationship of Scepticism to Philosophy* (never discussed by Lukács) and the chapter in the *History of Philosophy*, which is basically modelled upon the former, the argument regarding scepticism reappears in a series of decisive places. For example, in the paragraphs of the *Phenomenology* dealing with philosophy, Hegel states that with scepticism, 'thought becomes thinking which wholly annihilates the being of the world with its manifold determinateness'. Scepticism, he adds, is 'this polemical attitude towards the manifold substantiality of things'; it 'makes the objective as such disappear'.[9] In the first book of the *Science of Logic*, the same sophist 'elenchi' that can be regarded as an anticipation of the 'tropes' of scepticism (such as the elenchi of the 'bald man', the 'heap', etc.) are taken up and highlighted as 'proofs' of the passage from quantity into quality and vice versa. There Hegel states that these 'turnabouts' are not 'a pointless or pedantic joke but have their own correctness; they are the product of a mentality which is interested in the phenomena which occur in thinking'.[10] And finally, without considering many other examples, the relationship to scepticism has a crucial role in the first chapter of the *Phenomenology* on 'sense-certainty'.[11] The

8. G. Lukács, *Der junge Hegel*, op. cit., p. 651.

9. *Phen.*, pp. 246–8.

10. *L.*, p. 336.

11. Cf. also J. Hyppolite, *Genèse et structure de la Phénoménologie de l'Esprit de Hegel* (Paris, 1946), p. 84. Hyppolite points out that 'the critique that Hegel presents of this sense-certainty is in large part inspired by Greek philosophy', and that 'one cannot help but be struck by the resemblances between this first dialectic of the *Phenomenology* and that of the ancient Greek philosophers – Parmenides and Zeno. . .'. But despite these allusions (already broadly developed, moreover, by W. Purpus, *Die Dialektik der sinnlichen Gewissheit bei Hegel*, Nürnberg, 1905), Hyppolite only dilutes his remark in a series of more or less superficial notations. The best example of this lack of understanding

contents of this chapter are entirely drawn from ancient scepticism. In fact, the observations made there by Hegel concerning the 'Here', the 'Now', etc., are the same observations made by the sceptics on temporal determinations which we find cited in the *History of Philosophy*: ' ". . . This day is today, but tomorrow is also today, etc.; it is day now but night is also now, etc." '[12]

The great importance that Hegel attributes to ancient scepticism can also be seen in his way of counterposing it to modern scepticism. In subheading 39 of the *Encyclopedia* he says: 'The scepticism of Hume . . . should be clearly marked off from Greek scepticism. Hume takes as the basis of truth the empirical element, feeling and sensation, and proceeds to challenge universal principles and laws, because they are not justified on the basis of sense-perception. So far was ancient scepticism from making feeling and sensation the canon of truth, that it turned against the sensate first of all.'[13]

This question is taken up again in the second note to subheading 81. There Hegel states that ancient scepticism has nothing to do with its modern version. Whereas the latter – which 'partly preceded the Critical Philosophy, and partly sprung out of it' – consists, in fact, 'solely in denying the truth and certitude of the super-sensible, and in pointing to the facts of sense and of immediate sensations as what we have to keep to', ancient scepticism, contrariwise, has a full awareness of the 'nothingness of all finite existence (*der Nichtigkeit alles Endlichen*)'.[14]

Finally, in the *History of Philosophy* the simple observation of this difference is accompanied by explicit comment and an eloquent judgment of value. Having postulated once again that 'the older Scepticism must . . . be distinguished from the modern', Hegel

---

on Hyppolite's part of the meaning of Hegel's argument is that, whereas for the latter the 'dialectic of sense-certainty' has as its objective the destruction of the finite and all things, Hyppolite concludes that 'from now on we are no longer dealing with a "now" or a "here" that are *sui generis* and undefinable, but with a "now" or a "here" which are mediated within themselves, which are *things* (Colletti's emphasis) that contain within themselves both the unity of the universal and the multiplicity of the particular' (p. 98).

12. *H.P.*, pp. 333–4.

13. *En.L.*, p. 82 (translation modified).

14. ibid., p. 151.

specifies that only the former 'is of a true, profound nature; the modern more resembles Epicureanism', i.e. sensationalism, empiricism, or in the final analysis, materialism. Schulze and others 'make it fundamental that we must consider sensuous Being, what is given to us by sensuous consciousness, to be true; all else must be doubted . . . Modern Scepticism is only directed against thought, against the Notion and the Idea, and thus against what is in a higher sense philosophic; it consequently leaves the reality of things quite unquestioned, and merely asserts that from it nothing can be argued as regards thought. But that is not even a peasants' philosophy, for they know that all earthly things are transient, and that thus their Being is as good as their non-being.'[15]

This contraposition of the two scepticisms obviously does not mean that Hegel has no criticisms to make of ancient scepticism. It only means – but this difference is of enormous importance – that in relation to modern scepticism Hegel assumes a stance of total rejection, in the same way, moreover, that he rejects common sense, empiricism, and materialism. In relation to the ancient version, however, he recognizes and affirms the existence of a necessary and organic *relationship* with 'true' philosophy or idealism. In contradistinction to the modern kind, ancient scepticism does not oppose the Idea or Philosophy, but rather is directed against *Unphilosophie*, i.e. the 'dogmatism' of common sense and 'ordinary human understanding'. In his early writing, Hegel says that the contents of its tropes 'show just how far removed (ancient scepticism) is from any tendency opposed to philosophy and how it is solely directed against the dogmatism of everyday human understanding. Not one (of these tropes) strikes at reason and its knowledge, whereas all of them strike only at the finite and the knowledge of the finite, the understanding.'[16]

This orientation is sufficient, by itself, to confer on Greek scepticism a specific role and function. In fact, 'however trivial and commonplace these tropes may appear to be,' – above all the antique ones mentioned above – 'even more trivial and commonplace is the

15. *H.P.*, pp. 331–2.
16. Hegel, *Verhältnis des Skepticismus zur Philosophie*, op. cit., p. 242.

reality of the so-called external objects, that is, immediate knowledge, as when, for instance, I say "This is yellow". Men ought not to talk about philosophy, if in this innocent way they assert the reality of such determinations.' The merit of this scepticism is precisely that it 'was really far from holding things of immediate certainty to be true'; rather, it was precisely 'against the reality of things'[17] that it directed its attacks.

This function as destroyer of matter is exactly what, according to Hegel, establishes an organic relationship between scepticism and philosophy. More precisely, their relationship is this: 'that the former is the dialectic of all that is determinate. The finitude of all conceptions of truth can be shown, for they contain in themselves a negation, and consequently a contradiction. The ordinary universal and infinite is not exalted over this, for the universal which confronts the particular, the indeterminate which opposes the determinate, the infinite which confronts the finite, each form only the one side, and, as such, are only a determinate. Scepticism is similarly directed against the thought of the ordinary understanding which makes determinate differences appear to be ultimate and existent. But the logical Notion is itself this dialectic of Scepticism, for this negativity which is characteristic of Scepticism likewise belongs to the true knowledge of the Idea.'[18]

In other words, what links ancient scepticism to speculative philosophy or idealism and accounts for the fact that scepticism is at one with every true philosophy (*'mit jeder wahren Philosophie der Skepticismus selbst auf's innigste Ein ist'*[19]) or can be regarded as the introduction to and 'the first rung' of philosophy,[20] is the common presence of the dialectic of matter or the finite. 'The demonstration of the contradiction in the finite is an essential point in the speculatively philosophic method.'[21]

What is therefore important to understand is that every 'true' philosophy contains within itself scepticism, for the same reason that it 'necessarily has within itself, at the same time, a negative side,

17. *H.P.*, p. 347.
18. ibid., p. 330.
19. Hegel, *Verhältnis des Skepticismus zur Philosophie*, op. cit., p. 229.
20. ibid., p. 243.
21. *H.P.*, p. 366.

which is turned against everything that is circumscribed (*Beschränkte*) . . . , against the entire foundation of finitude . . . What more perfect and self-sufficient document and system of genuine scepticism could one find than the *Parmenides* in Platonic philosophy?' – that *Parmenides* 'which encompasses and destroys the entire area of knowledge founded on concepts of the understanding (*Wissens durch Verstandesbegriffe*)'. And Hegel concludes thus: 'This Platonic scepticism does not just bring into doubt [particular] truths of the understanding . . . , but arrives at a total negation of all truth derived from such a form of knowledge.'[22]

As far as scepticism true and proper is concerned, the essential operation that it carries out and that serves as an initiation to philosophy is easily described. Confronted with the mutual opposition of the principles of Stoicism and Epicureanism and opposed to the division into, on the one hand, the universal, i.e. abstract thought or the infinite, and on the other, the finite or sensate being – in the sense of an entity independent of and external to the former – scepticism dialecticizes these 'fixed extremes of determination'. In other words, it establishes a relationship between them, so as to 'revive' them and put them in motion until they finally dissolve, having passed over from one into the other.

Common sense and 'dogmatic philosophy' believe that a given thing *is* thus and is *not* otherwise? Well then, scepticism takes up that finite and conjoins it to the infinite, encompasses the individual thing and together with it *everything* that it *is not*, takes up *both* the particular object *and* its opposite. The consequence is that, whereas the infinite is no longer 'one of the two', but becomes a true infinite, i.e. unity of itself and the 'other', the finite, having been taken up with and into the infinite, disappears, i.e. loses its 'rigidity' and becomes 'unstable' – that is to say, it is no longer 'this', but 'both this and that'. It is no longer an external or real object, but only an object *penetrated by thought* (pensato); it is no longer being, but *thought* itself.

Nevertheless, the limitation of scepticism lies in the fact that it does not completely develop this dialectic of matter. As Hegel states,

22. Hegel, *Verhältnis des Skepticismus zur Philosophie*, op. cit., p. 230.

'In Scepticism we now really have an abrogation of the two one-sided systems that we have hitherto dealt with; but this negative remains negative only, and is incapable of passing into an affirmative.'[23] Further on he adds, 'Scepticism deduces no result, nor does it express its negation as anything positive.'[24] Its virtue, as we have seen, is that it represents the 'subjectivity of knowledge', i.e. that it redeems self-consciousness from all servitude to external reality. Except that if, on the one hand, one may say with scepticism, 'the mind has got so far as to immerse itself in itself as that which thinks; now it can comprehend itself in the consciousness of its infinitude as the ultimate';[25] on the other hand, it fails to understand that this final stronghold into which it withdraws is no mere accidental consciousness of the empirical individual, but the criterion and foundation of all reality. As Hegel says, 'In Scepticism we now find that reason has got so far that all that is objective . . . has disappeared for self-consciousness. The abyss of the self-consciousness of pure thought has swallowed up everything, and made entirely clear the basis of thought.'[26] Except that once this great work has been achieved and the freeing of Reason from all external constriction has been brought about, scepticism turns this unity of consciousness into 'something that is perfectly empty, and the actual filling in is any content that one chooses'.[27] It fails to see that, just as the work of destruction and annihilation is carried out by bringing the finite into the infinite, so the opposite of this negation is, at the same time, the expansion of the infinite into a true infinite, its interlinking with the 'other' and, therefore, a movement out from itself towards earthly existence. As Hegel makes clear, 'The speculative Idea . . . is in its nature nothing finite or determinate, it has not the one-sided character which pertains to the proposition, for it has the absolute negative in itself; in itself it is round, it contains this determinate and its opposite in their ideality in itself.'[28] But 'in so far as this Idea, as the unity of these opposites, is itself again outwardly a determinate, . . . it again places itself in unity with the determinates

23. *H.P.*, pp. 310–11.
24. ibid., p. 371.
25. ibid., pp. 371–2.
26. ibid., p. 371.
27. loc. cit.
28. ibid., p. 367.

opposed to it',[29] i.e. with that finite whose enclusion within the idea engendered the idea itself – not, however, in order to have the finite prevail *per se*, but rather to make it the *body* and vehicle for its (the Idea's) own incarnation or earthly 'exposition'.

In short, scepticism errs in not expressing its negation as something positive. This accounts for why, having dissolved everything in Reason and, therefore, in that 'logical Notion' which 'is itself the dialectic of scepticism', it is then unable to translate this negative into a positive, the logical into the ontological – i.e., it is unable to state that Reason *is*, or that the infinite, the Notion '*is* and *is there*, present before us'. Since in scepticism this repudiation, this negation of the world never becomes the epiphany of God, scepticism reveals itself to be only a part or the 'first rung' of philosophy, but not the true philosophy in its entirety. For if, as we have seen, it can be said that philosophy, in so far as it has a *negative side* turned against all that is finite, contains scepticism within itself, it is also true that it contains scepticism only in the sense that the convex contains the concave – since scepticism itself represents in philosophy 'the negative side of knowledge of the absolute', i.e. that side which 'presupposes in a direct way reason as the positive side'.[30] Which means that, whereas scepticism confines itself to pointing out the contradiction in the finite, 'Platonic scepticism' and together with it every 'true' philosophy recognize that 'the *non-being* of the finite is the *being* of the absolute', or that precisely 'because the finite is the inherently self-contradictory opposition, because it is *not* . . . the absolute is'.[31]

The dialectic of matter or the destruction of the finite is, therefore, the true initiation to philosophy. One cannot philosophize without having consciousness that the world is ephemeral and devoid of value. But in true philosophy, this scepticism towards everything that is earthly is only preparation for the highest bliss. The one cannot exist without the other. 'Thus although the Platonic *Parmenides* presents itself only from the negative side, Ficinus is quite

29. loc. cit.
30. Hegel, *Verhältnis des Skepticismus zur Philosophie*, pp. 230–1.
31. *L.*, p. 443.

right in observing that whoever takes up the holy study of the former must prepare himself in advance through a cleansing of the mind and a freeing of the spirit before he can hope to tap the holy secrets of the work.'[32]

We shall now leave Hegel and turn our attention to one of his interpreters. What in Plato, Ficinus, and Hegel (naturally with technical and historical differences that no one would dream of dismissing) is a negation of the world and an affirmation of God, becomes, in the hands of Marcuse a . . . *theory of revolution*. The 'understanding', i.e. common sense and science, which adhere to things and real factual data, represent positivism and the safe and sound world of the bourgeoisie; they stand for conformism and preservation, and that 'false' and 'self-assured' consciousness which sticks closely to objects, knowing full well that if 'this security disappears', it will be 'driven into unrest' and will undergo 'fear and anguish'. Contrariwise, Reason, which *denies* that things exist outside of thought and states that things are truly 'real' when they are no longer things but thoughts – this Reason represents the destruction of the established order. The 'intellect' is *positive thought*, thought that recognizes existing reality. Reason, on the other hand, which negates the world . . . for the sake of the Idea, is *negative thought*. The 'Understanding' (intellect) is Reaction – *Reason is Revolution*. As Marcuse says, 'Dialectical thought thus becomes negative in itself. Its function is to break down the self-assurance and self-contentment of common sense, to undermine the sinister confidence in the power and language of facts, to demonstrate that unfreedom is so much at the core of things that the development of their internal contradictions leads necessarily to qualitative change: the explosion and catastrophe of the established state of affairs.'[33]

As usual, it is the principle of non-contradiction that is the cause of all the trouble. The facts claim to be themselves and nothing else. They stubbornly refuse to embrace their opposite. Contrariwise, 'the liberating function of negation in philosophical thought

32. Hegel, *Verhältnis des Skepticismus zur Philosophie*, op. cit., p. 231.
33. Marcuse, op. cit., p. ix.

depends upon the recognition that the negation is a positive act: that-which-is *repels* that-which-is-not and, in doing so, repels its own real possibilities. Consequently, to express and define that-which-is on its own terms is to distort and falsify reality. Reality is other and more than that codified in the logic and language of facts. Here is the inner link between dialectical thought and the effort of avant-garde literature: the effort to break the power of facts over the word, and to speak a language which is not the language of those who establish, enforce, and benefit from the facts.'[34]

Just as in Hegel matter is the great enemy, so here it is the facts, the very data of actual experience. 'This power of facts,' Marcuse warns, 'is an oppressive power.'[35] And just as ancient scepticism was, for Hegel, the 'first rung' of philosophy because it was the liberation of self-consciousness from the 'servitude' of having to acknowledge that there exist things outside of us; similarly, for Marcuse, 'dialectical thought starts with the experience that the world is unfree. . . . The principle of dialectic drives thought beyond the limits of philosophy. For to comprehend reality means to comprehend what things really are, and this in turn means rejecting their mere factuality. Rejection is the process of thought as well as of action'.[36]

On the other hand, the evil genius who incarnates the principle of conservation is Hume. 'If Hume was to be accepted,' the facts had to be accepted; and if the facts had to be accepted, 'the claim of reason to organize reality had to be rejected', i.e. its claim to revolutionize the world and to destroy all things. Hegel was perfectly right, then, in criticizing and rejecting Hume's thought. The latter's philosophy 'confined men within the limits of "the given", within the existing order of things and events'. 'The result was not only scepticism but conformism.'[37]

As for Kant, he is a prisoner of the most antiquated kind of empiricism. 'Kant adopted the view of the empiricists that all human knowledge begins with and terminates in experience'; for him, 'experience alone provides *the material* for the concepts of reason'. 'There is no stronger empiricist statement than that which

34. ibid., p. x. 35. ibid., p. xiv. 36. ibid., p. ix. 37. ibid., pp. 19–20.

opens his *Critique of Pure Reason*. "All thought must, directly or indirectly, . . . relate ultimately to intuitions, and therefore, with us, to sensibility, because in no other way can an object be given to us."'[38] Contrariwise, 'Hegel's concept of reason thus has a distinctly critical and polemical character'[39] against reality in its entirety. Hegel's philosophy is 'a negative philosophy'. 'It is originally motivated by the conviction that the given facts that appear to common sense as the positive index of truth are in reality the negation of truth, so that truth can only be established by their destruction.'[40]

All of this is an extraordinary example of the heterogenesis of objectives. With Marcuse, spiritualistic disdain for the finite and the terrestrial world comes to life again as the philosophy of revolution, or, more exactly, as the philosophy of . . . revolt. One no longer struggles against determinant socio-historical institutions – such as, maybe, 'profit', 'income', 'monopoly', or perhaps even 'socialist bureaucracy'; rather one struggles against objects and things (*gli oggetti e le cose*). We are crushed by the oppressive power of facts. We suffocate in the 'enslavement' which forces us to acknowledge that there are things outside of us. 'Elles sont là, grotesques, têtues, géantes et . . . je suis au milieu des Choses, les innomables. Seul, sans mots, sans défenses, elles m'environnent, sous moi, derrière moi, au-dessus de moi. Elles n'exigent rien, elles ne s'imposent pas: elles sont là.'[41] Confronted with this spectacle of things, indignation wells up inside us and becomes Nausea. Only too easy to say glibly: 'there are the roots of a tree!' '*J'étais assis, un peu voûté, la tête basse, seul en face de cette masse noire et noueuse, entièrement brute et qui me faisait peur.*' Here is the absurdity that cries out to heaven for vengeance: '*ces masses monstrueuses et molles, en désordre – nues, d'une effrayante et obscène nudité* (p. 180).'[42] The absurdity is not Roquentin,

38. ibid., p. 21. 39. ibid., p. 11. 40. ibid., pp. 26–7.

41. J.-P. Sartre, *La nausée* (Paris, 1963), p. 177. English translation, *Nausea*, translated by Lloyd Alexander (New York, 1959), p. 169: 'They are there, grotesque, headstrong, gigantic and . . . I am in the midst of things, nameless things. Alone, without words, defenceless, they surround me, are beneath me, behind me, above me. They demand nothing, they don't impose themselves: they are there.'

42. ibid., pp. 171–2: 'I was sitting, stooping forward, head bowed, alone in front of this black knotty mass, entirely beastly, which frightened me. . . soft, monstrous masses, all in disorder – naked, in a frightful, obscene nakedness.'

trailing his poor petit-bourgeois self-indulgence about the public gardens, and giving consolation to Daladier or even to Laval – what is *absurd* are the roots of the tree. '*L'absurdité, ce n'était pas une idée dans ma tête, ni un souffle de voix, mais ce long serpent mort à mes pieds, ce serpent de bois. Serpent ou griffe ou racine ou serre de vautour, peu importe. Et sans rien formuler nettement, je comprenais que j'avais trouvé la clef de l'Existence, la clef de mes Nausées, de ma propre vie* (p. 182).'[43]

The revolution, then, lies not in an overturning and transformation of *social relationships*, but in the annihilation of *matter* and the destruction of *things*. In Hegel's original conception we know what was the meaning and function of this 'destruction': the world was negated in order to give way to the immanentization of God; the finite was 'idealized' so that the Christian *Logos* could incarnate itself and so that the infinite could pass over from the beyond into the here and now. In the case of Marcuse, however, who has quite lost the meaning of Hegel's 'secularization of Christianity', all that remains of the old theology is the nihilistic will to a destruction of the world.

The Revolution represents the annihilation of things. The Manifesto that proclaims this is in Hegel's early writings. It is the appeal, blatantly romantic and Schellingesque, to the 'Night' and 'Nothing' contained in his early writing on the *Differenz*.[44] In Marcuse's words: '. . . In his first philosophical writings, Hegel intentionally emphasizes the negative function of reason: its destruction of the fixed and secure world of common sense and understanding. The absolute is referred to as "Night" and "Nothing", to contrast it to the clearly defined objects of everyday life. Reason

43. ibid., p. 173: 'Absurdity was not an idea in my head, or the sound of a voice, only this long serpent dead at my feet, this wooden serpent. Serpent or claw or root or vulture's talon, what difference does it make. And without formulating anything clearly, I understood that I had found the key to Existence, the key to my Nauseas, to my own life.'

44. G. W. F. Hegel, *Differenz des Fichteschen und Schellingschen Systems der Philosophie*, in *Sämtliche Werke*, op. cit., vol. I, p. 49: 'The Absolute is the Night . . . ; – Nothing, the first element from which all Being, all the manifold of the finite has come forth.' And p. 50: 'Reflection annihilates itself, all Being and all that is circumscribed in so far as it establishes a relationship between them and the Absolute.'

signifies the "absolute annihilation" of the common-sense world. For, as we have already said, the struggle against common sense is the beginning of speculative thinking, and the loss of everyday security is the origin of philosophy.'[45]

In short, the revolution is the *sceptical* destruction of common sense and of its 'dogmatic' confidence in the existence of the world. 'The first criterion of reason', Marcuse states, referring explicitly to the writing on the *Relationship of Scepticism to Philosophy*, 'is a distrust of matter-of-fact authority. Such distrust is the real scepticism that Hegel designates as "the free portion" of every true philosophy'.[46]

On the other hand, the reappearance of Pyrrhonism in the first chapter of the *Phenomenology of Mind* (the dialectic of the 'Here' and the 'Now') and the entire course of the following chapters are also considered by Marcuse – in accordance with a habit of interpretation whose origins it will be worthwhile examining later on – as an anticipation of the very core of Marx's argument on the 'fetishism' and 'reification' connected with capitalist commodity production. 'The first three sections of the *Phenomenology* are a critique of positivism and, even more, of "reification" . . . We borrow the term "reification" from the Marxist theory, where it denotes the fact that all relations between men in the world of capitalism appear as relations between things', in that 'Hegel hit upon the same fact within the dimension of philosophy'. 'Common sense and traditional scientific thought take the world as a totality of things, more or less existing *per se*, and seek the truth in objects that are taken to be independent of the knowing subject. This is more than an epistemological attitude; it is as pervasive as the practice of men and leads them to accept the feeling that they are secure only in knowing and handling objective facts.'[47]

The conclusion is inescapable. 'Fetishism' and 'reification' are a product of common sense and 'traditional' scientific thought. The factory of these 'fetishes' does not reside in capitalism, but in the works of Bacon and Galileo.

Our excursus into Marcuse is concluded. To the extent that his

45. Marcuse, op. cit., p. 48. 46. ibid., p. 46. 47. ibid., p. 112.

argument makes sense, it reintroduces us to the Hegelian antithesis of 'intellect' and 'reason', 'dogmatism' and philosophy, materialism and idealism. For Hegel, Marcuse writes, 'the distinction between understanding and reason is the same as that between common sense and speculative thinking, between undialectical reflection and dialectical knowledge. The operations of the understanding yield the usual type of thinking that prevails in everyday life as well as in science.'[48]

This antithesis, as we have seen, is also the heart and nucleus of so-called 'dialectical materialism'. The only variant, in this case, is that, having identified dogmatism in Hegel's sense (*qua* the materialist principle of non-contradiction) with metaphysics (that is, with 'dogmatism' as understood by the materialist tradition), Engels is forced to conclude by ascribing the origin of metaphysics to science and common sense itself, i.e. to the way of thinking of 'everyday life'.

The chapter that deals with scepticism in the *Lectures on the History of Philosophy* was jotted down and commented upon by Lenin in his *Philosophical Notebooks*. Of the two notes that in this regard are worth bringing out, the first concerns Hegel's remark according to which 'Sceptical tropes . . . concern that which is called a dogmatic philosophy – not in the sense of its having a positive content, but as asserting something determinate. . . '.[49]

The meaning of this statement has already been amply explained and commented. Scepticism, Hegel says, liquidates the dogmatism of the 'intellect'. The 'intellect' is dogmatic because it makes the finite *absolute*. The meaning of this term is the same as its etymology: *solutus ab*. . . , freed from limitations, existing on its own, and therefore unrestricted and independent. The 'rational' Notion, for example, is termed by Hegel the *absolute* Notion or speculative Idea because, as opposed to the intellect or 'understanding', 'reason' is the Idea freed from all external limitations, the Idea 'round within itself', *independent* and self-subsisting, containing the 'other' within itself. This meaning is explicit (as in any number or other places) in the closing to subheading 60 of the *Encyclopedia*: '. . . The principle

48. ibid., p. 44.

49. *H.P.*, p. 363.

of independence of Reason, or of its absolute self-subsistence, is made a general principle of philosophy. . . .'[50]

In the same sense and in the same way, when Hegel says that the 'intellect' makes an absolute out of the finite, he means that the understanding takes up the finite as *independent* and *external* to the infinite; i.e. it conceives empirico-sense being as a *positive* being, existing on its own, not created or 'posited' by thought.

Now, Lenin's note to the passage cited above, in which Hegel is clearly polemizing with materialism, is the following: 'Hegel *against the absolute*! Here we have the germ of dialectical materialism.'[51] It is clear that the *Philosophical Notebooks* are what they are: notes and hasty notations, taken at the moment of his reading, without second thoughts and without going back to them. Nonetheless, for what it is worth, this first annotation indicates a singular habit and attitude on the part of a 'dialectical materialist': the belief that *dogmatism* is thinking in a determinate mode (*il pensare determinato*). This is an attitude – it hardly needs pointing out – that rests on the famous observation in *Anti-Dühring* that for the metaphysical, i.e. dogmatic, mode of thought, or 'so-called common sense', 'a thing either exists, or it does not exist' and 'it is equally impossible for a thing to be itself and at the same time something else'.[52]

The second annotation, which concerns Kant, is no less unsatisfactory. Lenin transcribes in the margin, with obvious agreement, Hegel's statement that 'criticism is the most wanton dogmatism of all' ('To the criticism which knows no implicit, nothing absolute,' Hegel says, 'all knowledge of implicit existence as such is held to be dogmatism, while it is the most wanton dogmatism of all . . .'[53]). It is true enough that Hegel's passage goes on, after the part cited by us, to call into question the Kantian theory of the 'thing in itself'. But, as is the case moreover throughout the *Notebooks*, it seems that Lenin is able to see only this aspect of Kant's thought, as if the *Critique* did not contain anything else. It is the same position –

50. *En.L.*, pp. 118–19.
51. Lenin, *Philosophical Notebooks*, op. cit., p. 301.
52. Engels, *Anti-Dühring*, op. cit., p. 28.
53. *H.P.*, p. 364.

rudimentary, but certainly more reasonable – adopted by him several years previously in the beginning of Chapter IV ('The criticism of Kantianism from the Left and from the Right') of *Materialism and Empirio-Criticism*: 'The principal feature of Kant's philosophy is the reconciliation of materialism with idealism. . . . When Kant assumes that something outside us, a thing-in-itself, corresponds to our ideas, he is a materialist. When he declares this thing-in-itself to be unknowable, . . . he is an idealist'; and again 'recognizing experience, sensations, as the only source of our knowledge, Kant is directing his philosophy towards sensationalism, and . . . under certain conditions, towards materialism'.[54] This very position is entirely abandoned in the *Notebooks*, where Lenin is always, or almost always, in agreement with Hegel against Kant.

It is not necessary to cite here the views of Engels (or of Plekhanov) on Hume and Kant, since they are so well known.[55] For them Hume and Kant represent, in general, the worst element – agnosticism, scepticism, idealism, etc. Finally, in Lukács this tendency – which in Engels and Lenin is at least mitigated by the 'non-professional' character of their 'philosophic' activity – assumes proportions defying all reason, or even ordinary good sense. Kant is at the origin of all error. Anything is better than his philosophy, even 'the attempt at a dialectical revival of the Platonic theory of the forms' made by Schelling.[56] Even 'this idealist objectivism represents an advance with respect to Kant'. In fact 'this change of direction gives Schelling the possibility of proclaiming anew the knowability of things in themselves on the basis of an objective idealism; thus, present in his work are tendencies towards objectivity – despite all the irrational mysticism – and a tendency to acknowledge the knowability of the external world that go far beyond Kant.'[57]

I must state right away that the possible accusation of a 'return to Kant' leaves me altogether indifferent. I am talking about the

54. V. I. Lenin, *Materialism and Empirio-Criticism* (New York, 1927), p. 200.

55. For the importance ascribed to Hume by the modern philosophy of science, cf. L. Geymonat, *Storia del pensiero filosofico* (Milan, 1956), vol. III, p. 321, who opposes Hume's concept of 'rationality' to that of traditional metaphysics, and, in particular, to that of Spinoza and Hegel.

56. G. Lukács, *Prolegomeni a un'estetica marxista*, op. cit., p. 35. 57. ibid., p. 55.

Critique of Pure Reason and not that of *Practical Reason.* In addition, this discussion is proceeding in a situation where the entire framework of traditional philosophical Marxism has been shattered. What matters to us here is that a crucial problem is at stake. What does 'dogmatism' mean? What is 'metaphysics'? Is there any 'critique' or *scepsis* that is salutary?

VI. Scepticism about Matter and Scepticism about Reason

The alternative, in this regard, is simple: either one assumes that the real objects to be known are *given*, or else it has to be that the known object is 'already' given *qua* knowledge itself (as 'innate' knowledge). With Hegel this alternative is absolutely clear: the negation of the possibility that thought could have a premiss in reality – which is the achievement of ancient scepticism – constitutes the 'negative side' that every 'true' philosophy has within itself; but this negative side 'presupposes in a direct way Reason as the positive side (*setzt unmittelbar die Vernunft als die positive Seite voraus*)'. Reason as a *positive*; i.e. as an entity existing on its own, independent, and therefore existing as an *individual* object – not as a category or *function* of another that has to be unified or thought out, but as a self-sufficient *reality* that is 'round in itself'.

Reason is 'round' because it 'already' contains the other within itself. It represents 'the identity of identity and non-identity'. It is, therefore, the *identity* of thought and being. But if the negation of premisses in reality, the negation of premisses that are external because independent, and independent because qualitatively (in reality) *different* from thought, implies the identity of thought and being, it is also clear that that negation leads to the assumption that knowledge is already formed 'from the beginning of time'. If indeed knowledge must issue forth from the synthesis or union of the two (thought and being), and these two are, however, identical with one another, i.e. forever united, that can only mean that their union has occurred *ab aeterno*, and that knowledge is already fully realized from the beginning of time. Knowledge has been produced before us, behind our backs. We find, at birth, that knowledge is *given* to us, just as in the other case we find that the world apprehended by our senses is given to us.

By whom is this knowledge given? The *exoteric* reply is that, on the whole, it is given by the parish priest. In the case of particularly unfortunate philosophers, it may even be given by their father. 'Why do you believe?' Jaspers asks himself. 'Because my father told me. Mutatis mutandis, this answer of Kierkegaard applies also to philosophy.' In general, however, Jaspers is right when he says: '*der philosophische Glaube ist in Überlieferung*' (philosophical faith is in tradition).[1]

The other reply, the *esoteric* one, is innatism: Knowledge is God, and the divine *Logos* is within us. As stated in the *Encyclopedia*: 'With reference to the *immediate knowledge of God*, of legal and *ethical principles*. . . , whatever form . . . we give to the original spontaneity. . . , it is a matter of general experience that *education* or development is required to bring out into consciousness what is therein contained. It was so even with the *Platonic recollection*: and the Christian rite of baptism, although a sacrament, involves the additional obligation of a Christian upbringing. In short, religion and morals, however much they may be faith or *immediate* knowledge, are still on every side conditioned by the *mediating process* which is termed development, education, culture.'[2]

Here, as one can see, immediate knowledge and its 'original spontaneity' are not at all negated; it is merely said that they require mediation. Hegel continues thus: '. . . One empirical objection was raised against the doctrine of *Innate ideas*. All men, it was said, must have these ideas; they must have, for example, the principle of contradiction present in their consciousness – they must know it; 'but this objection', he adds, which is 'completely valid against the theory of immediate knowledge,' i.e. against those like Jacobi who reject the mediation, 'can be laid down to a misconception; for the determinations in question, though innate, need not on that account have the *form* of ideas or conceptions of something known'.[3]

1. Karl Jaspers, *The Perennial Scope of Philosophy*, translated by Ralph Manheim (New York, 1949), p. 20.

2. *En.L.*, p. 130 (translation modified).

3. ibid., p. 131 (translation modified).

This is the place where innatism, i.e., the *presupposition* of ideas – which for Hegel, of course, are the Idea – has its truly correct formulation: knowledge is already given; mediation and development serve only to acquire 'consciousness (of) what is therein contained'. In other words – and here it is best to recall Kant's views on and against 'a priori analytic judgments' – the mediation, i.e. culture and philosophy, has merely the task of *explicating the implicit*. In fact, as Hegel states explicitly, 'the whole procedure of philosophizing, being a methodical, i.e. necessary one, is merely the explicit *positing* of what is already contained in a Notion'.[4] To suggest, however, that one should go back beyond the Notion or knowledge itself, i.e. pose the problem of their *origin*, would be absurd, since *the Notion was never born* (as Hegel states in a passage from the *Encyclopedia* previously examined: 'It is not *we* who frame the Notions. The Notion is not something which is originated at all . . . It is a mistake to imagine that the objects which form the content of our mental ideas come first and that our subjective agency then supervenes, and . . . frames Notions of them.'[5]).

One or the other, therefore: either one presupposes the world, or else one has to take as a presupposition knowledge itself. Hegel's philosophy, which begins without (external) presuppositions, begins, in actual fact, by presupposing itself, i.e. knowledge, the Idea, the *Logos* or God. 'The philosophy,' Feuerbach says, 'that begins with thought *without reality*, ends consequently *mit einer gedankenlosen Realität*', i.e. with a reality that is not mediated or verified by thought. It is altogether preferable, he goes on to say, 'to *begin* with *non-philosophy* (*Unphilosophie*) and end with philosophy than, contrariwise, like so many of Germany's "great" philosophers – *exempla sunt odiosa* – to *open* their careers with philosophy and to *conclude* them with non-philosophy'.[6]

These formulations clearly anticipate the remark made by Marx in the last manuscript of 1844: '. . . Despite its thoroughly negative and critical appearance, . . . there is already implicit in the *Phenomenology*, as a germ, as a potentiality and a secret, the uncritical

4. ibid., p. 163 (translation modified).

5. ibid., pp. 293–4.

6. L. Feuerbach. *Sämtliche Werke* (ed. Bolin und Jodl), Vol. II, p. 208.

positivism and uncritical idealism of Hegel's later works – the philosophical dissolution and restoration of the existing empirical world.'[7]

This is the high point attained by the materialist tradition in its critical consciousness concerning the nature of *dogmatism.* To deny the existence of premisses in reality (those premisses which are discussed at the beginning of *The German Ideology*: 'The premisses from which we begin are not arbitrary ones, not dogmas, but real premisses from which abstraction can only be made in the imagination'[8]), amounts to taking up the Notion or the Idea as that which is absolute and without limiting conditions, as an independent entity unto itself. But in order to be independent and therefore to count not just as reason but also as *reality*, the Idea must present itself as an individual object, i.e. it has to restore in an acritical fashion the sense phenomena previously transcended; it thereby turns the positive or individual, which is, properly speaking, the object to be understood and explained, into the body or 'vessel' of the absolute's exposition (for Hegel, Marx writes, 'not the logic of the thing, but rather logic's thing, is the philosophical moment. Logic does not serve as a proof of the State, but rather the State serves as a proof of logic').[9]

The dilemma outlined at the beginning of this chapter is formulated in explicit terms by Marx. If one denies that there exist premisses in reality for thought, then one is forced to take up knowledge itself as a *presupposed and given reality.* In so doing, those empirical premisses, previously negated and transcended, return acritically (i.e., not scrutinized and not mediated by thought) as mere predicates or incarnations of the Idea. Marx writes in *The German Ideology*: 'If for a moment Sancho' – i.e. Stirner – 'abstracts from all his rubbish about thought, . . . he has divested himself for a moment of all dogmatic presuppositions, but now for the first time the *real* presuppositions begin to exist for him. And these real presuppositions are also the presuppositions of his *dogmatic* presuppositions which, whether he likes it or not, will reappear to him

7. K. Marx, *Early Writings*, op. cit., p. 201.
8. K. Marx and F. Engels, *The German Ideology* (New York, 1947), pp. 6–7.
9. K. Marx, *Werke*, cit., Vol. I, p. 216.

together with the real ones so long as he does not obtain other real, and with them also other dogmatic presuppositions, or so long as he does not recognise the real presuppositions materialistically as presuppositions of his thinking, whereupon the dogmatic ones will disappear altogether.'[10]

The opposite natures of *dogmatism* and *critical thought* are here clearly specified. Dogmatism is the presupposition of the Idea, the assumption that knowledge is already *given* (as Feuerbach says, 'That philosophy which does not presuppose anything, presupposes itself'; it is 'that philosophy which begins directly with itself'[11]). This presupposition of the Idea means at the same time – obviously – the denial of premisses in reality and the affirmative statement that the *content* itself of knowledge is independent of experience, i.e. the assumption (as Kant says) of 'knowledge which transcends the world of the senses, and where experience can neither guide nor correct us, . . . knowledge which we possess without knowing whence it came, and (en)trust to principles the origin of which is unknown'.[12] Critical thought, contrariwise, is that thought which – precisely because it does not presuppose itself as a kind of 'original' knowledge or as having its contents 'already' within itself – can scrutinize both its own contents, preventing them from imposing themselves surreptitiously or 'sub rosa', and also scrutinize itself at work. That is, it can examine the way in which knowledge is produced and formed – which is, precisely, the fundamental critical problem of the formation and origin of the knowledge that we already possess.

Dogmatism is metaphysics; critical thought is materialism. The antithesis, with respect to Hegel, could not be more pronounced. Metaphysics is the *identity of thought and being*; its contents are 'already' within thought, they are independent of experience, i.e. supersensible. *Ergo*, form and content are forever united, knowledge is already formed, and it is impossible to pose the problem of the origin of the knowledge that we possess. Critical thought, contrariwise, identifies itself with the position that presupposes the *hetero-*

10. K. Marx and F. Engels, *The German Ideology* (Moscow, 1964), pp. 489–90.
11. L. Feuerbach, op. cit., Vol. II, p. 209
12. I. Kant, op. cit., p. 5.

geneity, i.e. a real and not formal (or purely "logical') difference, between being and thought. Thereby one can pose the 'critical' problem of the origin of our knowledge, inasmuch as knowledge itself is not already given. Which in turn presupposes that the two elements that are to be united have not always been united – presupposes, in a word, that the sources of knowledge are *two*: the spontaneity of the mind *and* whatever data are given to the receptivity of our senses.

In the first case, the relationship of thought to being coincides with the relationship of thought to itself. The passage from being to thought, from empirical reality to knowledge, from the concrete to the abstract, presents itself as a passage *within* knowledge: from the *cognitio inferior* to the *cognitio superior*; from implicit *knowledge* to explicit knowledge, from the obscure and confused ideas of the senses (remember Kant's critique of Leibniz and Wolff), to clear and distinct ideas. All of which means that *epistemology*, i.e. the theory of the relationship between the two elements of knowledge, is reduced to logic, i.e. to the theory of thought alone. In the second case, however, since thought is only *one* of the two elements, logic comes to fall within epistemology, i.e. presents itself as one of the two parts of that 'theory of elements' or *Elementarlehre*, into which the theory of knowledge of the *Critique of Pure Reason* is subdivided; for, as Lenin once saw clearly, it is crucial from the critico-materialist point of view 'to regard our knowledge (not) as ready-made and unalterable, but (to) determine how *knowledge* emerges from *empirical reality*, how incomplete, inexact knowledge becomes more complete and more exact'.[13]

Despite the unsolicited gift of a *Widerspiegelungstheorie*, which Lukács (as well as Kojève and Marcuse) have tried to make him, clearly Hegel's thought contains nothing of the kind. The pages of his *Science of Logic* are, as usual, of exemplary clarity (and the

13. V. I. Lenin, *Materialism and Empirio-Criticism*, op. cit., p. 99. The term *empirical reality* has been substituted for the term used by Lenin's translator, *ignorance*. Lenin's term, which is the equivalent of the German *Unwissen* and the Italian *non-sapere* (this is the term used by Colletti in his text), does not refer to the passage from ignorance to enlightenment – which is a pedagogic problem – but rather to the epistemological problem of how one moves from non-thought (empirical reality) to thought. (Trans.)

polemic against Kant is more than ever in evidence): 'Hitherto, the Notion of logic has rested on the separation, presupposed once and for all in the ordinary consciousness, of the *content* of cognition and its *form*, or of *truth and certainty*. First, it is assumed that the material of knowing is present on its own account as a ready-made world apart from thought, that thinking on its own is empty and comes as an external form to the said material, fills itself with it and only thus acquires a content and so becomes real knowing. Further, these two constituents – for they are supposed to be related to each other as constituents, and cognition is compounded from them in a mechanical or at best chemical fashion – are appraised as follows: the object is regarded as something complete and finished on its own account, something which can entirely dispense with thought for its actuality, while thought on the other hand is regarded as defective because it has to complete itself with a material and moreover, as a pliable indeterminate form, has to adapt itself to its material. Truth is the agreement of thought with the object, and in order to bring about this agreement – for it does not exist on its own account – thinking is supposed to adapt and accommodate itself to the object.'[14]

The reader has probably already grasped the point of the argument. If *scepsis towards matter* (Pyrrhonism, ancient scepticism) is a moment that is indispensable to philosophy *qua* idealism, the critico-materialist point of view cannot help but imply, contrariwise, a *scepsis towards reason*. The basis of this scepsis or 'critique of reason' lies in the very principle of materialism: the *heterogeneity* of thought and being, the extra-logical character of *existence*. Existence is not a predicate, it is not a concept. The conditions as a result of which something is given us to be known are not to be confused with the conditions as a result of which this something is taken up into thought; the *possibility in reality* is not identical with the *logical possibility*; 'logical process' is not to be confused with 'process in reality'.

This distinction between logical object and object in reality, between *Objekt* and *Gegenstand*, is properly termed a *scepsis* for it

14. *L.*, p. 44.

implies that reason is *per se* a *negative* (just as, contrariwise, for 'Platonic scepticism' the finite is a negative) – i.e. *devoid* of reality. Reason does not have reality 'already within itself'. Reason is a form, or more exactly, a function of something else. It itself is not a subject, but the predicate of a real subject. The signs of admiration and agreement with which all 'dialectical materialists' have always greeted the Hegelian polemic against Kant's 'formalism', only go to show that in order to be a modern materialist it is, unfortunately, not enough to make a simple decision of the 'will'. Hegel's claim to a form of thought that is 'rich in content', his statement that thought has the determinate or the 'difference' within itself, and is therefore the concrete, is the same thing as his proposition that 'the finite is ideal'. This explains – it may be said en passant – how Hegel's critique of 'logical formalism' is absolutely coherent even when it appears at first sight contradictory, due to the fact that at times it directs against 'formalism' the criticism of *absence of content* and, at other times, that of *absence of form*.[15]

15. Hegel's critique of so-called 'laws of thought' or of 'logical formalism' follows two lines that are apparently contradictory. The first line is that of the 'emptiness of logical forms'. Logical forms are 'abstract' because *devoid of content*. 'What is purely formal without reality is an *ens intellectus*, or empty abstraction without the internal diremption (or difference) which would be nothing else but the content' (*Phen.*, p. 329). This criticism returns again in the *Science of Logic*: 'the emptiness of logical forms' derives from the fact that they 'lack a substantial content – a matter which would be substantial in itself' (*L.*, p. 48). On the other hand, on the page following the one just cited of the *Phenomenology*, Hegel *appears* to grossly contradict himself. He now makes the objection that logical laws are *devoid of form*: '. . . It is not content that they lack, for they have a specific content; they lack rather form, which is their essential nature. In point of fact it is not for the reason that they are to be merely formal and are not to have any content, that these laws are not the truth of thought; it is rather for the opposite reason. It is because in their specificity, i.e. just as a content with the form removed, they want to pass for something absolute' (*Phen.*, p. 330). The contradiction is only apparent. In actual fact, Hegel's requirement that logic be a *science of reality*, and not a purely formal one, coincides with his requirement that what is recognized as true, objective content should not be a content external to thought, but within it (the ideal nature of the finite). 'When logic is taken as the science of thinking in general, it is understood that this thinking constitutes the *mere form* of a cognition, that logic abstracts from all *content* and that the so-called second *constituent* belonging to cognition, namely its *matter*, must come from elsewhere; and that since this matter is absolutely independent of logic, this latter can provide only the formal conditions of genuine cognition and cannot in its own self contain any real truth, nor even be the *pathway* to real truth because just that which is

Now, the two essential cornerstones of this critique of metaphysical or idealist dogmatism were laid down, for the first time, in the *Critique of Pure Reason.* The first of these emerges, as is known, in the claim that the sensate has a *positive* character (here, one need only look at the note that concludes section 7 of *Anthropologie in pragmatischer Hinsicht* with its violent polemic against Leibniz, who, as a 'follower of the Platonic school', 'considered sense data as merely a *void*', i.e. as something *negative* devoid of its own reality). What this means is, that by virtue of the heterogeneous or extra-logical nature of the sensate or existent, the relationship thought–being cannot be reduced to the simple coherence of thought with itself. The second emerges in that admirable act of theoretical destruction – a true monument of modern scepticism – which Kant carries out with respect to all the old metaphysics (the metaphysics that Hegel mourns in the preface to the *Science of Logic*). With respect to the 'productive use' of formal logic (formal logic treated as an 'organ' for the production of objective knowledge), Kant criticizes the transposition of the logical into the ontological, or the arbitrary and dogmatic upgrading of the mental or subjective into the 'essence' of the world, i.e. of the concept into the foundation or substratum of reality – a critique without which the very expression 'modern thought' would have no meaning whatsoever.

These two crucial critical propositions come together in the admirable pages that conclude the 'Analytic of Principles' – the pages in the 'Note to the Amphiboly of Concepts of Reflection'. The two complementary features of dogmatism's modus operandi – the idealization of the world and the transformation of logical ideas

---

essential in truth, its content, lies outside logic' (*L.*, pp. 43–4). In other words, logic is for Hegel a science of reality not simply because it has a content of its own, but because it is 'content alone which has absolute truth, or, if one still wanted to employ the word matter, it is the veritable matter – but a matter which is not external to the form, since this matter is rather pure thought and hence the absolute form itself' (*L.*, p. 50). The apparent contradiction is resolved, because the inclusion of content within logic coincides with the realization that form is itself and the 'other' at one and the same time; i.e., it coincides with that 'development' of form or expansion of Eleaticism (cf. the chapter on *Hegel and Spinoza*), the logical formalism of which is still deficient in that it maintains that form is only 'one of the two' and that content is external to or outside it.

into the objective essence of reality – are here taken up as two propositions that imply one another and are submitted to a unified critical argument.

First, the idealization or intellectualization of the world: '. . . The celebrated Leibniz erected an *intellectual system of the world.*' The basic considerations already examined by us return here once again. Leibniz 'believed that he could obtain knowledge of the inner nature of things by comparing all objects merely with the understanding and with the separated, formal concepts of its thought. . . . He compared all things with each other by means of concepts alone, and naturally found no other differences save those only through which the understanding distinguishes its pure concepts from one another. The conditions of sensible intuition, which carry with them their own differences, he did not regard as original, sensibility being for him only a confused mode of (logical) representation, and not a separate source of representations. Appearance was, on his view, the representation of the *thing in itself*. Such representation is indeed, as he recognized, different in logical form from knowledge through the understanding, since, owing to its usual lack of analysis, it introduces a certain admixture of accompanying representations into the concept of the thing, an admixture which the understanding knows how to separate from it.'[16]

Second, the transposition of logic into ontology, the upgrading of simple logical connections into connections in reality. In so far as 'Leibniz . . . compared the objects of the senses with each other merely in regard to understanding, taking them as things in general' and 'since he had before him only their concepts and not their position in intuition (wherein alone the objects can be given), . . . it inevitably followed that he should extend his principle of the identity of indiscernibles, which is valid only of concepts of things in general, to cover also the objects of the (*mundus phaenomenon*), and that he should believe that in so doing he had advanced our knowledge of nature in no small degree'.[17]

In other words, 'if a certain distinction is not found in the concept

16. I. Kant, *Critique of Pure Reason*, translated by Norman Kemp Smith (London, 1953), p. 282.

17. ibid., p. 283.

of a thing in general, it is also not to be found in the things themselves'; i.e. the *logical* indiscernibility is simply transposed into an indiscernibility in reality, that which is in thought is directly transformed into the substance of reality. And since 'in the mere concept of a thing in general we abstract from the many necessary conditions of its intuition, the conditions from which we have abstracted are, with strange presumption, treated as not being there at all, and nothing is allowed to the thing beyond what is contained in its concept'.[18]

Consider this conclusion for a moment; i.e. the indication of the error that lies in 'allowing nothing to the thing beyond what is contained in its concept'. If it is true, Kant says, 'that whatever universally agrees with or contradicts a concept also agrees with or contradicts every particular which is contained under it (*dictum de omni et nullo*);' . . . it would, however, be absurd 'to alter this logical principle so as to read: – what is not contained in a universal concept is also not included in the particular concepts which stand under it. For these are particular concepts just because they include in themselves more than is thought in the universal'.[19] The meaning of the argument could not be clearer; the individual or real thing contains *more* than the thing as a mere object of thought. Thought does not, within itself, exhaust reality. Logical possibility is not real possibility.

Now take up Hegel once again, and read those first pages of the *Science of Logic* which are so violent in their polemic against Kant. He states: 'Ancient metaphysics had in this respect a higher conception of thinking than is current today. For it based itself on the fact that the knowledge of things obtained through thinking is alone what is really true in them, that is, things not in their immediacy but as first raised into the form of thought, as things *thought*. Thus this metaphysics believed that thinking (and its determinations) is not anything alien to the object, but rather is its essential nature, or that things and the thinking of them . . . are explicitly in full agreement, thinking in its immanent determinations and the true nature of things forming one and the same content.'[20]

18. ibid., p. 289. 19. loc. cit. 20. ibid., p. 45.

This is the real basic dilemma: either the identity, or the heterogeneity, of thought and being – the choice that separates dogmatism from critical materialism. After having reduced being to thought by resolving the relationships of objects among themselves into a simple relationship of formal abstract concepts, Leibniz then carries out the inverse operation. He claims, that is, to 'extend his principle of the identity of indiscernibles, which is valid only of concepts of things in general, to cover also the objects of the senses', i.e., he claims 'to make these concepts valid for phenomena' or sense objects.[21] After reducing the relationship being-thought to a simple relationship of thought with itself, he claims to show this logical connection is a real and objective connection. He presents as a '*law of nature*' that which 'is only an analytic rule for the comparison of things through mere concepts'.[22] His entire philosophy is founded on this twofold *confusion*: the reduction of the *Gegenstand* to the *Objekt*, or the absorption of the finite into the 'ideal' (as Kant says, he 'sought for all representation of objects, even the empirical, in the understanding, and left to the senses nothing but the despicable task of confusing and distorting the representations of the former'[23]); and secondly, the transformation of the *Objekt* into the *Gegenstand*, i.e. of the logical idea into the structure and substratum of reality. Now, precisely this '*confounding*' is the amphiboly, which, according to Kant's own definition, is 'a confounding of an object of pure understanding with appearance (*Verwechslung des reinen Verstandesobjekts mit der Erscheinung*)'.[24]

And once again Kant's critique shows its incisiveness: 'These contentions would be entirely justified, if beyond the concept of a thing in general there were no further conditions (*etwas mehr*) under which alone objects of outer intuition can be given us – those from which the pure concept has (as a matter of fact) made abstraction. . . . But something is contained in intuition which is not to be met with in the mere concept of a thing; and this yields the substratum, which could never be known through mere concepts.'[25]

21. I. Kant, op. cit. (Müller translation), p. 211.
22. I. Kant, op. cit. (Kemp Smith translation), p. 284.
23. ibid., p. 286. 24. ibid., p. 282. 25. ibid., pp. 290–1.

It is something more, since the substratum, the existent, is not the concept itself; the substratum is extra-logical. With Hegel it is just the opposite: 'the demonstrated absoluteness of the Notion relatively to the material of experience . . . consists in this, that this material as it appears *apart from* and *prior* to the Notion has no *truth*; this it has solely in its ideality or its identity with the Notion. The *derivation* of the *real* from it. . . .'[26] The Idea is more real than reality. 'It is not the finite which is the real, but the infinite.'[27] With Marx, it is the opposite of this opposite: 'Hegel gives an independent existence to predicates and objects (*Objekte*), but he does so by detaching them from their real independency, from their subject. Subsequently the real subject appears, but as a development out of them, when actually one should take the real subject as one's point of departure and examine its objectification. Thus the mystical substance becomes the real subject, and the actual subject appears as something else, as a moment of the mystical substance. Precisely because Hegel takes as his point of departure the predicates of general determination rather than real being (*ὑποχείμενον*, subject), which must be nonetheless the vehicle of this determination, it is the mystical idea that becomes this vehicle.'[28]

One of Kant's basic conclusions in his critique of the logical-ontological confusion perpetrated by Leibniz and all the old metaphysical school is this: that *opposition in reality is something other than logical opposition.* 'If reality is represented only by the pure understanding (*realitas noumenon*), no opposition can be conceived between the realities, i.e. no relation of such a kind that, when combined in the same subject, they cancel each other's consequences and take a form like $3-3=0$. On the other hand, the real in appearance (*realitas phaenomenon*) may certainly allow of opposition. When such realities are combined in the same subject, one may wholly or partially destroy the consequences of another, as in the case of two moving forces in the same straight line, in so far as they either attract or impel a point in opposite directions, or again in the case of a pleasure counterbalancing pain.'[29]

26. *L.*, p. 591.
27. ibid., p. 149.
28. K. Marx, *Werke*, Vol. I, p. 224.
29. I. Kant, op. cit., p. 279.

Here is a further development and confirmation of this statement, so that the reader may have the essential terms of the argument before him: '... The principle that realities (as pure assertions) never logically conflict with each other is an entirely true proposition as regards the relation of concepts, but has not the least meaning in regard ... to nature.... For real conflict certainly does take place; there are cases where $A-B=0$, that is, where two realities combined in one subject cancel one another's effects. This is brought before our eyes incessantly by all the hindering and counteracting processes in nature, which, as depending on forces, must be called *realitates phaenomena*. General mechanics can indeed give the empirical condition of this conflict in an a priori rule, since it takes account of the opposition in the direction of forces, a condition totally ignored by the transcendental concept of reality.'[30] On the other hand, Leibniz and 'his disciples consider it not only possible, but even natural, to combine all reality in one being, without fear of any conflict. For the only conflict which they recognise is that of contradiction, whereby the concept of a thing is itself removed. They do not admit the conflict of reciprocal injury, in which each of two real grounds destroys the effect of the other – a conflict which we can represent to ourselves only in terms of conditions presented to us in sensibility.'[31]

The essential point to bear in mind in order to understand the meaning of this argument has already been indicated: *opposition in reality* is something other than *logical contradiction* or opposition.

Like Leibniz, Kant takes as his premiss that the rule governing thought is the principle of (non-)contradiction. A concept that contradicts itself negates itself. 'The object of a concept which contradicts itself is nothing, because the concept is nothing, is the impossible, e.g. a two-sided rectilinear figure (*nihil negativum*).'[32] In this sense, Kant and Leibniz's positions coincide. Both are still tied to the Eleatic principle; to both of them the revolution in logic brought about (or carried to fulfilment) by Hegel remains foreign – i.e. the expansion of Eleaticism, the recognition that reason is the 'identity of identity and non-identity', a tautoheterology or dialectic.

30. ibid., p. 284. 31. loc cit. 32. ibid., p. 295.

From this common basis, however, the paths of Leibniz and of Kant proceed in opposite directions. For Leibniz, the principle of thought is also the principle of reality: logical possibility is itself real possibility. Consequently, that which is logically impossible (opposition) is also impossible in reality. For Kant, contrariwise, the principle of non-contradiction is purely a *principium rationis*; the consistency of thought with itself is something other than the coincidence of thought with reality. Hence, the non-existence of logical contradiction must not lead to the conclusion of the non-existence of opposition in reality. '. . . There is no conflict in the concept of a thing unless a negative statement is combined with an affirmative; merely affirmative concepts cannot, when combined, produce any cancellation. But in the sensible intuition, wherein reality (e.g. motion) is given, there are conditions (opposite directions), which have been omitted in the concept of motion in general that make possible a conflict (though not indeed a logical one), namely, as producing from what is entirely positive a zero (=0). We are not, therefore, in a position to say that since conflict is not to be met with in the concepts of reality, all reality is in agreement with itself.'[33]

As to the difference between Leibniz and Hegel, this lies in their divergent way of understanding the principle of logic, which, for the former, is that of non-contradiction and, for the latter, that of dialectical contradiction. Beyond this difference, however, there is the continuity in metaphysics (that continuity which distinguishes them both from Kant): the identity of the principle of logic and the principle of reality, the elevation and transposition of logic into ontology. Leibniz, in denying logical contradiction, denies opposition in reality (extending thereby the principle of indiscernibles to the point of claiming it as a 'law of nature'). Hegel, who affirms logical contradiction, does so by making it the *substratum* of opposition in reality. Every thing is contradictory within itself, every thing 'is' and 'is not'; that is to say, opposition *in reality* is resolved into *logical* contradiction, i.e. into reason *qua* the union of sameness and otherness, 'being' and 'non-being' together. On the other hand, just as

33. ibid., pp. 289–90.

objects are only the incarnation of reason, so all objective or real oppositions, all *specific* oppositions, become the 'existence' or the 'phenomenon' of rational opposition, i.e. *generic* opposition.

This point, enough in itself to relegate all of 'dialectical materialism' to the museum alongside the stone axes, was seen with exemplary clarity by Marx.[34] In addition to the passage cited above from the *Poverty of Philosophy* dealing with 'movement', we find in the last of the 1844 manuscripts: Hegel's 'real interest . . . is the opposition of *in itself* and *for itself*, of *consciousness* and *self-consciousness*, of *object* and *subject*, i.e. the opposition *in thought itself* (Colletti's emphasis) between abstract thought and sensible reality or real sensuous existence. All other contradictions and movements are merely the *appearance*, the *cloak*, the *exoteric* form of these two opposites which are alone important and which constitute the *significance* of the other, profane contradictions'.[35]

Moreover, that the two ways of conceiving real conflicts are divergent is demonstrated by the fact that, whereas Kant, in the process of pointing out a *determinate* opposition, thinks immediately of the specific science that deals with it (cf. above: mechanics) for Hegel the science of contradictions is general *philosophy* or idealism. Just as for Engels it must be the always anticipated but never realized 'new' science – philosophical and dialectical by its very nature.

We have dwelt so long on this Kantian distinction between 'logical opposition' and 'opposition in reality' for two reasons –

34. Just as for Hegel, so for Engels, 'real' or specific oppositions are nothing other than 'manifestations' of the logical contradiction of reason with itself, always the same and thus eternal. The substratum of the finite is for him also the infinite. Consequently, he represents all knowledge as knowledge of the eternal and the absolute. Cf., for example, the *Dialectics of Nature*, p. 326: '. . . All real, exhaustive knowledge consists solely in . . . seeking and establishing the infinite in the finite, the eternal in the transitory.' And on p. 326 again: 'All true knowledge of nature is knowledge of the eternal, the infinite, and hence essentially absolute.' And in relation to the 'permanent' character of every true law of nature, cf. p. 239: 'By new discoveries we can give new examples of it, we can give it a new and richer content. But we cannot add anything to the law itself as so formulated. In its universality, equally universal in form and content, it is not susceptible of further extension: it is an absolute law of nature.'

35. K. Marx, *Early Writings*, op. cit., p. 201.

besides its obvious intrinsic importance – and we hope that the reader will pay particular attention to the first of these. It is possible that, having followed our critique of dialectical materialism and seen us at the same time uphold the principle of identity or material determination, the reader may have concluded that we wished to deny the existence of objective or material oppositions. Obviously, if such were the case, any claim to be reasoning with Marx (i.e. in accordance with his approach) would be destitute a priori of any foundation (which explains, parenthetically, why precisely this criticism of us was made by one subtle critic[36]). It is, however, precisely Kant's distinction between 'logical opposition' and 'opposition in reality' that shows (I believe) the incorrectness of this conclusion. That distinction, in fact, by implying the irreducibility of 'real' opposition to 'logical' opposition, or of existence (Kant's 'something more') to a concept, also implies the irreducibility of its particularity or *specificity* to a universal or *generic* opposition; i.e., it implies the fact that existence acquires its determinacy to be what it 'is' precisely through the exclusion or negation of *everything* that it *is not*. All of which confirms, I think – however much it may clash with ingrained habits of thought – that it is impossible to disregard the principle of *non*-contradiction precisely when one wants to point out *material* oppositions or contradictions, i.e. *specific* ones (for nothing is more poorly guaranteed by Hegel's dialectical logic than the specific 'species' of a thing, in other words natural or finite entities; it is a matter – and here Labriola comes to mind – of leaving 'open the question of the empirical nature of each particular formation'[37]). Vice versa, it also confirms that it is precisely the rejection or 'overcoming' of non-contradiction, its replacement by the so-called 'dialectic of matter', which implies the dilution or negation of *oppositions in reality*, i.e. their peaceful resolution within reason.

The second reason inclining us to emphasize Kant's argument is that, although some contemporary Marxists may have correctly grasped its importance (cf. the discussion 'On the Problems of

36. N. Badaloni, *Marxismo come storicismo* (Milan, 1962), pp. 201 ff.
37. Antonio Labriola, *Lettere a Engels* (Rome, 1949), p. 147.

Logic' in the *Deutsche Zeitschrift für Philosophie*, 1956, and C. Luporini in his *Spazio e materia in Kant*), they still run the risk, I believe, of throwing away its lesson when they tend to interpret it in a 'dialectical-materialist' sense.

Luporini, for example, who correctly sees that Kant's argument against Leibniz's 'intellectualization of phenomena' ('what resists this intellectualization is the opposition in reality between things, the forces which are operating one against the other and which are not reducible to a pure "logical" contradiction'[38]) hinges entirely on the antecedence and extra-logical character of existence, maintains that the significance of Kant's argument is to be sought in the fact that it 'is the germ, precisely, of a materialist dialectic'.[39] It should now be clear why we find it difficult to accept this opinion, given our line of reasoning. The 'materialist dialectic' is, in the strict sense, Hegel's own dialectic of matter. The latter, just as it presupposes the complete and total resolution of real conflict into logical opposition or contradiction (of being into thought), so it also presupposes, quite consistently, the rejection of materialism i.e. of that extra-logical 'something more' upon which Kant's entire argument is based – as Luporini sees clearly enough.

Now the paradox is this: whereas 'dialectical materialism', in order to be materialist, needed precisely that 'something more', it has instead adopted Hegel's 'dialectic of matter', i.e. the proposition that all things 'are' and 'are not', without realizing that the basis of that dialectic was precisely the *negation* (or the 'destruction') of that 'something more'. The absolute and irremediable theoretical insignificance of 'dialectical materialism' is all here: it has mimed idealism, thinking that it was being materialist; it has underwritten Hegel's liquidation of the 'intellect' and the principle of non-contradiction, without comprehending that this meant liquidating the very independence of the finite from the infinite, of being from thought.

Engels writes: 'The mind which thinks metaphysically is absolutely unable to pass from the idea of rest to the idea of motion,

38. C. Luporini, *Spazio e materia in Kant*, op. cit., pp. 73 and 112 ff.
39. ibid., p. 74.

because the contradiction pointed out above blocks its path.'[40] It would be interesting to know – if the 'understanding' is metaphysical – how Engels and all the 'dialectical materialists' after him manage to guarantee that irreducibility of being to thought, without which the contrasts of reality fade into mere *logical* contradictions, and materialism fades into mere pious intention.

The finite which does not 'pass over' into the infinite, being which does not 'pass over' into its opposite, is 'dead being'! In Hegel, this argument is meaningful. 'Dead being' is being which *remains* as the basis of thought, it is that 'something more' which Kant calls *das Substratum*. One understands then only too well why Hegel was concerned to get rid of all this. What one understands less well, or more exactly, what one understands not at all, is how Engels and Lenin could have attacked 'dead being' and claimed at the same time to be materialists.

In order to be a form of materialism, 'dialectical materialism' must affirm the heterogeneity of thought and being. To be able to put into practice the dialectic of matter, it must reduce all oppositions in reality to oppositions of 'being' and 'non-being', i.e. to logical contradictions (consider Engels's views on motion). In the first case, it needs the principle of non-contradiction; in the second, it needs to show, like Hegel, that this principle is sheer dogmatism. The way out of this impasse was to rethink in an organic fashion the meaning of non-contradiction, or material determinacy, and that of dialectical contradiction, or reason (precisely the path opened up by Della Volpe with his principle of tautoheterological identity). However, unable even to perceive the problem, 'dialectical materialism' has simply suffered the contradiction through and through. The consequence has been that wherever, as in *Materialism and Empirio-Criticism*, there is a clear statement of materialism and therefore of the heterogeneity of thought and being, there is lacking a theory of reason, i.e. of concepts and scientific law (this accounts for the metaphorical and fanciful character of the *Widerspiegelungstheorie* set forth in that work, as well as the 'primitive' level of the materialism it asserts). Vice versa, wherever there is a theory of dialectical

40. F. Engels, *Anti-Dühring*, op. cit., p. 133.

contradiction, this exists at the expense of the heterogeneity of the real and the logical, as in the *Philosophical Notebooks* and above all in Engels's *Dialectics of Nature* – works which are certainly rich in 'dialectic' but so poor in 'matter' as to become unconscious idealist metaphysics.

This radical discrimination has been lived out and impersonated in the most rigorous way – if it is possible to say such a thing – by Lukács. Having found in Hegel that 'dialectic of matter' and being convinced that this was a genuine form of materialism, he attempted at all costs to ascribe a *Widerspiegelungstheorie* to Hegel (being not unaware of the fact that it is difficult to imagine a form of materialism lacking a theory of truth as 'correspondence'). Afterwards, having adopted Hegel's premisses, and in particular that concerning the identity of logic and ontology (with the consequent *realism of concepts*!), he dedicated himself to a struggle without quarter against Kant, i.e. against the only classical German philosopher in whom it is possible to detect at least a grain of materialism. He was convinced that 'idealist objectivism represents an advance in relation to Kant' (even the objectivism of Schelling!) He was, however, altogether forgetful or unaware of the fact that this objectivism which he so ardently propounded had indeed been closely considered by the old man of Königsberg, in his appropriately titled *Dreams of a Visonary explained by the Dreams of Metaphysics.*

VII. Cassirer on Kant and Hegel

Let us attempt to carry the argument all the way through and push it to its uttermost 'limit'. If the crux, the vital nucleus of the *Critique of Pure Reason* (disregarding for a moment all its serious contradictions) lies in the argument that dogmatism is the transposition, the direct *confounding* of logic with ontology (and, hence, the realism of concepts), this means that in Kant one can find at least the beginnings – if only just the beginnings – of a critique of the processes of hypostatization. In a passage from the sceptic Schulze, the author of *Aenesidemus* – which is cited by Hegel in the *Relation of Scepticism to Philosophy* and explicitly referred to there as something written in a 'Kantian style' – this theme comes out clearly. Schulze writes thus: 'If there has ever been a beguiling attempt to link the realm of *objective reality* directly to the sphere of *Notions*, and to pass from the latter into the former merely with the help of a *bridge* which also is *made out of mere Notions*, this attempt has taken place in Onto-theology. Nevertheless, the empty sophistry and deception which was being practised have recently been completely uncovered'.[1]

This passage appears on the same page in which Hegel calls Kant's critique of the ontological argument a *Witz*, i.e. a witticism, almost a sarcastic joke, and gives us an idea of what 'germs' had been spread by Kant in the German culture of his age, which previously had been dominated by Onto-theology and after him was to be dominated by Hegel's Onto-theo-logic (cf. the essay by Löwith cited above). But – without turning our attention too far in that direction – important evidence concerning the lessons to be drawn from the *Critique* also comes to us from the milieu of Neo-Kantianism (in spite of the fact that in it the Kantian forest was extensively pruned and often reduced almost to a French-style garden). Exemplary, in this sense, is the chapter 'Critical Idealism

1. G. W. F. Hegel, *Verhältnis des Skepticismus zur Philosophie*, op. cit., p. 255.

and Absolute Idealism' in *Das Erkenntnisproblem* where Cassirer compares the two greatest German thinkers. Here, indeed, together with a series of accurate but (from a Neo-Kantian perspective) relatively obvious remarks, one finds others that cannot help but make one realize the critical effectiveness retained by Kantianism even when one attempts to apply to it Hegel.

The 'obvious' (but nonetheless interesting) remarks alluded to above are those which concern the thought-being relationship in the two philosophers. Cassirer bases his argument on Kant's distinction between *intellectus archetypus* and *intellectus ectypus*, intuitive intellect and discursive intellect. The latter, which is the intellect dealt with in the *Critique*, i.e. ordinary human intellect, has 'before itself a diverse sensate manifoldness to which it can gradually give determinacy through the pure categories of thought, but which it can never completely resolve into these categories'. Thus this understanding does indeed posit the object as determinable through thought, but it finds that being and concept are constantly separating from one another. The other one, however, which is the intuitive intellect or 'the intellect's intuition', about which Hegel often talks as a synonym for 'reason', not just in his early writings (which were still under the influence of Schelling's terminology), but also in his mature works – this other mode of understanding 'knows every manifold only as an unfolding and more specific determination of the original unity which it itself is'. Thus, 'thought and the object of thought have become a single thing, such that even the barrier which our empirical intellect must necessarily set up between the real and the merely possible has ceased to exist for it'.[2]

Hegel's logic, Cassirer continues, 'is the logic of the intuitive intellect, of an intellect that has outside itself only that which it itself has produced. This logic is not familiar with the refraction or blurring which the intellect would undergo if it had to avail itself of an extraneous means, a sense-world (*Sinnlichkeit*) posited next to or below itself.'[3] All this is obvious enough but comes, nonetheless,

2. Ernst Cassirer, *Storia della filosofia moderna* (Turin, 1953), Vol. III, pp. 457–8.
3. ibid., p. 458.

as a breath of good sense after Lukács's dronings about a *Widerspiegelungstheorie* in Hegel's philosophy.

We cannot explore here other interesting observations, such as the one in which Cassirer points out that 'the form of the speculative treatment of nature' created by Hegel, which disdains 'the path that passes through the mathematical and empirical *science* of nature', has given rise to 'a new form of penetration into the "inwardness of nature" understood as spiritual inwardness' (he goes on to note that 'the exposition of Hegel's philosophy of nature has certainly shown how this apparent change of direction towards a more concrete mode of treating things leads in actual fact only to a dialectical volatilization of the content of nature, such that the laws proper to nature and experience are dissipated'). And we must also leave aside his very significant allusion to the aversion felt by Goethe for Hegel's 'philosophy of nature' because it represented a 'conversion of organic becoming into the form of logical becoming' ('The propositions of Hegel's logic – in which it is stated that buds disappear with the blossoming of flowers and that therefore one can say that the former are contradicted by the latter, and also that the fruit defines the flower as a "false existence of the plant" – seemed simply grotesque to him; they gave him the impression that one wanted to destroy the eternal reality of nature with a bad, sophistical joke.')[4]

We are only concerned here to point out how Cassirer, developing his analysis from a strictly Kantian point of view, ends up nonetheless, almost inadvertently, by formulating his critical judgment of Hegel in terms analogous to, or even identical with those used by Marx in his *Kritik des Hegelschen Staatsrechts* or in the last of the 1844 manuscripts – a fact all the more significant when one considers that *Das Erkenntnisproblem* appeared a number of decades before the posthumous publication of these writings.

Typical in this sense is the remark that Hegel's procedure 'is forced to elevate to an absolute that which is an individual or contingent element'; and that 'here in actual fact absolute idealism finds itself before its systematic opposite, absolute empiricism, and

4. ibid., pp. 472–3.

threatens to convert itself into it', because, 'with the pretext that reason is "everything that is real", any reality that has taken shape and determinacy is declared *ipso facto* rational'. The mind of the reader cannot help but turn to Marx's formula of the coexistence in Hegel of an 'acritical idealism and of a positivism equally devoid of criticism'.[5] Typical also is the remark that 'a particular empirical present is always threatening to introduce itself surreptitiously into the present of the pure idea and its unfolding, as an appropriate realization and expression of the latter'; or that 'a determinate *temporal* present threatens to substitute itself for the "substance which is immanent and the eternal which is present" '.[6] Here one can see the corrupt and surreptitious way in which the positive is smuggled back whenever it serves to give *body* to the Idea, i.e. to the *realization* of the 'principle of idealism' and so to the 'positive exposition of the absolute'. All this not only vividly calls to mind analogous remarks by Marx, but leads one to a comparison (not without its disenchantments) with the equivocations and confusion of many contemporary Marxists concerning the nature and meaning of Hegelian 'objectivism'.

Finally, no less significant, there is Cassirer's notation that 'the language of Hegelian pan-logism turns into the language of myth' and that 'in this way of representing the idea . . . there re-echo, in actual fact, ancient mythico-religious themes and descriptions of the becoming of the world created by God's original being'.[7] Here comparison is inevitable with the 'manipulated' statements of Marcuse and also of Lukács concerning the irreligiosity and atheism of Hegel, but so is the recollection of Feuerbach's and Marx's remarks on the 'rational mystique' or 'logical mysticism' of Hegelian philosophy.

Although Cassirer was undoubtedly unfamiliar with Marx's comments in writing that chapter, he may well have known Feuerbach's or, perhaps, those of Trendelenburg.[8] However this may be,

5. K. Marx, *Early Writings*, op. cit., p. 201.

6. Cassirer, op. cit., pp. 464–5.

7. ibid., p. 471.

8. For Trendelenburg's anti-Hegelian critique, see the very important pages in M. Rossi's *Marx e la dialettica hegeliana* (Rome, 1963), pp. 66 ff.

the one certain and incontrovertible fact is that the initial guide and immediate stimulus to formulating his thoughts came from direct contact with Kant's work. It was from the latter that he most keenly felt an admonition against metaphysics *qua* a 'general tendency of thought to transform the pure means of knowledge into just so many objects of knowledge',[9] categories into 'essences' or the structures of reality; in short, metaphysics as an 'apparently irrepressible tendency to transform the functions of knowledge into concepts (i.e. into knowledge that is already formed) and (logical) preconditions into things'.[10] All of which explains Cassirer's capacity to throw light on an often ignored aspect of the *Critique* – i.e., how the 'thing in itself', being the mere *Objekt* of pure thought without a counterpart in experience, has above all the function (together with all the others that it certainly has in the general economy of Kant's thought) of representing not a truer and more profound 'reality' in relation to simple 'phenomenal' existence (as is so widely believed), but rather the unknowable, because *illusory*, *reality* of metaphysics. It is, in other words, that imaginary and unreal 'object' into which 'we only hypostatise the *structure*' of our own subjective consciousness.[11] The concept of 'noumena', Cassirer writes, means 'not the particularity of an *object*, but the attempt to set apart a determinate *function of knowledge*' in order to turn it directly into a reality as such.[12] The 'thing in itself', he adds, emerges 'as a correlative term, i.e. as the "counterpart" of the function of synthetic unity. It comes into effect whenever we regard the *x* which in actual fact is only the unity of a connective conceptual rule as a particular objective content, and claim to identify it as such. The "non-empirical" or transcendental object of representations, this *x* in other words, certainly cannot be perceived by us – not, however, due to the fact that it is something totally unknown and self-subsisting which hides behind the representations, but rather due to the fact that it constitutes only the form of their unity, ascribed to them by thought, without possessing, however, a concrete and independent existence apart from this.'[13]

9. Cassirer, op. cit., Vol. II, pp. 792–3.
10. ibid., p. 793.
11. ibid., p. 810.
12. ibid., p. 808.
13. ibid., pp. 810–11.

All of which means that the limitation of our knowledge to the world of 'appearances' and 'phenomena' – not the 'illusory beings' of Hegel, but simply empirical objects themselves, i.e. *phenomena* or natural events precisely in the sense in which Newton talks about them – does not imply for Kant 'anything whatsoever of that sceptical resignation'[14] which often appears in the 'positivism' of a d'Alembert or a Maupertuis. It represents, on the contrary, a barrier or, more exactly, a 'limitation' imposed on the supersensible (and hence illusory) use of our powers of knowledge. This is precisely what Kant himself says – but with the admirable forcefulness and sobriety of the *Critique*'s language – when he writes that 'if by the complaints – *that we have no insight whatsoever into the inner (nature) of things* – it be meant that we cannot conceive by pure intellect what the things which appear to us may be in themselves, they are entirely illegitimate and unreasonable. For what is demanded is that we should be able to know things, and therefore to intuit them, without senses, and therefore that we should have a faculty of knowledge altogether different from the human, and this not only in degree but as regards intuition likewise in kind – in other words, that we should be not men but beings of whom we are unable to say whether they are even possible, much less how they are constituted'[15] – not men, but Gods Almighty, like the metaphysicians of that age and those of today.

Of course Kant's *Critique* also has other sides to it: e.g., the distinction between *denken* and *erkennen*, between thinking and knowing. As a consequence of this distinction a relationship of thought to itself, which is not at the same time a relationship to reality, does become possible. The preservation of the logical 'a priori' is also possible. This latter, even without positing itself as reality, nevertheless legitimates the *metaphysica naturalis*, as an aspiration at least – an aspiration to the knowledge of the 'absolute object', i.e. of the *Objekt* of pure thought, whereby the 'thing in itself' becomes indeed the 'unknowable' of agnosticism, and the

14. ibid., p. 797.
15. I. Kant, *Critique of Pure Reason* (Kemp Smith translation) op. cit., pp. 286–7.

phenomenon becomes the mere subjective 'appearance' of phenomenalism. However, our concern here is to point out the real and effective presence in Kant's thought of that other *tendency* which (moreover) it was a merit of Hegel's to have brought out so forcefully, if only in order to oppose it. And to point out, also, how Marxism ought to have less interest than anyone in obfuscating that tendency or in relegating it to oblivion.

Obviously this does not exhaust the complex question of the relationship of Marxism with Kant on the one hand and with Hegel on the other. The argument, so far, concerns only the theory of knowledge. And it is certain that whatever Hegel may lose in this particular area, he regains in large measure on that plane where (in the final analysis) Marx's thought truly and properly comes to life: history. Nevertheless, those apparently simpler concepts of historical materialism are in fact by far the most difficult. The most difficult of all is that of the 'social relations of production', which calls, at this point, for another pause and detour.

VIII. Kant, Hegel, and Marx

As far as I know, no significant discussion of the *Critique of Pure Reason* exists in the works of Marx. One finds a rapid but essential *prise de position* on the *Rechtslehre*, the writing in which Kant traced the basic outlines of that *Rechtsstaat* which was to be a major feature of the real state with which the bourgeoisie governed in Europe throughout the nineteenth century. But on the *Critique* as such, an analysis is lacking.

In a certain sense the question is analogous to (and perhaps even more serious than) that of Marx's relationship to Rousseau. It is impossible to understand the *Judenfrage* apart from Rousseau's critique of the rift of modern man into *bourgeois* and *citoyen*; and impossible to understand the critique of parliamentary representation contained in the *Kritik des Hegelschen Staatsrechts* or even in the *Civil War in France*, without reference to Rousseau's anti-parliamentarianism and his theory of popular sovereignty as inalienable sovereignty. Yet on the few occasions that Marx mentions Rousseau it is only in order to criticize his (presumed) contractualist natural right theory.

The problem is a striking one, but it is neither uncommon nor impossible to explain. A thinker makes certain 'discoveries' – which in part are, as always, 'rediscoveries' – and remains nonetheless unable to clearly account for their genealogy. His consciousness fails to give a full account of his being. Furthermore, certain influences acted on Marx indirectly, through the mediation of other writers. In my view Kant's influence, for instance – especially as concerns what Marx needed – undoubtedly reached him *via* the mediation of Feuerbach. Finally, one must consider the historical climate in which a thinker is formed (not excluding fashions and fads, which are not an exclusive privilege of today): the polemics among the various Hegelian 'schools', for instance, the debates within the Left itself, the imposing and august presence in the background of Hegel's great thought itself. And – last but not least – one crucial fact: the strong historico-political orientation and interest which Marx displayed from the outset, and the 'indifference' which he always showed towards epistemological problems as such. This should not be taken to mean an epistemological nihilism or a disdainful 'turning of his back' on philosophy, as it has sometimes been vulgarly misunderstood; it means, rather – and this is much harder to grasp – that precisely because this philosophical or epistemological problem had been settled for him, it was shifted in his mind to another level, where everything – both categories and subject matter – changed name and nature.

Especially in cases like these, the motto of the historian must evidently be: *zu den Sachen selbst* (to the things themselves)! To count the number of times that Kant's name recurs in the writings of Marx would be a pointless undertaking. All one can do is go directly to the problems themselves and there, in the thick of the actual question, come to terms with the historical 'give' and 'take' it implies – whatever may have been the awareness or self-consciousness of the individual thinker as such.

In the case of the relationship to Kant, I think there exists a place where the experiment can be carried out with a high degree of precision: the first pages of subheading 3 of the 1857 Introduction to the *Grundrisse der Kritik der politischen Ökonomie*. There, Marx discusses and criticizes the thought of Hegel. I believe that the passage in the *Science of Logic* which Marx had in mind can be located (it does not matter whether he had the text before him or whether it was only present to his memory). Hegel's text contains a critique of Kant. Marx, in turn, criticizes this text of Hegel's. Thus, there exist reasonable conditions for attempting to examine the relationships among the three of them.

The passage is in the *Science of Logic*, Volume II, p. 588: 'A capital misunderstanding which prevails on this point', i.e. in the theory of the Notion, 'is that the *natural* principle or the *beginning* which forms the starting point of the *natural* evolution or in the *history* of the developing individual, is regarded as the *truth*, and the *first* in the *Notion*. Now in the order of nature, intuition or being are undoubtedly first, or are the condition for the Notion, but they are not on that account the absolutely unconditioned; on the contrary, their reality is sublated in the Notion and with it too, the illusory show they possessed of being the conditioning reality.' Consequently, even if philosophy 'assumes the stages of feeling and intuitive perception (*Anschauung*), of sense-consciousness, etc. as precedent to the understanding', one must bear in mind – Hegel concludes – that 'they are postulated as conditions for the coming-into-being of the understanding (intellect) only in the sense that the Notion comes forth out of *their dialectic* and *nothingness*, as the ground of their being, and not in the sense that it (the Notion) is conditioned by their reality'.[1]

The question, it can be seen at once, is one that we have already dealt with several times. The process of development 'according to nature' is the process of reality; the process of development 'according to the Notion' is the logical process. The first gives us the situation as viewed by the 'intellect': empirical-sensate being is the *prius*, it places limiting conditions on thought. The second gives us the situation as depicted by 'reason': thought *cancels out* – by dialecticizing them – the limiting conditions or premisses in reality upon which it appeared to depend. It includes the 'other' within itself; and in so doing, just as it transforms itself from that which has limiting conditions placed upon it into that which establishes those conditions, so it also transforms the empirical being on which it appeared to depend into one of its own effects or consequences. The first process of development gives us the relationship that characterizes the progress *towards* knowing: the passage from being to thought, from empirical reality (*non-sapere*) to knowledge. The second gives us the process *of knowing*. In the process of development 'according to nature', the Notion comes second and reality first. In the logical process, it is the other way round, the Notion first

1. *L.*, p. 588. Miller's translation has unaccountably left out an entire line from Hegel's text; hence, in this instance Miller's otherwise excellent translation has had to be altered. (Trans.)

and reality second; that is to say, reality is deduced and derived from the Notion.

It is a fact that Hegel (like any other genuine thinker) cannot simply do away with either of these two processes. Nevertheless, when taken together they represent the cross which his theory of *mediation* has to bear. The process of development 'according to nature' is indispensable to him so that the Notion may appear as a result, i.e. as something *mediated* ('For to mediate is to take something as a beginning and to go onward to a second thing; so that the existence of this second thing depends on our having reached it from something other than itself'[2]). If it were not mediated, the Notion would be mere subjective *faith*, it would be precisely the *immediate knowledge* of Jacobi. On the other hand, Hegel must also free himself from this process of development 'according to nature', in order to affirm the principle of idealism: i.e., that the Notion has no limiting conditions or premisses outside itself, but is rather the *unconditional* and the absolute. As stated in the *Encyclopedia*: 'If mediation is represented as a state of conditionedness (*Bedingtheit*), and this is brought out in a one-sided fashion, it may be said – not that the remark would mean much – that philosophy owes its origin to experience (the *a posteriori*). (As a matter of fact, thinking is always the negation of what we have immediately before us.) With as much truth however we may be said to owe eating to the means of nourishment, since we could not eat without them. If we take this view, eating is certainly represented as ungrateful: it devours that to which it owes itself. Thinking, in this sense, is no less ungrateful.'[3]

Torn between these opposing necessities, Hegel's solution was to downgrade the process of development 'according to nature' into an *apparent* process. The process of development 'according to the Notion', on the other hand, is upgraded into a *real* process. In other words, the process in reality or according to nature is reduced to an 'appearance' or manifestation of the logical process, the process according to the Notion.

As was perceptively observed by A. Moni (that obscure but

2. *En.L.*, p. 20 (translation modified).
3. ibid., pp. 20–1 (translation modified).

remarkable Italian Hegel scholar, whose translation of the *Logic* has no parallel, not even when compared with Croce's version of the *Encyclopedia*), Hegel's solution is the same as Aristotle's, only in reverse. The distinction between logical process and process in reality, he writes, 'is the well-known Aristotelian distinction between πρῶτον καθ'ἡμάς and πρῶτον φύσει', with the reservation, however, 'that what Hegel states later, i.e. that perception and being are first according to nature (*der Natur nach*), is to be understood in the sense that they are first *secundum generationem*, whereas here the Notion corresponds to φύσις'.[4]

Now, it is precisely on these grounds that the clash between Hegel and Kant occurs. One can in fact trace out the two processes indicated above in the *Critique of Pure Reason*: the process according to which the intellect is something on which limiting conditions are placed, and the process (vice versa) according to which reality appears as a *product* of thought. Quite apart from the 'transcendental schematism', wherein 'productive imagination' determines pure perception (*Anschauung*) and thereby establishes the passage over into experience, the *logical process* is stressed in the very theory of the 'original synthesis of apperception' (as Hegel says, 'The connection of these two is . . . one of the most attractive sides of the Kantian philosophy', for 'pure sensuousness and pure understanding, which were formerly expressed as absolute opposites, are now united', and, because 'there is thus . . . present an understanding that perceives and a perception that understands'[5]). Hegel says, again: 'Since Kant shows that thought has synthetic judgments *a priori* which are not derived from perception, he shows that thought is so to speak concrete in itself', i.e. something that already has the other within itself.[6] As stated in the *Logic*: 'This original synthesis of apperception is one of the most profound principles for speculative development; it contains the beginning of a true apprehension of the nature of the Notion', because it does not represent the Notion as something empty and one-sided, but as a

4. G. W. F. Hegel, *Scienza della logica*, translated by A. Moni (Bari, 1925), Vol. III, p. 25 n.

5. *H.P.*, Vol. III, p. 441 (translation modified).

6. ibid., p. 430.

unity that has the other within itself.[7] Here, Hegel emphasizes, 'the idea which is present . . . is a great one'. But, he adds, 'on the other hand, quite an ordinary signification is given it, for it is worked out from points of view which are inherently rude and empirical, and a scientific form is the last thing that can be claimed for it. In the presentation of it there is a lack of philosophical abstraction, and it is expressed in the most commonplace way; to say nothing more of the barbarous terminology, Kant remains restricted and confined by his psychological point of view and empirical methods.'[8]

In other words, despite the great idea of an 'original synthesis of apperception', 'the further development . . . does not fulfil the promise of the beginning'. 'The very expression *synthesis* easily recalls the conception of an *external* unity and a *mere combination* of entities that are *intrinsically separate*. Then, again, the Kantian philosophy has not got beyond the psychological reflex of the Notion and has reverted once more to the assertion that the Notion is permanently conditioned by a manifold of intuition.'[9]

Let us now see more closely where the argument leads. Hegel discovers both of the processes in Kant: the logical process as well as the process in reality. In the former, the Notion appears as the *totality*, i.e., as the 'original synthesis', or unity of self and other together; and here, since it already contains the particular or the differentiated within itself, the Notion itself is the concrete. In the latter, on the other hand, the Notion or thought appears only as 'one of the two', having the 'other' *outside* itself. In the one case reality is a *product* of thought; in the other thought has limiting *conditions* placed on it by empirical being. From this basis in what (broadly speaking) constitutes a common problematic, Hegel and Kant then proceed in opposite directions. Kant, while allowing that thought is an 'original synthesis', maintains the distinction between *real* conditions and *logical* conditions; so that, having recognized that thought is a *totality*, he considers it (precisely because this totality is only of *thought*) to be only *one* element or one part of the process of *reality*. Hegel, however, carries out the reverse operation: he absorbs the process of reality within the logical process, he reduces the relation-

7. *L.*, p. 589. 8. *H.P.*, Vol. III, pp. 430–1. 9. *L.*, p. 589.

ship in which thought is only 'one of two' to one in which it is the 'totality'. With the consequence that, whereas the Notion is transformed by him from a pure logical condition or *ratio cognoscendi* into a *ratio essendi*, i.e. into the *raison d'être* or limiting condition of reality, the latter, on the other hand, becomes a mere product or manifestation of the Idea.

It is clear what the problem is, stirring at the root of this distinction. There can be no thought unless something is previously *given* to be thought; which means that the objectivity of reality – or in other words the condition for there being a *content* to knowledge – is a condition for the existence of thought (since there can be no thought except thought with a determinate object). On the other hand, if in this sense reality is the *cause* and thought the effect, it is also true that, in so far as what is 'thought' (*pensato*) is inevitably a *product* of thought (*pensiero*), what was at first cause now becomes *effect* and what was effect becomes the cause of its cause. Any attempt to evade this twofold process, in which reality and thought appear alternately as limiting condition and that which has limiting conditions placed upon it, is only an illusion. Reality, in fact, is that which is *objective*, and the objective – contrary to idealism – is precisely that which is external to and independent of thinking subjectivity. It is no less true, however – contrary to empiricism or 'primitive' materialism – that an indispensable condition for discriminating the objective from the subjective and, therefore, reality from illusion, is, most assuredly, thought – in a word, *subjectivity* itself. All of which means that *induction* and *deduction* here reciprocally imply and mutually require one another; for, just as reality is anterior and independent, and thought in relation to it is something on which limiting conditions are placed, so it is also true that we can only arrive at a *recognition* of that reality *deductively*, i.e. through a process from which reality emerges as the *result* of a sifting and a selection carried out by thought.

The intertwining of receptivity and spontaneity, of causal determination and subjective creativity, which previously had only been inadequately sketched out by the different versions of *Widerspiegelungstheorie* (with the well-known argument that 'reflexion' is no mere mirror image, but implies a project and initiative), begins here to take on a definite shape. Reality or the concrete is first; materialism remains, in this sense, the point of departure. On the other hand, in so far as we can only arrive at the *recognition* of what is concrete through thought, i.e. by means of those 'abstract determinations' which are precisely what 'lead to the reproduction of the concrete in the course of thinking', the concrete itself, as Marx says, 'appears in thought'.[10]

Reaching the most vital part of his reply to the *Science of Logic*, Marx continues:' Hegel fell into the illusion, therefore, of conceiving reality as the result of self-propelling, self-encompassing, and self-elaborating thought; whereas, the method of advancing from the abstract to the concrete is merely the way in which thought appropriates the concrete and reproduces it as a concrete that has assumed a mental form (*geistig*). This is by no means, however, the process which generates the concrete itself. For consciousness, then – and philosophical consciousness is such that contemplative thought is conceived as real man and thus the contemplated world as such is conceived as the only reality – for this consciousness the movement of categories appears as the real act of production (which unfortunately receives only a stimulus from outside), the result of which is the world. All of this is correct, in so far as – and here again we have a tautology – the concrete totality, *qua* totality made up of thought and concrete made up of thought, is in fact a product of thinking and comprehending. In no sense, however, is this totality a product of a concept (*Begriff*) which generates itself and thinks outside of and above perception and representation; rather, it is a product of the elaboration of perception and representation into concepts. The whole, as it appears in our minds in the form of a whole made up of thought, is a product of a thinking mind, which appropriates the world in the only way possible for it. . . '. Nevertheless, Marx concludes, 'the real subject still remains outside the mind, leading an independent existence'; so that 'even in the case of the theoretical

10. K. Marx, *Introduction to the Critique of Political Economy*, in *A Contribution to the Critique of Political Economy*, translated by N. I. Stone (Chicago, 1904), p. 293 (translation modified).

method', it 'must constantly be kept in mind as the premiss from which we start'.[11]

The essential argument that interests us is all contained in this one page. Like every genuine thinker, Marx recognizes the irreplaceable role of the logico-deductive process.[12] He knows full well that the concrete, in so far as it is 'thought' (*pensato*) and arrived at only *through* thought (*pensiero*), is itself a *product* of thinking and knowing; that is, not a point of departure, but a point of arrival. But, as opposed to Hegel, Marx upholds the process of reality side-by-side with the logical process. The passage from the abstract to the concrete is only the way in which thought appropriates reality; it is not to be confused with the way in which the concrete itself originates. If, therefore, in the logical process the concept is *prius* and reality is only a particular *deduced* or derived from the former, one must bear in mind, Marx cautions, that the concept does not generate itself, nor exist as thinking outside and above perception and representation. It is itself the *outcome* (note the profoundly Kantian overtone of this statement) of the 'elaboration of perception and representation into concepts (*Verarbeitung von Anschauung und Vorstellung in Begriffe*)', and precisely for this reason one must bear in mind that implicit in the logical process is a process of reality which works in the opposite direction: here the concept, which in the logical process came first, now comes second, and reality, which in the logical process was a resultant, is in actual fact the point of departure rather than the point of arrival.

What was said above of Marx's relationship to Hegel and Kant is, I believe, amply confirmed here. From Hegel, Marx derives above all the theory of reason, i.e. certain lessons concerning the role and structure of the logico-deductive process (a process which was never

11. ibid., pp. 293–5 (translation modified).

12. The importance of the logico-deductive process in Marx, as against any possible misunderstanding or empiricist interpretation of his early critique of Hegel, was properly pointed out by M. Dal Pra, *La dialettica in Marx* (Bari, 1965), pp. 114 ff. On the whole I share the basic orientation of this work, except for its interpretation of the *Einleitung*. My reconstruction of the latter's argument also departs somewhat from Della Volpe's essay of 1962, *Sulla dialettica*, published in the appendix to *Libertà communista* (Milan, 1963).

fully developed in Kant). He derives, we might add (although this is perhaps only another way of saying the same thing), a profound sense of the unity of logical process and real process, i.e. the principle of that *unity* of thought and being which in Hegel, however, was so imperious as to jeopardize from the very beginning their *real* distinction. From Kant, on the other hand, Marx clearly derives – whether he was aware of it or not, and whatever may have been the process of mediation – the principle of real existence as something 'more' with respect to everything contained in the concept; a principle which, while it makes the process of reality irreducible to the logical process, also prevents us from forgetting that, if the concept is logically first, from another angle it is itself a resultant – the result, precisely, of the 'elaboration of perception and representation into concepts', i.e. the point of arrival of that passage from empirical reality to knowledge (the process of the *formation* of knowledge) which has been, of course, *the* critical problem par excellence.

A further insight offered by these pages of the 1857 *Einleitung* is that there is complete homogeneity (contrary to all the fatuous *rêveries* current today concerning the so-called *coupure*) between its critique of Hegel and the critique which Marx launched against Hegel in 1843 in his *Kritik des Hegelschen Staatsrechts.* In both writings, the critique hinges on the same argument. Hegel reduces the process of reality to a simple logical process; he turns the Idea into the subject or substratum of reality. Subsequently, just as empirical reality becomes for him the phenomenal appearance or 'illusory being' of the Idea, so the process by which one comes to *know* reality must necessarily be transformed into the process of the *creation* of reality. The logical universal, or the category, which should be the predicate, is transformed by him into the subject; and vice versa, the particular – which is the true subject of reality – becomes the 'predicate of its predicate', i.e. the manifestation or incarnation of the logical universal, which has thus been substantified.

It would be possible to conclude our discussion of the *Einleitung* at this point. But since we sense only too well the vagueness and uncertainty which may still surround the 'unity of deduction and induction' in the reader's mind it may be useful, next, to examine the concrete problem Marx adduces as an example in the initial pages of the section on 'The Method of Political Economy'. Thus we shall be able to show, in the particular, how the logico-deductive process and the inductive process, or process of reality, are intertwined and combine with one another. The focal point, which one must start from, is what has been brought out already a number of times: the twofold nature (let us use this phrase for the moment) of thought, i.e. thought as 'intellect' and thought as 'reason', thought as 'one of two' and thought as the 'totality' of relationships. This simple distinction gives us immediate access to a fundamental statement by Marx, contained in the section of the *Einleitung* mentioned. 'The simplest economic category, say, exchange value, implies the existence of population, population that is engaged in production under certain conditions; it also implies the existence of certain types of family community, or state, etc. It can have no other existence except as an abstract *one-sided* relation of a concrete and living whole that is already given. As a category, however, exchange value leads an antediluvian existence',[13] so antediluvian that all treatises on economics *begin* their exposition with this category, rather than with population, which is (nonetheless) its *premiss*. This is similar to the way in which 'Hegel, for instance, rightly starts out his *Philosophy of Right* with possession, as the simplest legal relation of the subject', although, as is evident, 'there is no such thing as possession before the family or the relations of lord and serf, which are relations that are a great deal more concrete'.[14]

In these lines, if one reads them closely, *abstraction* is discussed in a twofold way: as totality or mental *generalization*, and as *one* aspect or analytic feature of the *particular* object under consideration; as abstraction from the point of view of logic and as abstraction from the point of view of reality.

Exchange value, Marx says, 'can have no other existence except as an abstract *one-sided* relation of a concrete and living whole that is already given'. What strikes us here with great clarity is undoubtedly the second meaning. Abstraction is (or expresses) *one* aspect, a one-sided *feature*, which has been separated (or, more precisely,

13. Marx, op. cit., p. 294 (translation modified).

14. ibid., p. 295.

'abstracted') from a concrete and real object; an object which, as always, has more than one side to it. Exchange value, for example, presupposes a population that exchanges; but the category, 'exchange value', gives us only one characteristic, only *one* way of being (a '*one-sided* relation') of this 'object', the population.

On the other hand, the other aspect according to which the category, besides being one side of the *particular* concrete object, is a mental *generalization* or an idea, emerges clearly from the lines that open this section. In scientific analysis or exposition, Marx says, 'it seems to be the correct procedure to commence with the real and concrete, with the real premiss; in the case of political economy, to commence with population which is the basis and the subject of the entire social act of production. Yet, on closer consideration it proves to be wrong. Population is an abstraction, if we leave out, for instance, the classes of which it consists. These classes, again, are but an empty word, unless we know what are the elements on which they are based, such as wage-labour, capital, etc. These imply, in their turn, exchange, division of labour, prices, etc. If we start out, therefore, with population, we do so with a chaotic conception of the whole. . .'.[15]

What has to be pointed out immediately is that the presupposition under discussion here is the opposite of the one mentioned above. The population is the premiss *in reality*, it is the basis and the subject of the entire social act of production. But in reality this premiss presupposes, in its turn, a whole series of conditions without which it does not *mean* anything, it would be a word devoid of sense, a chaotic representation. The population has no *meaning* without the classes of which it is composed; in their turn, these classes mean nothing, 'unless we know the elements on which they are based', i.e. wage-labour and capital; finally, the latter presuppose exchange value, the division of labour and prices.

It is clear that whereas the first is a presupposition *in reality*, the second is a *logical* presupposition. Exchange value 'presupposes the population'; it 'can have no other existence except as an abstract *one-sided* relation of a concrete and living whole that is already

15. ibid., p. 292.

given'. On the other hand, this population which is the premiss and basis in reality of everything presupposes, in its turn (from the point of view of logic), a whole series of categories without which it (the population) would have no *meaning* – whence the impossibility of beginning a scientific analysis or exposition with it. At the top of this series of categories one finds that of exchange value. The population, which is *prius* from the point of view of reality, is last from the point of view of logic. On the other hand, exchange value, which *realiter* is only a *one-sided* characteristic, is, from the point of view of logic or as a mental generalization, the most comprehensive *generality*, in relation to which all the other categories appear merely as derived particularities.

The argument, as one can see, has led us back to the basic problem: i.e., *causa cognoscendi* and *causa essendi*, deduction and induction, process of development 'according to the Notion' and process of development 'according to nature'. Or, to use Marx's terminology in the *Afterword* to the second German edition of *Capital*: *Darstellungsweise* and *Forschungsweise*, i.e. the method of setting forth thought and the method of researching the material (from which that thought is formed). '. . . The method of presentation must differ in form from that of inquiry. The latter has to appropriate the material in detail, to analyse its different forms of development, to trace out their inner connexion. Only after this work is done, can the actual movement be adequately described. If this is done successfully, if the life of the subject-matter is ideally reflected as in a mirror, then it may appear as if we had before us a mere a priori construction. My dialectic method is not only different from the Hegelian, but is its direct opposite. To Hegel, the life-process of the human brain, i.e., the process of thinking, which, under the name of "the Idea", he even transforms into an independent subject, is the demiurgos of the real world, and the real world is only the external, phenomenal form of "the Idea". With me, on the contrary the ideal is nothing else than the material world reflected by the human mind, and translated into forms of thought.'[16]

16. K. Marx, *Capital*, translated by S. Moore and E. Aveling (New York, 1967), 'Afterword to the Second German Edition', vol. I, p. 19.

Hence, in the case under examination – a population which produces capitalistically – exchange value presents itself to us in two different respects: on the one hand, as the most comprehensive and broadest *generality* from which all the other categories are *deduced* and from which a scientific exposition must begin; on the other hand, as an *objective characteristic*, as the last (in the inductive chain) and therefore most *superficial* and abstract characteristic (the most *generic* and indeterminate element, if taken by itself) of the concrete object in question. As the latter, one cannot help but refer it back to the more concrete, *internal* relations which are its basis, and from which it is *derived* – a mere mode of being and articulation of those relations.

Now, the situation delineated here is precisely the one found at the beginning of *Capital.* The work begins its analysis by studying the 'form of value', the 'commodity form' assumed by the labour product when it is produced for exchange. Marx takes this as his starting-point because, as he explains, 'the value form of the labour product is the most abstract, but also the most highly generalized, form taken by that product in the bourgeois system of production'.[17] It is the broadest and most comprehensive form for the simple reason that there is nothing (or almost nothing) in bourgeois society which does not have the form of value and does not present itself as a commodity. The 'form of money' and the 'form of capital' itself are only its more *particularized* or specified forms – derived forms which would be absolutely unintelligible if previously one had not clarified the value or commodity form from which they derive.

It is from this that the logico-deductive course of the work proceeds. Beginning with the 'form of value' or commodity form, one descends to the 'form of money' and from this to the 'form of capital', just as, in *logic*, one passes from the universal to the particular, and from the particular to the individual. First of all one begins with the commodity; then money, which is itself a commodity, although it has a particular function; finally capital, which is itself money, designed for a particular use. All of the links of the deductive

17. K. Marx, *Capital*, translated by Eden and Cedar Paul (London, 1930), Vol. I., p. 55 (I have sometimes used this later translation in preference – Trans.).

chain appear to be suspended from the logical *prius* from which they started, so that, as Marx says, 'it may appear that we had before us a mere a priori construction'. In actual fact, what prevents any a priorism is that the category, besides having its meaning as a generality or idea and therefore as a logical *prius*, is here grasped in relation to the *particular object* from which it was abstracted. In other words, it is taken as the most generic and superficial characteristic, the *last* element which has been reached in the course of the inquiry or the analytic dissection of the object (hence the crucial importance of the process of the *formation* of concepts).

All of which means that the work develops, together with the deductive process descending from the commodity to money, and from the latter to capital, as an inductive process *going back* from the *generic* or secondary features of the object in question to its *specific* or primary ones, from subordinate elements to dominant ones – in short, from the 'particular phenomenal forms'[18] of commodity and money to *capital* itself, which is their basis and which alternately assumes those forms in the course of its life cycle.

One must not misunderstand this argument concerning the inverse order of the logical process and of the process of reality. It does not mean that our knowledge gives us an upside-down image of the world, as if we were condemned to seeing the world standing on our heads. Rather, it means that thought by itself is not knowledge; that knowledge is the congruence *between* thought and reality; and that, if anything, it is precisely the person who does not take account of this difference that is condemned to seeing the world upside-down.

Commodity – money – capital: the logical order is to be viewed in this way. Thought passes from the universal to the particular. This is its procedure. However, in so far as the universal which one takes as a starting-point is not a self-contained universal but is only the *simplest* feature of a *complex* object, the expository formula, commodity – money – capital, shows itself to be also the exposition *best-suited* to the procedure by which analysis gradually penetrates the object in question, departing from the non-essential or *generic*

18. ibid., p. 139.

aspects and going back to the fundamental or *specific* ones, from effects to causes, and (in short) from the most superficial phenomena to the real basis implicit in them.

It is clear that everything said at the beginning of *Capital* concerning commodities is valid for commodities in whatever historical conditions they may appear. 'The wealth of societies in which the capitalist method of production prevails, takes the form of "an immense accumulation of commodities", wherein individual commodities are the *elementary units.* Our investigation must therefore begin with an analysis of the commodity.'[19] But since the commodity, even when it is not the 'elementary unit' of bourgeois wealth, is always made, *qua* commodity, in the same way (as a unity of use-value and value), the analysis given in *Capital* is also valid for the commodity as it appears, e.g., in the Greek society of the Odyssey. The same could be said for money. Furthermore, inasmuch as the commodity appears in the logico-deductive process as the *condition* for the genesis of money, and money as the *condition* for capital, it is evident that that logical process itself is none other than the synthetic-rational résumé of the entire historical road that *preceded* the birth of modern capital – starting from that moment, lost in the darkness of time, in which the labour product first acquired the 'form of value' and so became a commodity. 'The circulation of commodities is the starting-point of capital. Commodity production and that highly developed form of commodity circulation which is known as *commerce* constitute the *historical premisses* upon which it rises. The modern history of capital begins in the sixteenth century with the establishment of a worldwide commercial system and the opening of a world market.' Similarly, 'from the historical outlook, capital comes in the first instance to confront landed property in the form of money; it appears as *money property*, merchants' (mercantile) capital and usurers' (moneylenders') capital'. Hence, even if 'we have no need to look back into the origin of capital in order to recognise that money is its first phenomenal form', because 'this history is repeated daily under our own eyes' and because 'every new aggregate of capital enters upon the stage, comes into the market

19. ibid., p. 3.

(the commodity market, the labour market, or the money market), in the form of money',[20] it remains true that the *logical deduction* from money to capital represents the essence of the *historical movement* which preceded the birth of modern capital. (In this regard it may be noted en passant that our argument concerning Marx's derivation from Hegel of the logico-deductive process is also beginning to take shape, together with our argument concerning the role played by this inheritance in the formulation of his thought as *historical thought*.)

It is certainly true that the process by which, in analysing modern capitalism, we depart from its most superficial and abstract aspects and go back to its inward-most and essential ones, is at the same time also a recapitulation of the *historical premisses* which preside over the birth of modern capitalism; on the other hand, it is no less crucial to grasp the *differentiation* of the two processes together with this unity, and – in short – to hold fast more than ever to the idea that deduction is not induction, nor the logical process the process of reality itself. Once the foundations of modern production based on capital have been laid, the cause of the entirety is to be sought, Marx says, in the real premiss itself, i.e. in the present datum that *is and exists*, and not in the historical premisses which by now *no longer exist* and have disappeared. The cause, the foundation in reality, is, in short, capital, and not the commodity or money, which appear rather as its prerequisites from a logical point of view. The deductive process which derives money from commodities and capital from money, just because it sums up the history which preceded the birth of modern capital, will enable us to explain (e.g.) the fact that the money with which the first capitalist bought labour-power could not itself have been the result of wage-labour, but had to have as its prerequisite the simple production of commodities. However, such logical premisses give us, in more precise terms, the 'antediluvian conditions of capital'; they represent 'its historical prerequisites (*Voraussetzungen*), which already as such are past, and thus belong to the history of its development and not in any way to

20. ibid., p. 131 (translation modified).

its contemporary history, i.e. not to the real system of the mode of production which it controls'.[21]

Marx continues thus: 'The conditions and prerequisites of the development, of the *coming into being*, of capital thus in fact imply that it does not yet exist, but that it will; thus they disappear as capital becomes reality, as capital itself, proceeding from its reality, establishes the conditions for its realisation.' These prerequisites, 'which were originally conditions of its formation – and thus could not yet arise from its action *as capital* – now appear as the results of its own realisation, its own reality, as established by it – *not as the condition of its coming into being, but as the result of its existence*'. Those who, contrariwise, mistake the logical process for the process of reality, such as the 'bourgeois economists, who consider capital to be an eternal, *natural* (and not historical) form of production, are always seeking to justify it, in that they portray the conditions of its formation as the conditions of its present realisation. They present the conditions in which the capitalist (because he is still developing into a capitalist) still has a non-capitalist mode of appropriation as the very conditions of capitalist appropriation.'[22]

Let us turn aside from the main argument for a moment, and look at some of its implications. The total lack of understanding of this relationship between the logical process and the process of reality – which is the crucial link that must be examined if one wants to give a rigorous meaning to Marx's concept of *history* – enables us to explain one of the most conspicuous 'oddities' which has characterized theoretical Marxism till now. That is, its tendency to mistake the 'first in time' – i.e. that from which the logical process departs as a *recapitulation* of the historical antecedents – with the 'first in reality' or the actual foundation of the analysis. The consequence has been that whereas Marx's logico-historical reflections culminate in the formulation of the crucial problem of the *contemporaneity of history* (or as Lukács once aptly said, the 'present as

21. K. Marx, *Grundrisse der Kritik der politischen Oekonomie* (Berlin, 1953), p. 363. An English translation of this passage is to be found in *Selections from the Grundrisse*, translated by David McLellan (London and New York, 1970), p. 106.

22. ibid., pp. 363–4. in *Selections*, op. cit., p. 107.

history') traditional Marxism has always moved in the opposite direction of a *philosophy of history* which derives its explanation of the present from the 'beginning of time'. This enables us to understand two things: firstly, the indefatigable yearning for a universal history which would take its starting-point in Epimenides's 'egg' and come right down to the present day (perhaps with the aid of well-known 'general laws') – whence many pensive assertions that, for there to be 'a theoretical substantiation of historical materialism', a truly exhaustive justification of it, one must have, as Plekhanov wrote, 'a brief manual on world history written from the materialist viewpoint'[23] (the wish was subsequently realized by Kautsky with his *Die materialistische Geschichtsauffassung*). Secondly, it also helps us to understand that thinly veiled note of presumption with which Marxism has always judged *Capital* as an analysis of one *particular*, historical phenomenon or as simply one 'example' of the application of a 'general conception' whose justification, however, must remain precarious and uncertain until steps are taken to 'found' it by reconstructing the whole of history.

But the most significant documentary proof of this lack of understanding is offered by writings in which Marxist authors undertook to reconstruct Marx's line of argument in the first two parts of *Capital.* In them one finds that what in Marx's work is a concise recapitulation of *logico*-historical antecedents selected out as a *function* of the *present* – which is the premiss *in reality* to be explained – becomes diluted into a (more or less colourful) narration or description of mercantile relationships as such. In such descriptions, since commodity and money are taken by themselves (rather than as the most general and abstract form *of* the capitalist mode of production), the argument ends up not as the beginning of the analysis of *capital* but as a digression upon an age with ill-defined limits in time, when there may indeed have been commodities and money, but there was not even a trace of capital. Typical in this sense (and all the more so if one takes into account the incisive intelligence of the author) is Luxemburg's *Einführung in die Nationalökonomie* – a work full, moreover, of interesting insights. Or, to come to the

23. G. V. Plekhanov. *Fundamental Problems of Marxism* (New York, 1969), p. 86.

present day (and descending somewhat from past heights), the second and third chapters of E. Mandel's *Marxist Economic Theory* – he too, of course, is a 'dialectical materialist' – with its pathetic paragraphs on 'silent barter and ceremonial gifts' and all its irrelevant padding about how in Papua, or among the Todas, the Karumbas, and the Badogas exchange and money developed little by little out of barter.

It is no accident that the root of these errors lies in their mistaking the logical process for the process of reality, or, in other words, in an abstract *dialectization* of the *finite* (of the concrete object in question). Thus, the determinate relationships which constitute the object itself – such as, e.g., the fact that commodity and money represent the alternate modes of being of capital, which, in investments, passes from the money form to the *commodity* form (means of labour, raw materials, labour-power) and then back again through the realization of the value produced, from the commodity form to that of *money* – these determinate relationships are then all turned and dissolved into abstract rational relationships. Consequently the categories (in this case, the commodity, money, and capital), rather than being grasped in the relations and meaning they have *within modern bourgeois society*, are instead conceived in accordance with the place and meaning which they have in the *succession of the various forms of society* – in other words, according to that succession which is more or less recapitulated in the logico-deductive movement of the 'succession "in the Idea" '.[24]

This accounts for two profoundly different ways of seeing things. On the one hand, there is the thesis of the *Anti-Dühring* that 'political economy, . . . as the science of the conditions and forms under which the various human societies have produced and exchanged and on this basis have distributed their products – political economy in this wider sense has still to be brought into being'; with the corollary observation that 'such economic science as we have up to the present is almost exclusively limited to the genesis and development of the capitalist mode of production'.[25]

24. Marx, *Introduction to the Critique of Political Economy*, op. cit., p. 304 (translation modified).

25. Engels, *Anti-Dühring*, op. cit., p. 166.

On the other hand, there is Marx's thesis, which caps his argument concerning the transformation of the 'historical premises' from *conditions* for the rise of capital into *consequences* of its existence. Here he not only states that 'therefore it is not necessary, in order to analyse the laws of the bourgeois economy, to write the actual history of production relationships'; but he also adds that it is the 'deduction of them as historically developed relationships' which 'always leads us to draw comparisons (*Gleichungen*) based on the past history of this system; and that it is precisely 'these allusions' or comparisons which, 'together with a correct grasp of the present day, . . . also offer a key to the understanding of the past'.[26]

Returning now to the main argument, let us conclude with a restatement which takes the argument back to its epistemological foundations. With an extreme effort of conciseness, one could reduce the entire question of the relation between deduction and induction, logical process and process of reality, to a single two-fold statement of Marx's: that 'every capital is a sum of commodities, i.e., of exchange values, and, on the other hand, that 'not . . . every sum of commodities, of exchange values, is capital'.[27] To paraphrase Kant, this means simply that: (a) whatever agrees in general with a concept – in this case, the commodity or exchange-value – also agrees with every particular which is contained under that concept – in this case, capital; (b) that, nonetheless, it is 'absurd to alter this logical principle so as to read: – what is not contained in a universal concept is also not included in the particular concepts which stand under it. For these are particular concepts just because they include in themselves more than is thought in the universal'; whence the error of those for whom 'nothing is allowed to the thing beyond what is contained in its concept'.[28]

If we have understood it correctly, this means three things. First, that the deduction, commodity-money-capital, is indispensable for understanding capital, in that capital also is a commodity. Second, that the deductive passage from the abstract to the concrete, which is

26. Marx, *Grundrisse*, op. cit., pp. 366–7. In *Selections*, op. cit., pp. 109–10.
27. Marx, *Wage-Labour and Capital* (New York, 1933), p. 29.
28. Kant, *Critique of Pure Reason* (Kemp Smith translation), op. cit., p. 289.

carried out 'in the course of thinking', always remains itself *within the abstract*, such that the concrete or the particular is only a *particularization* of the universal, and not something heterogeneous in relation to that universal (and, in point of fact, that passage tells us that capital also is a commodity, but not what it is that makes any given commodity into capital). Hence the inevitable tautology which is the fate of whoever asserts the validity of the deductive process alone, and hence the forced, surreptitious recourse to experience which they are constrained to make in order to obtain that 'something more' which is indispensable if one wants to break out of the tautology – the something (experience) which thought alone can never succeed in giving us. Third, that the *actual* passage from the abstract to the concrete is not a passage 'within the abstract', but goes from the latter to the concrete of reality (or is the conversion of deduction into induction); so that here one is dealing not with the relationship 'thought-being' *within* thought, but rather with the relationship *between* thought and reality. Once again one confronts the need to consider thought not only as the 'totality' of the relationship but also as 'one of two'.

All this means that deduction or reason – with their demonstration that capital too is a commodity – give us that element indispensable to historical analysis which is the *continuity* of the present with regard to the past. The other point of view – no less indispensable to historical analysis – while considering history as a continuity of events, also sees events as always *discontinuous* among themselves; for this point of view the present has meaning precisely to the degree that it is *not* reducible to the past. And this viewpoint can only be furnished by the domain of matter, which supplies the 'something more' whereby a sum of commodities or exchange-values becomes capital.

Hence there is both continuity and differentiation. There is, for example, inclusion of the particular present to thought, so that the particular fact which is modern capital is connected to the *logical recapitulation* of its historical antecedents and becomes a differentiation within the concept of commodities (Hegel would say: 'the negative of the negative', the finite as a moment within the infinite).

On the other hand, there is also differentiation *in reality*, for the particular fact, far from being reduced to a moment of the logical universal, affirms itself in its *heterogeneous* nature as a thing going beyond the universal, and therefore as the *exclusion* of all the preceding moments summarized in thought. The basis for this is precisely that principle of the non-contradiction of matter which is articulated in Marx's profound remark that, whenever *there exist* the historical prerequisites and premisses for capital, the latter does *not* yet *exist*, and that, contrariwise, whenever capital exists, those historical premisses must have disappeared.

The ultimate sense of this argument is that the principle of reason or dialectical contradiction is insufficient not only in scientific knowledge but also in historical knowledge – and, moreover, is so in the latter precisely because it is itself a form of scientific knowledge. Hence another principle, that of material identity or non-contradiction, is also necessary. In short, it is a question, in Marx's words, of a 'dialectic whose limits are to be determined and which does not sublate concrete differences',[29] those differences which are given to us precisely from consideration of the particular, not just as a moment within the universal, but also as the *exclusion* of *everything* that it (the particular) *is not*.

It is true, then, that the commodity and money, which at first were the prerequisites for the rise of capital, reappear later within capital itself, so that the latter is not an unarticulated identity, but rather a complex or multi-dimensional object. Except that, between the initial phase and the later phase, i.e. between the commodity and money as *prerequisites* for the birth of capital and as the *consequences* of its existence (consequences *posited* by capital itself), there is a fundamental difference, which was extremely important in the difficult elaboration of the theory of value – not as a theory that is valid for the 'primitive and crude state' discussed by Smith, but as a theory valid for the particular conditions of modern capitalist development. This is the difference that exists between simple mercantile production and the capitalist production of commodities.

29. Marx, *Introduction to the Critique of Political Economy*, op. cit., p. 309 (translation modified).

The former is a secondary and subordinate branch of production for direct consumption (and in which the appropriation on the part of the non-producers is not mediated by exchange and the market: the levy on grain for the feudal lord, the grain of the tithe for the priest, the direct appropriation of the product on the part of the slave owner). The capitalist mode of production, on the other hand, is characterized by the *elimination* of everything previously dominant, and by the fact that what was once marginal and secondary has now established itself as the basic element. Thus, value, by becoming the '*overbearing subject*' of the entire productive process, *is no longer* commodity value or money value, but *surplus value*, i.e. capital; and 'presents itself as a substance endowed with independent motion of its own, a substance of which commodities and money are themselves merely forms', such that 'instead of representing relations of commodities, it enters, so to say, into a *private relation to itself*'; and 'it differentiates itself as primary value (investment) from itself as surplus value, much as God the Father distinguishes himself from himself as God the Son; yet both, in fact, form only one person; . . . as soon as the Son, and by the Son the Father, is begotten, the difference between the two vanishes, and both become one. . .'.[30]

If, therefore, one does not wish to repeat the error of those economists who confuse the historical premisses of capital with its present conditions of existence, or (what is the same thing) confuse simple mercantile production with capitalist production, one must clearly grasp three things. First, that the *difference* between these two modes of production has its basis in that principle of the identity of matter which enables the *particular* (in this case, the capitalist mode of production) to win out *to the exclusion* of its opposite, the universal, in which *everything* that it (the particular) *is not*, is recapitulated; in a way, then, which is diametrically opposed to the dialectic of matter or 'dialectical materialism', for which the particular or the finite must have as its essence the 'other', i.e. the infinite or the negative. Second, that precisely this principle of the exclusion of the opposite (the principle of non-contradiction), nonetheless has

30. Marx *Capital* (Eden and Cedar Paul translation), op. cit., p. 140 (translation modified).

need of the principle of *dialectical contradiction* in order to be able to fully realize itself; for, in order to be able to gauge the difference of one thing from other things, it is necessary to compare them with one another (cf. Marx's remark that it is precisely these comparisons which, 'together with a correct grasp of the present day, . . . also offer a key to the understanding of the past'). Third and finally, that the real oppositions or contradictions found within the concrete datum *qua* multi-dimensional object (such as, e.g., the contradiction which arises with labour-power in the passage of capital from the money form to the commodity form, or the contradiction of the conversion crises associated with the reconversion of capital from the commodity form into the money form) are all contradictions which *constitute* the object itself – i.e., contradictions in reality, and for that very reason *particular* or historically determinate ones. In short, they are contradictions which, precisely in so far as they establish the specificity of the capitalist mode of production in relation to all other socio-economic formations, contribute to defining its (capitalism's) *identity*, and thus turn out to be irreducible to the terms of a simple rational contradiction.[31]

31. Marx's entire critique of the method of political economy hinges on this theme of the irreducibility of opposition in reality to logical opposition; that is, the impossibility of taking up the unity of opposites or their inclusion within reason apart from the exclusion of opposites or their antithesis in reality. The argument is developed particularly in this examination of the ways in which political economy attempts to deny crises. We give below some of the most significant passages. 'Where the economic relation – and therefore also the categories expressing it – includes contradictions, opposites, and likewise the unity of the opposites, he [James Mill] emphasizes the aspect of the *unity* of the contradictions and denies the *contradictions*. He transforms the unity of opposites into the direct identity of opposites. For example, a commodity conceals the contradiction of use-value and exchange-value. This contradiction develops further, presents itself and manifests itself in the duplication of the commodity into commodity and money. This duplication appears as a process in the metamorphosis of commodities in which selling and buying are different aspects of a single process and each act of this process simultaneously includes its opposite. In the first part of this work, I mentioned that Mill disposes of the contradiction by concentrating only on the *unity* of buying and selling; consequently he transforms circulation into barter, then, however, smuggles categories borrowed from circulation into his description of barter' (*Theories of Surplus Value*, Part III, London, 1972, p. 88). And again on p. 101 of Part III, op. cit.: 'The logic is always the same. If a relationship includes opposites, it comprises not only opposites but also the *unity* of opposites. It is therefore a *unity without opposites*. This is Mill's

logic, by which he eliminates the "contradictions".' And in Part II of *Theories of Surplus Value* there is this rather significant passage: 'Thus the apologetics consist in the falsification of the simplest economic relations, and particularly in clinging to the concept of unity in the face of contradiction. If, for example, purchase and sale – or the metamorphosis of commodities – represent the unity of two processes, or rather the movement of one process through two opposite phases, and thus essentially the unity of the two phases, the movement is essentially just as much the separation of these two phases and their becoming independent of each other. Since, however, they belong together, the independence of the two correlated aspects can only *show itself* forcibly, as a destructive process. It is just the *crisis* in which they assert their unity, the unity of the different aspects. The independence which these two linked and complimentary phases assume in relation to each other is forcibly destroyed. Thus the crisis manifests the unity of the two phases that have become independent of each other. There would be no crisis without this inner unity of factors that are apparently indifferent to each other. But no, says the apologetic economist. Because there is this unity, there can be no crises. Which in turn means nothing but that the unity of contradictory factors excludes contradiction. In order to prove that capitalist production cannot lead to general crises, all its conditions and distinct forms, all its principles and specific features – in short *capitalist production* itself – are denied. In fact it is demonstrated that if the capitalist mode of production had not developed in a specific way and become a unique form of social production, but were a mode of production dating back to the most rudimentary stages, then its peculiar contradictions and conflicts and hence also their eruption in crises would not exist.' (pp. 500–01) or again on p. 519: 'The apologetic phrases used to deny crises are important in so far as they always prove the opposite of what they are meant to prove. In order to deny crises they assert unity where there is conflict and contradiction.' And one last citation from the *Grundrisse der Kritik der politischen Oekonomie*, p. 161: 'For example, the relationship between capital and interest is reduced to the exchange of exchange-values. Once it has been learned from empirical reality that exchange-values exist not only in this simple determinacy, but also in an essentially different one, as capital, the latter is again reduced to the simple concept of exchange-value; and interest, which now expresses a determinate relationship of capital as such, is also wrenched from its determinacy and equated with exchange-value, abstracted from the entire relationship in its specific determinacy and carried back to the undeveloped relationship of the exchange of one commodity for another. *To the extent that I abstract from what differentiates a concrete datum from its abstraction, the former is naturally that abstraction and does not at all differentiate itself from it.*' (Collett's emphasis.)

IX. Hegel and Jacobi

The importance of this theory of Marx's of the twofold nature of abstraction (as being at once a form, a *generality*, and, *realiter*, a *particularity* of the concrete object in question) cannot be fully appreciated (just as the element which it undeniably derived from Kant cannot be appreciated) until the argument has been expanded. It must be broadened to include – however briefly – that essential moment of the history of modern and contemporary irrationalism which is represented by the struggle to bring about the *destruction of the intellect*. This struggle, which is certainly not lacking in opaque and obscurantist aspects, is still under way today (not without the complicity of 'dialectical materialism' itself, as we shall see). It is not to be confused in any way with the destruction described in Lukács's famous *Die Zerstörung der Vernunft* ('The Destruction of Reason'); for the 'reason' adopted as the standard in his work is not the Enlightenment's *raison* but, on the contrary, Hegel's 'dialectical reason'; and thus 'reason' itself turns out to be contaminated by mystical elements. In Hegel's own words, in the *Zusatz* to subheading 82 of the *Encyclopedia*: '. . . There is mystery in the mystical, only however for the understanding which is ruled by the principle of abstract identity; whereas the mystical, as synonymous with the speculative, is the concrete unity of those propositions, which understanding only accepts in their separation and opposition.' He concludes that thus, 'the reason-world may be equally styled mystical, – not however because thought cannot both reach and comprehend it, but merely because it lies beyond the compass of understanding'.[1]

Now, in this as yet unwritten history of the 'destruction of the intellect', one insight of great interest is offered us by Jacobi's critique of Kant; that Jacobi whom (as we have seen) Hegel held in

1. *En.L.*, p. 154.

such high esteem and so often referred to – despite constant criticisms of him (criticisms harsher, moreover, in the early *Glauben und Wissen* than in his mature works). Hegel even placed him before Kant, as Croce correctly points out: 'In the preliminary remarks to the *Logic* of his *Encyclopedia*, when he indicated the progressive ordering of the "three positions of thought with regard to their objective truth", [Hegel] placed Jacobi's theory of immediate knowledge third and highest.'[2]

The principal argument made by Jacobi's philosophy is, once again, the critique of the 'intellect'. In his first phase, i.e. the phase in which *Über die Lehre des Spinoza* (1785) and the discourse on *Idealismus und Realismus* (1787) were written, the 'intellect' is identified with all of thought; whereas later, as in *Von den göttlichen Dingen* (1811) or in the long *Introduction* of 1815 to the publication of his works, Jacobi explicitly distinguishes 'intellect' from 'reason'.[3] Now, this line of argument immediately shows an important point of contact with Hegel. Thought, Jacobi says (the difference from Hegel is that at this point Jacobi still does not distinguish 'intellectual' from 'rational' thought), is always a knowledge of the *finite*. To think, to understand, to explain is *scire per causas*, i.e. to adduce the conditions for something to exist, the cause and foundation from which the thing itself derives. But that means, Jacobi says, that 'in so far as we think in conceptual terms, we remain within a chain of *conditioned conditions*', in which everything appears to us 'as a consequence of mechanical connexions, i.e. as merely something which is *mediated*', and, in short, as something which is dependent on and the effect of something else (remember Hegel's definition of 'mediation' as a process of arriving at something by starting from another). 'Everything that reason can produce through analysing, making connexions, judging, reasoning, and reflexive knowing are mere things of nature, and human reason itself, as a limited essence, also belongs to these things. But all of nature, the whole of deter-

2. Benedetto Croce, *Considerazioni sulla filosofia del Jacobi*, in 'La Critica', Vol. XXXIX (Naples, 1941), pp. 320–1.

3. F. H. Jacobi, *Idealismo e Realismo*, edited by Norberto Bobbio (Turin, 1948), pp. 10 and 159 (for the original of this and all other Jacobi quotes, see his *Werke*, 5 vols, Leipzig, 1812–20).

minate beings, cannot manifest to the inquiring understanding more than what is contained in nature, i.e. manifold existence, changes, a play of forms – never a *real* beginning, never a real start of some *objective* existence.'[4]

Now, Jacobi says, this mediated nature of our logico-intellectual knowledge, characterized by the principle of causality, accounts for the fact that not only can thought not conceive of 'the concept of an *absolute beginning or origin* of nature' – the concept of the *unconditional* – but also for the fact that whenever it attempts to conceive of this, it cannot help but undermine its own meaning. For, 'if a concept of this unconditional and unlinked – and therefore of the *extra-natural* – becomes possible, it too must be subjected to certain conditions'. This accounts, Jacobi continues, for 'the irrationality of the claim to a *proof* for the existence of God'. Because no sooner do our understanding and will ('for both of them are enmeshed in co-existence, i.e. in dependency and finitude') venture to deal with the 'first cause' than they change it from first to second – proof of the deep-seated contradictoriness of the old metaphysics, which never realized that, in its claim to prove God *by logical means*, 'the natural *had been posited as the basis* of the supranatural, and nonetheless the former had to be conceived as inferior to the latter'. And Jacobi concludes thus: 'Since everything that lies outside the chain of the causally conditioned and of that which is *mediated as a natural fact*, is also outside the sphere of our clear knowledge and cannot be understood through concepts; the supranatural cannot be acknowledged by us in any way other than as it is given to us, i.e. *as fact* – IT IS.'[5]

The argument, as one can see, carried us back – and indeed it is one of its sources – to Hegel's critique of precritical metaphysics

4. F. H. Jacobi, *Lettere sulla dottrina di Spinoza*, in op. cit., pp. 224, 226 and 222.

5. ibid., pp. 224, 225 and 227. Cf. also *Idealismo e Realismo*, p. 246: 'Whenever one has to give the proof of something, it is always necessary to have an argument on which to base the proof. This argument encompasses the thing to be proven as something subordinate to itself, such that the thing's truth and certitude derive therefrom, and such that it receives its own reality from the argument . . . Similarly, if we had to prove the existence of a living God, it would be necessary that God could be explained, deduced, and unravelled from His beginning, from something which we could grasp as His foundation and which would be antecedent and external to Him.'

(in particular, Descartes, Spinoza, and Leibniz). The principle of that philosophy was idealism, i.e. the proposition that the sense-world is nothingness and dross. The content of that metaphysics was the absolute, i.e. the proposition that God and God alone is the truth. Nevertheless, the method of 'intellectual demonstration' used by that philosophy forced it to contradict itself in spite of itself. In the passage from the world to God, God – who had been declared the creator and therefore *primus* – became *secundus*; whereas the world, which had been declared non-being and ephemerality, became the 'fixed being' which is the foundation of things.

Hegel's reference to Jacobi on this point is unequivocal. In a very important page of Volume II of the *Science of Logic* (cited above) Hegel distinguishes between the attack waged on the old metaphysics by Kant *with regard to its contents* (i.e. criticizing its claim to have removed the suprasensible and the absolute – God, the soul, etc. – from the empirical object) and that waged by Jacobi, who 'has attacked it chiefly on the side of its method of demonstration, and has signalized most clearly and most profoundly the essential point, namely, that a method of demonstration such as this is fast bound within the circle of the rigid necessity of the finite, and that *freedom*, that is the *Notion*, and with it *everything that is true*, lies beyond it and is unattainable by it'.[6]

The high esteem for this fundamental theme of Jacobi's thought reappears in the paragraphs of the *Encyclopedia* devoted to him. Hegel writes thus, explaining his thought: 'To *comprehend* an object . . . can only mean . . . to grasp it under the form of something *conditioned* and *mediated*. Consequently, if the object in question be the True, the Infinite, the Unconditioned, it is changed into a finite and conditioned; whereby, instead of apprehending the truth by thought, we have inverted it into untruth.'[7]

Hegel's critical reservations are never lacking, of course. Even in this paragraph which concludes by approving Jacobi's polemic against science and materialism, one glimpses the basic cause of disagreement. Jacobi's critique is effective against the 'intellect'; but it is wrong about 'reason'. Jacobi's concepts of intuition, faith

6. *L.*, p. 816.

7. *En.L.*, pp. 121–2 (translation modified).

and 'immediate knowledge' contain major equivocations. Sometimes that intuition shows traces of a subjectivist sensationalism, while at other times – as when 'intuition and belief . . . are taken in a higher sense, (as) belief in God' – intuition is none other than 'intellectual intuition' and, therefore, thought itself.[8] Here too there are still some of the sarcastic remarks about Jacobi's 'wild vagaries of imagination and assertion', which abound in Hegel's early writing; just as there is not lacking the grave warning that 'philosophy does not permit mere assertion, nor flights of the imagination, nor fanciful somersaults of ratiocination'.[9] The expression 'Faith', Hegel observes, 'brings with it the special advantage of suggesting the faith of the Christian religion. . .'. However, 'we must not let ourselves be deceived by appearances. . . . The Christian faith comprises in it an authority of the Church: but the faith of Jacobi's philosophy has no other authority than that of one's own subjective revelation.'[10] For 'immediate knowledge', 'all superstition or idolatry' can very well be 'allowed to be truth': 'It is because he believes in them, and not from the reasoning and syllogism of what is termed mediate knowledge, that the Hindoo finds God in the cow, the monkey, the Brahmin, or the Lama.'[11]

Nevertheless, admitting all this, Croce was still correct when – basing himself on Hegel's 1817 review of the third volume of Jacobi's *Werke*, as well as on these paragraphs from the *Encyclopedia* – he pointed out that Hegel, after his earlier 'lively critique' of Jacobi, 'made amends in the maturity of his genius for that initial judgment, and assigned him a very high place in the formation of philosophic logic'. He also stressed that 'Hegel praised and approved of Jacobi for having pointed out, with all possible forcefulness and resoluteness, the capital importance of the immediacy of divine knowledge, that He is a living God, Spirit and eternal love, and that, by differentiating Himself within Himself, He is knowledge of Himself'.[12] The two were allied in some academic controversies, while Jacobi's clarification of his own philosophy – his incorporation

8. ibid., p. 124.
9. ibid., p. 141 (translation modified).
10. ibid., p. 125 (translation modified).
11. ibid., p. 136.
12. Croce, art. cit., p. 320.

of the distinction between 'intellective' (*Verstands-*) thought and 'rational' thought (e.g.) and his final recognition that his 'intuition' or faith was nothing other than 'speculative reason' itself – also contributed to the change in Hegel's attitude. The latter arrived, in fact, at a fuller understanding of the real nature of Jacobi's philosophy.

Without fear of exaggeration, one can say that one of the best proofs of how Hegel still remains *malgré tout* the greatest historian of philosophy is offered precisely by the extraordinary acuity with which he grasped the place of Jacobi's philosophy in the history of thought. Just think: Jacobi, as a critic of Spinoza! One of the first remarks on Jacobi in the *Encyclopedia* is that the arguments of his polemic against the 'intellect' were 'borrowed from the philosophy of Spinoza himself'. And as for Jacobi's 'realism' (!) that realism that has so often given rise to ill-founded remarks about his supposed materialism (such as those who say: if you want materialism, you have to refer back to Jacobi and not to Kant!) – here too Hegel shows an admirable incisiveness. 'This immediate knowledge', he writes, 'consists in knowing that the Infinite, the Eternal, the God which exists in our representation (*Vorstellung*), really *is*; or, that in our consciousness there is immediately and inseparably bound up with this representation the certainty of its actual being.'[13] Or again: Jacobi's 'intuition', which has so often served to represent materialism as an act of faith! Hegel's reply here is that this intuition, this 'immediate knowledge' (an ecstasis towards the on-high and not downwards to the baseness of matter) is the very intuition with which modern idealism begins: the immediate *identity* of thought and being, the *Cogito ergo sum* of Descartes – 'the founder of modern philosophy', on whose proposition 'may be said to hinge the whole interest of Modern Philosophy'. Hegel adds immedately thereafter with delightful irony that, in fact, 'one need know little more about the nature of syllogism than that in a syllogism the word *Ergo* appears, in order to regard that proposition as a syllogism. But where is the *medius terminus* supposed to be? It is more essential to the nature of syllogism than the word *Ergo*. If, however, one attempts to

13. *En.L.*, p. 126 (translation modified).

justify the use of the term by calling that connexion established by Descartes an *immediate* (*unmittelbar*) syllogism, then this superfluous form of syllogism is nothing but a *connexion* of *different* determinations, *mediated by nothing*. But then the connexion of being with our representations, as expressed in the maxim of immediate knowledge, is neither more nor less than a syllogism.'[14]

It could not be better stated. At the basis of modern idealism lies 'immediate knowledge', *innatism*, or the presupposition of the idea – not the syllogism, which would be a form of reasoning, but rather an 'intellectual' *intuition*, or in simple terms, *faith*. Hegel's merit is that he was at least aware of this.[15]

Hegel is not deceived as to the real stature of Jacobi: he is a second-rank thinker (in comparison with Descartes's expressions, 'so vivid and distinct', concerning the 'inseparability of the thinking ego from being', 'the modern statements of Jacobi and others . . . can only pass for needless repetitions').[16] But he correctly grasps the true meaning of Jacobi's philosophy: the revival – so important in his eyes – of the very 'principle' of classical metaphysics (the identity of thought and being), as against and *after* the philosophy of Kant.

Whatever may be the enormous differences separating Hegel from Jacobi, it is beyond doubt that – at least in the critico-negative part of their thought and especially in the critique of Kant, of materialism, of the 'scientific understanding' and the principle of causality – there exists in their arguments a broad area of convergence.

In the *Critique of Pure Reason*, Jacobi says, 'the intellect, although it is termed the second source of knowledge, is not in actual fact such a source, for objects are not posited, but only thought by it'.[17] 'Without the data of either pure or empirical intuition, the understanding . . . cannot develop itself, nor attain an actual existence. Thus it is conditioned by the sense-world; and, in the mode of thought that is characteristic of it, the intellect relates to it (the

14. ibid., p. 127 (translation modified).

15. Cf. G. W. F. Hegel, *Differenz des Fichteschen und Schellingschen Systems*, op. cit., pp. 67–8: 'Similarly, transcendental knowledge and transcendental intuition are one and the same.'

16. ibid., p. 128.

17. Jacobi, *Idealismo e Realismo*, op. cit., p. 19.

sense-world) in everything and for everything as a means.'[18] Not only this, but since 'the intellect cannot find in nature what is not there, i.e. its creator', it ends by 'formulating the thesis that nature exists on its own, self-sufficient. . . , and one concludes that nature alone exists and that outside and above it nothing exists'.[19]

The consequence, Jacobi continues, is a radical 'reversal'. Intellect and science represent a view of reality which is the opposite of that proffered by philosophy. 'Proceeding from sensory intuition' and 'developing itself primarily within it', the intellect cannot take as a premiss for this intuition the Notion of the true as it is formulated by reason', i.e. the Notion of the *unconditional*. On the contrary, 'the understanding poses the question of the substratum of this Notion – without which there is no way of verifying its (the Notion's) reality –, and searches for it on the level of phenomena, in which it believes that it is able to find the being-in-itself of all beings and their manifold properties'.[20] The consequence is that, in Kant's philosophy, 'objective validity' is denied 'to the idea of the unconditional', according it only 'a merely subjective validity', such that 'there takes place in man's cognitive faculty a total reversal as a result of this contrived transformation of the unconditional from a real being into a merely ideal one; reason is degraded to the level of mere understanding, and the philosophy of absolute nothingness has its beginning'.[21]

Here, as the reader himself can see, the link with Hegel becomes very evident. Straining at the very limits of his own *intuitionist* philosophy, Jacobi comes to the point of formulating his argument on the process of development 'according to nature' and the process of development 'according to the Notion'. Kant's mistake was to have made the Notion, which should have been the *unconditional*, something secondary and dependent. With him, the finite *is* and the infinite *is not*: 'The revelation of nothingness is placed on the side of God and of the suprasensible or supranatural; truth and reality, contrariwise, on the side of that which can be apprehended with the senses, on the side of nature, which alone unfolds itself objectively.'

18. ibid., p. 20.
19. ibid., p. 66.
20. ibid., p. 57.
21. ibid., p. 269.

In other words, Kant's error was to have sustained the process of development 'according to nature'; whereas, Jacobi argues, 'if one wants to leave even a single way open for giving an objective meaning to the ideas of pure notions of reason, one must above all deny objective meaning to the initial notions of the understanding (i.e. the categories), deny the reality of nature and its laws, and deny to the 'intellect the property of being in some way a faculty suited for knowing the true'. In the *Critique*, however, Kant 'counterposes the interest of science (or of the intellect) to that of reason, Epicureanism to Platonism, and presents himself as a representative of science, of Epicureanism against Platonism, of naturalism against theism'.[22]

The project for the 'destruction of the intellect' – the *Annihilation des Verstandes* which Hegel too discusses in *Glauben und Wissen*[23] – is here laid down very resolutely. In order to give 'an objective meaning to the ideas and pure Notions of reason' (the 'objectivism' so ardently championed against Kant by 'dialectical materialism' as well, that objectivism in the name of which Lukács did not fear to appeal even to Schelling) 'one must deny objective meaning to the intellect and, therefore, one must deny the reality of nature and its laws'.

Destruction of nature and, together with it, destruction of the intellect and of science, this is Jacobi's project. And one can well understand why, in spite of his reservations, Hegel should not disapprove of it. As Jacobi writes: 'The understanding and reason act like the flesh and the spirit, which, according to Paul's saying, oppose one another because they desire different things. And just as the flesh is the manifest element, . . . and the spirit is the concealed element', so we tend to think, blinded as we are by external appearances, that 'the faculty of our mediated knowledge is superior to that of immediate knowledge, conditioned knowledge superior to unconditional, the faint echo to the vibrant voice which announces the spirit, the intellect to reason.'[24] Whereas in fact science is only an 'echo of an echo',[25] illusory knowledge, an empty play-thing.

22. ibid., pp. 250, 247 and 249.
23. G. W. F. Hegel, *Glauben und Wissen*, op. cit., p. 334.
24. Jacobi, op. cit., p. 267.
25. loc cit.

'Our sciences, taken simply as such, are toys which the human spirit has made for itself as a diversion. By making these toys, it has organized its own ignorance without even coming a hair's breadth closer to knowledge of the true.'[26]

Jacobi's conception of the world is not only – and it takes little effort to grasp this – a religious conception of the world, but also (as often happens) one in which frankly superstitious elements weigh quite heavily. And nonetheless, despite this (or perhaps precisely because of this) Jacobi's place in the history of thought is a significant one. Not only on account of his resolute and ferocious polemic against science and the principle of causality, which made him the archetypal representative of an all too flourishing family tree; but also (and above all) as the consequence of an argument – not 'discovered' by him, but perhaps first given full expressive force by him – which he added onto that polemic. The argument, that is, that science is the *abstract* and philosophy the *concrete*; every *naturalistic* conception is abstract, while spiritualism is concrete.

The theme is already familiar to us. We came across it while analysing the thesis which lies at the centre of Hegel's entire thought: i.e., the thesis that the finite is *ideal* and the infinite *real*; abstract the knowledge of the 'part', concrete the knowledge of the 'totality'. Nevertheless, whereas Hegel continues in spite of this to term his own philosophy 'idealism', with Jacobi the idea receives a considerably more radical formulation. This formulation derives directly from the accusation of *abstractness* directed at 'finite knowledge', *qua* knowledge of the particular, and from the counterposing of 'rational' or infinite knowledge as the only *concrete* form of knowledge. It consists in a turning upside-down of the meaning of the terms *idealism* and *realism*; whereby what, by traditional usage, would be called naturalism or materialism, is instead termed 'idealism'; and, vice versa, what would usually be called idealism or spiritualism is termed 'realism'.

Idealism is science, causal determinism, naturalism, or what Jacobi calls generically 'Spinozism'; because, as it never leaves the 'closed circle of the conditioned', logico-intellectual knowledge can

26. ibid., pp. 183–4.

only put us in the presence of the world of nature and its laws – a 'manifest' world, like the flesh, but 'in truth' unreal like a dream. Realism, on the other hand, is mystical feeling, the immediate 'certainty' which lies in the spirit, the *faith* in the existence of God that bursts forth from consciousness. As Croce writes: 'In the various and contradictory Spinozist philosophers Jacobi perceived "idealism", as he called it, in the original meaning of this word in polemical usage: to consider as truth or as the sole truth accessible to man, the abstractions of the physico-mathematical sciences and of the causalist and determinist metaphysics modelled after them; and claiming to be a realist and only a realist, he remained on guard against any encroachment of the intellect or any recourse to it.'[27]

Science, therefore, is *nothingness* because it implies abstraction, and abstraction implies a honing down, almost a rarefaction of being. Science is nothingness because it reveals to us an accidental, contingent, and phenomenal world (and here, of course, Jacobi attempts to make capital from Kant's phenomenalism). The full and true reality, however, is what is presented to us by 'faith' or the 'unmediated authority of reason', whose knowledge – being 'a form of knowledge that has no need of proofs, an original, superior knowledge which does not depend on particular characteristics'[28] – escapes verification and the process of selection which is carried out by thought. 'Reason is the consciousness of the spirit. But the spirit can only be in so far as it derives directly from God. Thus to possess reason and to have consciousness of God are one and the same thing, just as it is one and the same thing not to have consciousness of God and to be an unreasoning brute.'[29]

Once again: 'because the finite is *not*, for this reason the absolute *is*'; 'the *non-being* of the finite is the *being* of the absolute'. Once account has been taken of all the very real differences between Hegel and Jacobi, there remains something in common. The philosophy which begins without (external) presuppositions begins, in actual fact, by presupposing itself; i.e., it begins by taking up the Idea as something that is 'already' given, knowledge as something preconstituted 'from the beginning of time', the *Logos* as a *fact*.

27. Croce, art. cit., p. 323. 28. Jacobi, op. cit., p. 246. 29. ibid., p. 262.

Jacobi of course also refers to 'a form of knowledge that has no need of proofs', to 'an original, superior knowledge which does not depend on particular characteristics', and wherein the Notion is not conditioned by a finite that is its *substratum*; he says that 'the supranatural cannot be acknowledged by us in any way other than as it is given to us, i.e. *as fact* – IT IS'. This Jacobi is certainly not to be confused with Hegel; nonetheless, he has in common with him the identity of thought and being.

He has in common this identity and (consequently) in common also the aversion for 'causal explanation', the famous *Erklären* (see the second chapter of the third section of Volume II of the *Logic*; this same *Erklären*, it should be noted, will later be the object of the attack launched by the irrationalist polemic of Dilthey and Rickert).

Here what one can and must acknowledge is a single fact: the point is not that there exists common ground, at least in a critical-negative sense, between Hegel's idealism and the mystical spiritualism of Jacobi, but that with the course of time all of the major reservations which idealism – following Hegel – has maintained in regard to Jacobi's intuitionism have been little by little lessened and diminished. So that idealism and spiritualism, united in the 'fatal embrace' of their common opposition to materialism and science, have seen the barrier separating them gradually diminish and the difference between one and the other grow more and more blurred.

Croce writes of Kant that he 'never ventured to declare the science of the intellect non-science or non-truth, and the science of reason the only true science and philosophy, but regarded the former one as the sole, true science, the only one that is given to man'. – Then this same Croce not only finds that Jacobi 'was more radical and better inspired in that regard'; he goes on to justify Jacobi's mysticism as a salutary reaction 'to the philosophic ideal of his time, i.e. materialism, naturalism, determinism, intellectualism, and logicism, which elevated the exact science of nature into a metaphysics and introduced this metaphysics into the area of philosophic truths' (as if the German Enlightenment had consisted of so many Lamettries). He not only presents in a sympathetic light 'his (Jacobi's) critique of the philosophizing done with the causal and determinist method of the physico-mathematical science of nature', agreeing with him that 'the principle of causality does not transcend nature, the realm of the finite and that as a result we are coming moreover to realize that such a realm does not exist'; he goes on to conclude by outrightly espousing Jacobi's cause, and even turns against Hegel himself in the name of Jacobi. Croce writes: 'In point of fact, Hegel, although he arrived at a thought as important and fecund as that of the dialectic, i.e. of the logic which is intrinsic to philosophy and history, left standing the constructs of the intellect, as a result of a sort of compromise with the Hellenic and Scholastic philosophic traditions as well as with Cartesian and Spinozist rationalism; he refrained from doing anything other than to correct these constructs and to elevate and complete them by means of the dialectic, which, being used in this way, necessarily became extrinsic; as a consequence, he retained a great deal of the framework of the old metaphysics, even though he filled it with new thoughts, which logically should have broken and swept away that old framework.'[30]

There is no need to deal here with this somewhat hasty and summary interpretation of Hegel's critique of the old metaphysics. That critique was not simply a work of 'correction' but a much more complex process: the process of the transformation of the Substance into the Subject, the shifting of God from the 'beyond' into the here and now of subjective *self-consciousness* and, in short, to use Feuerbach's formula, it was the passage from theism or 'ordinary theology' to 'speculative theology' or immanentism (a transformation, as we shall see, of profound historical significance). More important here, one can hardly fail to be struck by how even in this philosopher of so many 'distinctions' (*i distinti*), the spiritualist *raptus* acts with such force as to make him judge insufficient even Hegel's 'destruction' of the finite and the intellect. Hegel did not carry out his work thoroughly enough. The 'constructs of the intellect', the 'framework' of determinate logical thinking, must be still further 'broken' and 'swept away'; so that the spirit may be freed from all concepts that are definite, determinate, and non-'fluid', or as Bergson would call them, *figés* – those same 'fixed'

30. Croce, art. cit., pp. 320, 317, 318 and 323.

concepts exorcized (above) in the introduction to the *Anti-Dühring*. And since metaphysics is precisely the 'constructs' of the intellect, Croce – who does not care for metaphysics – is in a position to correct Hegel with Jacobi. 'As against "idealism", which is tied against its will to the knowing process as *Verstand* and to naturalistic schema, even though it strives to perfect them with the dialectic, Jacobi affirms the innocent truth of visible or sensible things unaltered by abstractions'[31] – i.e. the innocent truth of the 'poor in spirit' to whom the portals of heaven are open, the 'sensible things' which Jacobi discusses in *Von den göttlichen Dingen und ihrer Offenbarung* ('On Divine Things and Their Revelation').

These lines critical of Hegel are rich in points of reference. There recurs in them the theme, basic in Hegel and in his relationship to Spinoza, of the transcendence of Eleaticism, i.e. of the broadening of the principle of Parmenides into the 'identity of identity and non-identity' (here, indeed, a theme that constitutes one of the strengths of Hegel's logic is ungenerously turned against him). There is also, as an ongoing development of this first theme, another which is a sort of corollary to it: the great antithesis between *Christian realism and Greek idealism*, an antithesis popularized at the beginning of the century by the Abbé Laberthonnière, a modernist and follower of Blondel, in a book of the same title. But long before it became the main argument of Christian spiritualism, this theme had its roots in German romantic philosophy and in Hegel's thought itself. The antithesis is between Greek naturalistic intellectualism and the principle of infinite Subjectivity (which is nonetheless individual and concrete spirit) introduced into the world by Christianity with the idea of the God-man. As Hegel writes in his discussion of Spinoza: 'The difference between our standpoint and that of Eleatic philosophy is only this, that through the agency of Christianity concrete individuality is in the modern world present throughout in spirit.'[32] However, this is precisely what is lacking in Spinoza: 'the principle of subjectivity, individuality, personality, the moment of self-consciousness in Being'.[33]

The importance of this theme and the role that it has played in

31. ibid., p. 325. 32. *H.P.*, Vol. III, p. 258. 33. ibid., p. 287.

Italian neo-idealism can hardly be discussed here. It must suffice to point out how the antithesis between 'intellect' and 'reason', thus developed as the antithesis between Greek *naturalistic* idealism and Christian *spiritualist realism*, was taken up as the basic principle of the *Sistema di Logica*, in Gentile's '*attualismo*' (Actualism). To quote Gentile: 'All of philosophy, which for us is encompassed in the history of its development from Thales to our day, is divided into two clearly distinct periods. In the first one, which can be termed that of *Greek philosophy*, intelligible reality or the concept of reality is constructed in a naïve fashion; and for this reason philosophy is not aware of the subjective character of this intelligibility of the real, and therefore of the subjective character of the real itself; and it fully develops this position out to its extreme conclusions by bolstering, so to speak, to the highest degree possible the concept of a reality in itself. In the second period, which must be termed the *Christian* epoch because of its original and most powerful inspirational motif, philosophy gradually acquires a critical and reflective awareness of the workings of the spirit in the production of reality. Thus, it can be said that there have been two philosophies which have been delineated in history: the first one definable as the concept of reality; the second one as the concept of the spirit; or, in other words, the first one as the concept of the spirit as reality and the second one as the concept of reality as spirit.'[34]

Thus, the logic of the *finite* is 'the logic of the abstract'; while the logic of the *infinite* is 'the logic of the concrete'. Naturalism is *idealism* and spiritualism is *realism*. 'Greek philosophy, which was naturalistic before Socrates, idealistic from Socrates to Aristotle, and naturalistically idealistic afterwards, shows itself to be, in point of fact, entirely naturalistic to whomever considers its unchanging character, which consists in the fact that it always sought the spirit in the antecedent of spirit, nature; and as such, it was not philosophic, but a part of the nature proper to the individual sciences.'[35]

Just as in Hegel then, materialism and science belong to *Unphilosophie*. The 'true' philosophy is always and only *idealism* – the

34. Giovanni Gentile, *Sistema di logica*, Vol. I (Florence, 1940), p. 22.
35. ibid., p. 30.

philosophy of the 'concrete'. To contrast idealist with realist philosophy is therefore meaningless. Any philosophy which ascribes true being to finite existence as such does not deserve the title of philosophy. And since, as Gentile says, the method of science is 'implicitly committed to the principle of dogmatically presupposing its own object'[36] (Gentile's pathetic belief is that the greatest possible insult to thought is to suggest that the ink-well exists outside of us!), science is *dogmatism*; whereas idealism, which asks us to accept as *data* a list of much more imposing presuppositions (God, the soul, the Idea, etc.) is *critical thought*. That Kant wrote his *Refutation* of all this is of no account. Hence the monotonous refrain from which no one today appears to escape: science is *idealism*, formalism; the idealist dialectic is *realism*; the *part* is the abstract, the *totality* the concrete. The principle of identity or material determination, the principle which gives us the particular *to the exclusion* of its opposite, is *metaphysics*. Contrariwise, idealism, the 'dialectic of matter' – i.e. the assumption that the finite does not have reality in and of itself, but has as its essence and foundation the infinite and, consequently, *everything* that it (the finite) *is not* – this idealism is genuine *science*. What recent times have added to this is only a bit of naïveté; the extraordinary naïveté of believing that the 'rational' totality which Hegel discusses – i.e. that Idea, 'round in itself', which, as he says, is *this* just as much as *that*, precisely because it is a *Weder–Noch*, i.e. *neither* this *nor* that – is . . . simply the totality of the *natural world*.

'Scientific experience', Kojève writes, 'is thus only a pseudo-experience. And it cannot be otherwise, for vulgar science is in fact concerned not with the concrete real, but with an *abstraction*. To the extent that the scientist thinks or knows his object, what really and concretely exists is the *entirety* of the Object . . . The isolated Object is but an abstraction'. That means, Kojève continues, that, e.g., due to its limited and one-sided character, 'the (verbal) physical description of the Real necessarily implies contradictions: the "physical real" is simultaneously a wave filling all of space and a particle localized in one point, and so on. By its own admission, Physics can never attain Truth in the strong sense of the term. – In

36. loc. cit.

fact, Physics does not study and describe the concrete Realm but only an artificially isolated aspect of the Real – that is, an abstraction . . . there is no Truth in the domain of Physics (and of science in general). Only philosophic Discourse can achieve Truth, for it alone is related to the *concrete* Real – that is, to the *totality* of the reality of Being. The various sciences are always concerned with abstractions.'[37]

And again (because it is as well for the reader to have a complete idea of this type of argument): 'Let us consider,' Kojève says, 'a *real* table. This is not *Table* "in general", not just *any* table, but always *this concrete* table right here. Now, when "naïve" man or a representative of some science or other speaks of *this* table, he isolates it from the rest of the universe: he speaks of *this* table without speaking of what is not this table. Now, *this* table does not float in empty space It is on *this* floor, in *this* room, in *this* house, in *this* place on Earth, which Earth is at a determined distance from the Sun, which has a determined place within the galaxy, etc., etc. To speak of this table without speaking of the rest, then, is *to abstract* from this rest, which in fact is just as real and concrete as this table itself. To speak of this table without speaking of the whole of the Universe which implies it, . . . is therefore to speak of an *abstraction* and not of a *concrete reality*.' 'In short,' Kojève concludes, 'what exists as a *concrete reality* is the spatial-temporal *totality* of the natural world: everything that is *isolated* from it is by that very fact an *abstraction*, which exists as isolated only in and by the *thought* of the man who thinks about it.'[38]

The quotation is rather long, but it deserved to be presented. Following this line of reasoning, an Italian '*attualista*' thinker stated a number of years ago that, since the *particular* which is science's object of study is incomprehensible outside of the *totality*, the problem of science was identical with the *theological problem*. It is legitimate to doubt whether this point of view was 'enlightened' or, more simply, at all acceptable to scientists. There is no doubt, however, that, in comparison with Kojève's thesis or, in point of

37. A. Kojève, *Introduction to the Reading of Hegel*, op. cit., pp. 177–8.
38. ibid., pp. 210–11.

fact, with that expounded by Stalin at the beginning of his well-known essay *On Dialectical Materialism and Historical Materialism* (and of which Kojève's is only a rhetorical amplification),[39] the Italian philosopher's argument enjoyed one undeniable superiority: the superiority of one who really knew what he was talking about.

39. The reference is to the definition of metaphysics as 'knowledge of the part' at the beginning of Stalin's essay, *On Dialectical Materialism and Historical Materialism.*

X. From Bergson to Lukács

Examining Bergson's critique of science in his *Logica come scienza del concetto puro*, Croce makes this illuminating remark: 'All of this criticism directed against the sciences does not sound new to the ears of those who have already heard the critiques of Jacobi, Schelling, Novalis, and other romantics, and in particular the extraordinary one made by Hegel of the abstract (i.e. empirical and mathematical) intellect and which runs through all of his books, from the *Phenomenology of the Mind* to the *Science of Logic*, enriched by examples in his comments on the paragraphs of the *Philosophy of Nature*.'[1]

In point of fact, Bergson is just that: the high point of the convergence between the modern 'idealist reaction against science'[2] and certain major themes of romantic philosophy. 'Life' is movement, becoming, being and non-being together, continuity and reciprocal interpenetration of opposites. The 'intellect', contrariwise, is the abstraction which isolates the *particular* from its opposite, which takes the determinate object to the exclusion of everything that it *is not*. It is sufficient to hold fast to these two themes in order to arrive directly at the heart of Bergson's thought. The intellect – '*et je dis*', Bergson specifies, '*l'intelligence, je ne dis pas la pensée, je ne dis pas l'esprit* (I say the intellect, I do not say thought, I do not say mind)'[3] – 'dislikes what is fluid, and solidifies everything it touches'.[4] 'Of

1. Benedetto Croce, *Logica come scienza del concetto puro* (Bari, 1942), p. 359.

2. This expression, which was originally used by Aliotta in a positive sense in a well-known book of 1912, has been adopted again, and rightly so, by F. Lombardi – although this time in the sense of a regressive phenomenon – in *Il senso della storia* (Rome, 1965), pp. 137 ff.

3. Henri Bergson, *La Pensée et le Mouvant* (Paris, 1946), p. 102. English translation by M. L. Andison, *The Creative Mind* (New York, 1946), p. 110 (translation modified).

4. H. Bergson, *L'évolution créatrice* (Paris, 1914), p. 50. English translation by Arthur Mitchell, *Creative Evolution* (New York, 1944) pp. 52–3.

immobility alone does the intellect form a clear idea'; it is incapable of conceiving '*la continuité vraie, la mobilité réelle, la compénétration réciproque et, pour tout dire, cette évolution qui est la vie* (true continuity, real mobility, reciprocal penetration – in a word, that creative evolution which is life)'.[5] The 'insoluble difficulties' into which the intellect falls whenever it 'speculates upon things as a whole', derive simply from the fact that 'the intellect is especially destined for the study of a part, . . . we nevertheless try to use it in knowing the whole'.[6]

Common sense, which concerns itself only with self-contained objects (*objets détachés*) and 'science, which considers only isolated systems', both persist in 'treating the living like the lifeless and think all reality, however fluid, under the form of the sharply defined solid. We are at ease only in the discontinuous, in the immobile, in the dead. *The intellect is characterized by a natural inability to comprehend life.*'[7]

However, beneath 'these clear-cut crystals and this frozen surface' which the intellect and science present to us as reality, there lies, in actual fact, '*une continuité d'écoulement* (a continuity of flow)': 'It is not the "states", simple snapshots we have taken . . . along the course of change, that are real; on the contrary, it is flux, the continuity of transition, it is change itself that is real.'[8] Philosophy cannot grasp this profounder reality of 'becoming', except when 'it goes beyond the concept, or at least when it frees itself of the inflexible and ready-made concepts and creates others very different from those we usually handle, I mean flexible, mobile, almost fluid representations, always ready to mould themselves on the fleeting forms of intuition'.[9] When, in short, it succeeds in raising itself to 'fluid concepts, capable of following reality in all its windings and of adopting the very movement of the inner life of things'.[10] If, however, we attempt to grasp the 'profound meaning of movement' with the aid of ordinary concepts (concepts that are '*figés, distincts,*

5. ibid., pp. 169 and 175. English translation, pp. 171 and 178.
6. H. Bergson, *The Creative Mind*, op. cit., p. 44.
7. H. Bergson, *Creative Evolution*, op. cit., pp. 12 and 182.
8. H. Bergson, op. cit., p. 16.
9. ibid., pp. 192 (translation modified) and 198.
10. ibid., p. 224.

immobiles'), we get nowhere; for 'in vain we force the living into this or that one of our moulds. All the moulds crack. They are too narrow, above all too rigid'.[11]

We shall forgo here any comparison with Hegel, and the more complex argument this would entail. But certain analogies with Engels present themselves as a matter of course. Identity is inertia, stillness, '*dead being*'; '*life*', movement, are by contrast 'becoming', unity of being and non-being together, the contradiction and reciprocal interpenetration of opposites. And, just as for Engels, common sense or the 'metaphysical way of viewing things' may be 'justifiable and even necessary' in the everyday *practice* of life, they end by falling into 'insoluble contradictions'. This is so because in considering individual things common sense loses sight of their connections; 'in contemplating their existence it forgets their coming into being and passing away; in looking at them at rest it leaves their motion out of account; because it cannot see the wood for the trees';[12] similarly, for Bergson 'it is incontestable that in following the usual data of our senses and consciousness we arrive in the speculative order at insoluble contradictions';[13] for, whereas 'the intellect is especially destined for the study of a part, . . . we nevertheless try to use it in knowing the whole'.

So it follows for the rest of the argument. The intellect is unable to conceive of life. Life, Engels says, is contradiction; life itself is the refutation of the principle of identity. Jankélévitch, a follower of Schelling, echoes Engels quite involuntarily in his exposition of Bergson: 'Life jeers at the contradictions which are the despair of the intellect. Becoming, a mélange of being and non-being, is the escape from the principle of the excluded third.'[14]

Or again, motion is a form of contradiction. A body in motion, states *Anti-Dühring*, 'is' and 'is not', and 'the continuous assertion and simultaneous solution of this contradiction is precisely what motion is'.[15] Changing slightly the subject, which in this case is not

11. H. Bergson, op. cit., p. xx.
12. F. Engels, *Anti-Dühring*, op. cit., p. 28.
13. H. Bergson, *The Creative Mind*, op. cit., p. 165.
14. V. Jankélévitch, *Henri Bergson* (Paris, 1959), p. 17.
15. F. Engels, op. cit., p. 132.

motion *tout court* but time, Jankélévitch, who knows Bergson but may never have read Engels, observes in practically the same words that 'time is not simply the absence of contradiction, but is rather contradiction overcome and endlessly resolved; or, better stated, it is this resolution itself, regarded from its transitive side'.[16]

We shall leave aside minor but nonetheless significant similarities; such as, e.g., the 'dialectical' interpretation made by Bergson of infinitesimal calculus, or his allusions to the 'law' of the transformation of quantity into quality – '*la quantité est toujours de la qualité à l'état naissant* (quantity is always nascent quality)'. Or his exaltation of the 'new science' which, 'the more it progresses the more it resolves matter into actions moving through space, into movements dashing back and forth in a constant vibration so that mobility becomes reality itself'[17] – this is also (it will be remembered) a characteristic theme in Engels's thought; i.e. his hope that science will cease to be a science of *things* (or, as he says, a *metaphysics*) in order to become at last a science of movement alone.

What we are concerned to point out here, beyond the analogous formulae, is the paradox they conceal. It is a fact that Engels's general philosophic *programme* has nothing at all to do with Bergson's. The aim, the 'spirit' of the two philosophies is radically different; the two mentalities are far removed from one another (which explains, moreover, why the similarity between their statements has never been noticed till now). And yet, despite the difference in 'programme', despite Engels's materialist *intention*, it is beyond doubt that the convergence of the two philosophies is more than merely formal. The basis of the convergence is, in actual fact, a shared theoretical nucleus: the critique of intellect, the critique of the principle of non-contradiction. And what differentiates the two philosophies is only that they draw opposite conclusions from this same critique.

In Bergson's case, the critique of the scientific understanding is the critique of materialism itself. Just as in Jacobi or Hegel, the intellect and materialism here appear to suffer the same fate. The concepts of the intellect and science are 'determinate' and 'distinct'

16. V. Jankélévitch, op. cit., p. 38. 17. H. Bergson, op. cit., pp. 225 and 175.

in relation to one another, for they are the subjective equivalent of the assumption that objective reality is space and matter. In Bergson's words: 'The intellect is in the line of truth so long as it attaches itself, in its penchant for regularity and stability, to what is stable and regular in the real, that is to say to materiality.'[18] 'Thus the same movement by which the mind is brought to form itself into intellect, that is to say, into distinct concepts, brings matter to break itself up into objects excluding one another. *The more consciousness is intellectualized, the more is matter spatialized.*'[19]

In Engels's case, vice versa, since he mistakenly concluded that the intellect was metaphysical because 'dogmatic' (whereas with Hegel it is dogmatic precisely because it is materialistic), the critique of the understanding and the transcendence of the principle of non-contradiction appear as the foundation of materialism.

In both cases the content is the same; what changes is only the way of describing it. In both cases there is at work a *vitalist metaphysics* with a strong irrationalist bent. Except that, whereas Bergson knows full well what is at stake – '*l'intelligence est faite pour utiliser la matière*'; '*à la science la matière et à la métaphysique l'esprit* (the intellect has been made in order to utilize matter'; 'to science let us leave matter, and to metaphysics, mind)'[20] – Engels believed instead that the intellect was spiritualist metaphysics and that by contrast metaphysics or dogmatism was a higher form of materialism. The consequence is that the same vitalist biologist, De Vries, whom Bergson used in order to give his metaphysics a 'scientific' attire, can be cited by Plekhanov as proof and confirmation of 'dialectical materialism'.[21]

But perhaps even more significant is their evaluation of common sense and science. Just as for Jacobi the sciences were only 'toys' that the human spirit has made for itself as a 'diversion', similarly for Bergson (and, needless to say, also for Croce), science has no cognitive, but only *practical* value. It does not show us true reality.

18. ibid., p. 112.

19. H. Bergson, *Creative Evolution*, op. cit., p. 207.

20. H. Bergson, *La Pensée et le Mouvant*, op. cit., pp. 35 and 44. English translation, pp. 43 and 50.

21. G. V. Plekhanov, *Fundamental Problems of Marxism*, op. cit., pp. 46–7.

It is only a *fiction* useful to us in our practical conduct. We have access to the true reality by means of intuition, or – given that Bergson, like Jacobi, sees intuition and speculative reason as the same thing – by means of concepts of a 'higher order' than those we usually handle.

Now, this same conception is present *in nuce* in Engels as well. The principle of identity works all right in everyday practice; common sense is a trustworthy companion as long as it stays within the confines of the 'four family walls'; the 'metaphysical way of viewing things' is justifiable and even necessary in everyday, petty usage. The difference is that in Engels this critique is based on an error of interpretation, on the notion that everyday practice is the realm of metaphysics (a quite peculiar misunderstanding for a materialist thinker). For Bergson, however, who knows very well that *practice* is the realm of materialism *par excellence*, the critique is carried out (as with Jacobi) on the basis of the Pauline distinction between the world of the 'flesh' and the world of the 'spirit' – the former seems 'firm' and 'manifest', but in actual fact is fictitious and unreal like a dream; the latter seems impalpable and 'fluid', but is nonetheless 'true'.

Certainly, Engels did not live to experience in full the period when Europe was swept by the great wave of the 'idealist reaction against science'. The moment in which 'philosophy takes its revenge posthumously on natural science'[22] is, in the *Dialectics of Nature*, more a matter of prophecy than of observation. Nevertheless, the extent to which the old romantic philosophy of nature that lies at the basis of 'dialectical materialism' was to render theoretical Marxism a helpless witness of that 'reaction', if not an out and out accomplice of its involution and obscurantism, is demonstrated – to take only the most striking example – by the case of Lenin. In his *Philosophical Notebooks*, Lenin uncritically adheres to and takes over Hegel's destruction of the intellect and of the principle of non-contradiction; to the point of reinventing for himself the very formulae of Bergson's spiritualist irrationalism. 'We cannot imagine, express, measure, depict movement, without interrupting con-

22. F. Engels, *Dialectics of Nature*, op. cit., p. 164.

tinuity, without simplifying, coarsening, dismembering, strangling that which is living. The representation of movement by means of thought always makes coarse, kills, – and not only by means of thought, but also by sense-perception, and not only of movement, but *every* concept.'[23]

Here, as so often in the *Notebooks*, what is set forth is, in point of fact, a collection of all the most representative themes of vitalist irrationalism, in the illusory belief that they are a new and higher form of materialism. The theme of the intellect's *morcelage* for instance: 'From the totality of the existent', Simmel writes, 'our intellect cuts out individual fragments which are separated from the restless mobility of the All'; 'the intellect carves up the matter of life and of things in order to turn them into instrumental means, systems, and concepts'.[24] Or the theme of the principle of identity and of non-contradiction as a principle of inert and dead being: 'Our logic,' Simmel says, 'is the logic of solid bodies'; 'it is based essentially on the fundamental concepts of identity and otherness, but precisely these concepts are completely devoid of validity in relation to states of mind (*für seelische Zustände*), in analogy to which Bergson conceives of the world'; 'the opposition between identity and otherness disappears in the continuity of change'.[25] And lastly the theme that 'Life' cannot be grasped, is *unbegreiflich*, by thought because it is contradiction, unity of opposites, and therefore totality, whereas thought, or at least the *Verstandsbegriffe* (intellectual concepts) are one-sided and incomplete concepts, unable thus to 'know the pure essence of cosmic life'.[26]

But in Bergson's philosophy there is even more. His theory of the merely *practical*, non-cognitive function of science is also the birthplace of that particular concept of 'reification' which, subsequently, was to leave its impression on a large part of so-called 'Western Marxism'. If reality is fluid becoming, 'life', and spiritual *durée*, and the intellect gives us instead the solidified, the inert, the lifeless – then from what does the *world of things* derive its origin?

23. V. I. Lenin, *Philosophical Notebooks*, op. cit., pp. 259–60.

24. Georg Simmel, 'H. Bergson' (1914), in *Zur Philosophie der Kunst* (Potsdam, 1922), pp. 135–7.

25. ibid., p. 137.

26. ibid., p. 140.

Things are the 'abstract', the 'one-sided'; they have the *appearance*, as has been seen, of positive and independent beings, whereas, in actual fact, they are 'moments' that are *unreal* outside the totality, fleeting glances which the intellect 'congeals' and 'solidifies' in the very act in which it cuts them out of the 'uninterrupted flow' of life. As Bergson says, '*tout ce qui apparaît comme* positif *au physicien et au géomètre*', is in actual fact '*un système de négations, l'absence plutôt que la présence d'une réalité vraie*' ('All that which seems *positive* to the physicist and to the geometrician is actually a system of negations, the absence rather than the presence of a true reality')[27]. Who then conjured up this *world of things*? Who conferred on them this illusory existence as inflexible 'crystals' if not the intellect and science? Our intellect, Bergson says in *Creative Evolution* has a function that is 'essentially practical, made to present to us things and states rather than changes and acts. But things and states are only views, taken by our mind, of becoming. There are no things, there are only actions.' Therefore if 'the *thing* results from a solidification performed by our understanding', and if 'there are never any things other than those that the understanding has thus constituted',[28] that means that the *material world*, which science presents to us as reality, is in fact only an illusion and contrivance inspired by science itself.

Matter is merely a creation of the intellect. 'Things' are the crystals into which our tendency to reify coagulates and congeals, i.e., our tendency to 'solidify' the world in order to act in it practically and to change it. *Reification is the product of science and technology.* And science and technology, in their turn, arise from the requirements of 'everyday life', i.e. that need for 'regularity' and 'stability' which is characteristic of common sense. They derive from our purely 'corporeal' and outward penchant for acting under safe and predictable conditions; that is to say, our penchant for acting in a solid and stable world, where the original élan and jubilation of Life is inverted and petrified into a mass of inert 'objects' with well-defined features.

27. H. Bergson, *L'évolution créatrice*, op. cit., p. 228. English translation, p. 228.
28. H. Bergson, *Creative Evolution*, op. cit., pp. 270–1.

This theme is, of course, still only in its early stages in Bergson. (It does reappear later in his work, but only obscurely and incompletely, in the description of the instinctual and 'automatic' circularity characterizing the 'closed society' of *Les deux sources.*) Nonetheless, even in this first beginning it is not difficult to identify the seeds of the future development. The reified world is the physico-natural world presented to us by science. It is the solid yet inconsistent reality which caters for both our propensity to 'dominate nature, i.e. to arrange things, have them at hand, and use them as tools and means of labour (the *Zuhandenheit* which Heidegger will discuss later), and our need for the security which characterizes 'inauthentic' existence (the *Alltäglichkeit* of *Sein und Zeit*). That is, existence that is completely immersed and absorbed in things, adrift in the 'cares' of the world, i.e. 'bourgeois' or civic existence.

Science is a form of positivism. And since positivism is the typical mentality through which the need for 'bourgeois security' expresses itself, the triumph over reification can come about only with the destruction of that reified world which is the artificial contrivance of science. Thus the argument goes back to the pages of Marcuse previously examined (it is no chance that Marcuse was originally a pupil of Heidegger). The overcoming of reification depends upon the destruction of things. The dialectic of the 'Here' and the 'Now', with which at the beginning of the *Phenomenology*, Hegel annihilates all objects, and his *sceptical* destruction of 'sense certainty' – these are actually 'a critique of positivism and, even more, of "reification" '; for reification is nothing other than common sense and scientific thought, which 'take the world as a totality of things, more or less existing *per se*, and seek the truth in objects that are taken to be independent of the knowing subject'. Because, in short, what alienates and dehumanizes men is precisely this way of seeing things characteristic of science, which is considerably 'more than an epistemological attitude', being 'as pervasive as the practice of men and leading them to accept the feeling that they are secure only in knowing and handling objective facts'.[29]

However, the argument goes back well beyond Marcuse. It takes

29. H. Marcuse, op. cit., p. 112.

in a complex variety of themes developed above all in Germany during the first years of this century. These tendencies developed partly on the crest of Bergson's original inspiration; but in large part they were independent of him and constituted a direct revival of the themes of romantic philosophy (one need only, to give just one example, think of the concept of 'nature' as *versteinerte* [petrified] *Intelligenz* in Schelling). Gradually, these tendencies made up the outlines of that particular theory of *reification* which is our present object of attention. It is clear that to give even a vague idea of the complex interlacing of these themes – at times developed by quite different and contrasting theoretical orientations – would be absolutely impossible in this context. Apart from Dilthey, the intensity of the anti-intellectualist and irrationalist impetus that engulfs German philosophy at the beginning of the century (forming the *humus*, the direct preface to the critique of science as reification) is testified to, perhaps most spectacularly, by the dissolution of even a philosophy as 'academic' as Neo-Kantianism. One need only recall the two characteristic *Antrittsreden* dedicated by Windelband in 1910 to the 'revival of Hegelianism' (*Die Erneuerung des Hegelianismus*),[30] and to the 'mysticism of our times' (*Von der Mystik unserer Zeit*),[31] – two documents without which it is difficult to get an idea of what that particular philosophy of the 'age of imperialism' was. In them the horror for every notion of the world as a plural universe with manifold determinations, and the aversion for any form of objectivity or materialist 'exteriority', are elevated into the distinguishing feature of the entire epoch. The character of this philosophy of the moment is described as 'the impulse towards unity and the urge towards inwardness (*Drang nach Verinnerlichung*)'.[32] This, as Windelband says, is a question of advancing and redeeming 'a spiritual unity to life as against its fragmentation in the culture that deals with the outwardness of matter'.[33] In a certain sense, he adds, 'we are living through . . . the same revolution in modes of thought which was carried out around 1800 in all of Europe, but especially in Germany, in the passage from

30. W. Windelband, *Präludien* (Tübingen, 1921), vol. I, pp. 273–89.
31. ibid., pp. 290–9.
32. ibid., p. 290.
33. ibid., p. 291.

the Enlightenment to Romanticism'. Consequently, 'even now the irrational is again proclaimed as the holy secret of all reality, as the foundation of life that lies beyond all knowledge; and thus even the religious impulse, which is at work in the need for a *Weltanschauung*, once again gladly takes on the form of mysticism'.[34] 'Just as Romanticism once brought honour again to the forgotten Jacob Böhme, similarly the father of all philosophical mysticism, the great neo-Platonic Plotinus, has again, like a new star in the sky, ascended to a place in the history of philosophy.'[35] The period, Windelband states, hungers for a '*Weltanschauung*', following the long neo-Kantian interlude. Everywhere the cry goes up for a 'philosophy of action and the will'. And it is precisely 'this hunger for a *Weltanschauung* which has taken hold of our younger generation and which seeks satisfaction of this hunger in Hegel.'[36]

In addition to Windelband, some other names must be mentioned. An important moment in the critique of the intellect was Rickert's analysis of the 'limits of conceptualization in the natural sciences'.[37] This analysis is all the more significant if one considers the influence that Rickert had on the young Lukács and on Heidegger. Here one need only refer to the development in his *Grenzen* of the critique of *Erklären*, i.e. of knowledge as 'causal explanation', as it is produced by the naturalistic intellect; one could refer also to the major emphasis that is given to 'intuition' and, in general, to the need for the 'transcendence of the limits of what is conceptually knowable (*das Ueberschreiten der Grenzen des begrifflich Erkennbaren*)',[38] in his description of that mode of knowledge which deals with the historically specific (*Verstehen*). All of which leads, on the one hand, to the revival of the openly irrationalist themes of *Erleben*, *Einfühlen*, etc., themes which, in so far as they imply a 'sympathetic penetration' of subject and object, presuppose the *identity* of the two (whence Dilthey's explicit reference to the 'theory of the sciences of the spirit');[39] and on the other hand, to the representation of philosophy as a 'science of the totality'.

34. ibid., pp. 291–2. 35. ibid., p. 293. 36. ibid., p. 278.

37. H. Rickert, *Die Grenzen der naturwissenschaftlichen Begriffsbildung*, 4th edition (Tübingen, 1921). 38. ibid., pp. 265–8. 39. ibid., p. 412.

To enter into a detailed analysis of the crucial role played by Heidegger in developing this theory of the reifying function of science, is impossible here. The theory is a central theme in all his works. According to it the determinations of the world arise together with the activities of the 'intellect' (understanding and 'judging'), which culminate in science. *Sein und Zeit* insists at great length on how the *being* of things means their *being used* by man, and how the 'judgment', in its turn, transforms what is usable into a 'corporeal-thing' (*Körperding*).[40] The 'reifying' nature of science and its at once 'formalist' and 'empirical' character (cf. also Croce on Hegel) emerges with particular clarity in the last part of the book. 'The classical example,' Heidegger writes, 'for the historical development of a science and even for its ontological genesis, is the rise of mathematical physics. What is decisive for its development does not lie in its rather high esteem for the observation of "facts", nor in its "application" of mathematics in determining the character of natural processes; it lies rather in *the way in which Nature herself is mathematically projected*. In this projection something constantly present-at-hand (matter) is uncovered beforehand. . . .'[41] It is therefore like the horizon, the *a priori* in virtue of which *things* come to exist for us.

The place, however, where this particular conception of reification has one of its most important turning-points is in the extension of its critique of the understanding into a critique of 'culture' and 'society'. Lukács referred to this 'philosophic-bourgeois critique of culture' in his 1967 preface to the new edition of *History and Class Consciousness*. This deals with the focal position which – upon the background of the great German-philosophical antithesis between *Kultur* and *Zivilisation*, organicist-romantic culture and rationalist-enlightenment culture – was then assumed by the problem of the *estrangement* of man in technological-industrial society, in the mass society of modern capitalism. The question, as Lukács recalls, was then 'in the air'. It presented itself as the outcome and point of

40. Martin Heidegger, *Sein und Zeit* (Tübingen, 1949), pp. 71, 84, 106, and 156.

41. ibid., p. 362. English translation, by J. Macquarrie and E. Robinson, *Being and Time* (London, 1962), pp. 413–14.

arrival for diverse currents of thought. And this was 'recognized ... by both bourgeois and proletarian thinkers, by commentators on both right and left'.[42] In addition to Heidegger, naturally the most important name in this context, one should at least mention *Der Konflict der modernen Kultur* by Simmel[43] – a thinker, like Rickert, whom one cannot ignore whenever the early writings of Lukács are under consideration. The critique of science and the related disdain for technical-practical action – the world of work and production – are here extended to a critique of modern civilization, whose conflicts are not explained in the light of particular socio-historical causes, but on the basis of an irrepressible antithesis between the principle of the organic totality of 'Life' and the purely 'external' principle of mechanical or causal connection. The conflict in modern civilization consists, for Simmel, in the fact that the 'forms' engendered by 'Life' are solidified into *objective institutions* separated from it, that these objective institutions acquire an autonomy of their own and set themselves over against the becoming that generated them originally. Thus, whereas Life continually tends to resolve and dissolve within itself the forms in which it has momentarily objectified itself, these forms become solidified and rigidified into permanent entities which oppose and impede the process of re-establishing the original unity, i.e. the recomposition of the identity of the finite and the infinite.[44] This is the source of the conflict, i.e. the state of internal division and laceration which characterizes modern civilization and the latter's tendency to overturn and reverse the meaning of reality. The forms originally engendered as forms and functions *of* Life, by solidifying themselves into objective institutions, tend to subordinate and constrain Life, their own origin, into alienated routine and mechanical repetitiveness. The finite, which in reality is a momentary projection of Life's infinity, becomes the foundation of the real; whereas Life, which was the

42. George Lukács, *History and Class Consciousness*, translated by Rodney Livingstone (London, 1971), p. xxii.

43. George Simmel, *Der Konflikt der modernen Kultur* (Munich and Leipzig, 1918).

44. Cf. P. Rossi, *Lo storicismo tedesco contemporaneo* (Turin, 1956), p. 258, in which it is clearly seen that this identity of the finite and the infinite is the 'fundamental presupposition of romantic philosophy'.

real beginning and the unconditional, becomes something subordinate and secondary.

One's mind cannot help but return here to the basic themes of Hegel's thought and to that subversion of reality which he attributed to the intellect. 'Ordinary human understanding' transforms that which is first into that which is second, and vice versa. In the 'intellectual proof', the finite, which *is not*, becomes a 'fixed being', the positive or the foundation; whereas the infinite, which is the true positive and the unconditional, becomes the infinite 'made finite', the negative, the unreal. But the juxtaposition immediately reveals an essential difference. With Hegel, the healing of the 'split' engendered by the intellect is guaranteed. The reinstatement of the world turned upside-down by common sense is the self-conscious and self-confident programme of his entire philosophy. Unity has to be re-established. The principle of idealism is *realized*. So that already the *Phenomenology* can proclaim that the new philosophy is the *verkehrte Welt*, the world 'stood on its head' in relation to how common sense saw the world. With Simmel, however (not to mention many other differences), the same metaphysical event takes place under a less favourable sign of the zodiac. For him as well life's process is the infinite's positing of itself as finite. But whereas in Hegel this 'alienation' (besides being momentary) is regarded as necessary to the ends of the self-explication which the spirit must carry out in order to recapitulate itself and so enjoy itself as self-conscious Spirit, in Simmel the need of the infinite to posit itself as finite is described as a 'tragic fate',[45] i.e. as a 'split' which opens a permanent crisis, putting in jeopardy the 'return' to Unity. This different *Stimmung* is highly significant.

Under the guise of an analysis of 'modern society', in reality what is put forth is once again a critique of the intellect, of materialism, and of the principle of causality. The conflict in modern civilization derives from the fact that the 'forms' of its life take on the nature of 'institutions'. The 'tragedy' of modern society is that it is a public sphere, an *objective* world – the realm of *Allgemeingültigkeit*, i.e. of

45. ibid., p. 262. Rossi's remarks concern Simmel's *Lebensanschauung*, which we have not examined.

the universal and *impersonal* validity common both to the statements of science and to behaviour and 'rules' of social life.[46]

46. Bergson's *L'Essai sur les données immédiates de la conscience* (published in Paris, 1914, but the work dates from 1888; English translation, *Time and Free Will*, by F. L. Pogson, London, 1910) already develops the relationship between the solidification or 'reification' carried out by the intellect and the requirements of language and social life. Intersubjective communication and society presuppose the translation-falsification of *durée* (whether psychological or real) into terms of externality-spatiality. Two different subjects also correspond to the two *durées*, one of them 'fundamental' and the other 'superficial' and fictitious: 'Below homogeneous duration, which is the extensive symbol of true duration, . . . a duration whose heterogeneous moments permeate one another; . . . below the self with well-defined states, a self in which *succeeding each other* means *melting into one another* and forming an organic whole. But we are generally content with the first, i.e. with the shadow of the self projected into homogeneous space. Consciousness, goaded by an insatiable desire to separate, substitutes the symbol for the reality, or perceives the reality only through the symbol. As the self thus refracted, and thereby broken to pieces, is much better adapted to the requirements of social life in general and language in particular, consciousness prefers it, and gradually loses sight of the fundamental self . . . In other words, our perceptions, sensations, emotions and ideas occur under two aspects: the one clear and precise, but impersonal; the other confused, ever changing, and inexpressible, because language cannot get hold of it without arresting its mobility or fit it into its common-place forms without making it into public property' (pp. 128–9). Here, as the reader can see, there is already delineated a theory of 'true' and 'false' consciousness, of 'personal' existence and 'impersonal' existence. And the world of society is the world of 'banality'. These antitheses are not, however, to be directly identified with Heidegger's. For the latter – at least during the early period of *Sein und Zeit* and *Vom Wesen des Grundes* – the romantic-spiritualist premisses upon upon which Bergson's argument is based have no validity (if to anyone, Bergson should here be compared to Jaspers). Returning to the *Données*, the solidarity of the 'intellect' with language and social life is confirmed throughout: 'We instinctively tend to solidify our impressions in order to express them in language' (p. 130). The reason is 'that our outer and, so to speak, social life is more practically important to us than our inner and individual existence'. And again, on the connection between language, society, and impersonality: 'the word with well-defined outlines, the rough and ready word, which stores up the stable, common, and consequently impersonal element in the impressions of mankind' (p. 132). '. . . The intuition of a homogeneous space is already a step towards social life' (p. 138). Concerning the two subjects, of authentic-personal existence and of social-impersonal existence – 'two different selves, one of which is, as it were, the external projection of the other, its spatial and, so to speak, social representation' – Bergson observes (p. 231) that: 'The greater part of the time we live outside ourselves, hardly perceiving anything of ourselves but our own ghost, a colourless shadow which pure duration projects into homogeneous space. Hence our life unfolds in space rather than in time; we live for the external world rather than for ourselves.' Or again, on the socializing function performed by the intellect and the reification which it carries out: 'This intuition of a homogeneous medium . . . enables us to externalize our concepts in

It need hardly be pointed out that this anonymous validity has its place of origin in the *objektive Gültigkeit* (validity) of judgment and technical-scientific practice. No less than the subject of science, the protagonist of social life is *man* (the German impersonal pronoun – *Trans.*), the impersonal 'one' of 'one says' or 'one does', i.e. the subject of *anonymous existence* as the existence of every one and no one.

In *Sein und Zeit*, of course, this existential analysis operates at another level. Although the theoretical presuppositions of the work prevent it from becoming concrete, Heidegger's argument is not *only* a critique of *democracy* and of the advancing society of the 'great masses'; it is also, if only secondarily and at the level of mere phenomenological description, the perception of that much more specific process of 'depersonalization' linked to the advent and domination of modern *monopolistic* capitalism and its great 'anonymous corporations'. Despite the difficult, philosophically technical appearance of the book, *Sein und Zeit* is a work upon which are indelibly stamped the signs of the crisis of the German society of the period. The realm of impersonal existence which it describes – the individual's fall under the sway of uncontrolled, 'objective' forces – appears to evoke in places that other process of 'depersonalization' discussed by Rathenau in his analytic sketch in 1918 of the great 'joint stock companies' (though Heidegger was, of course, never conscious of this distinction, either then or later). Here the 'depersonalization' of property means that property itself acquires an autonomous existence in relation even to the very holders of property rights. The 'enterprise' takes on an independent life, as if it belonged to no one – the object becomes the subject, and the subject becomes the object of its object.[47] The uncontrolled forces of society

---

relation to one another, reveals to us the objectivity of things, and thus, in two ways, on the one hand by getting everything ready for language, and on the other by showing us an external world, quite distinct from ourselves, in the perception of which all minds have a common share, foreshadows and prepares the way for social life' (p. 236). And finally on p. 138: 'Our tendency to form a clear picture of this externality of things and the homogeneity of their medium is the same as the impulse which leads us to live in common and to speak.'

47. Walther Rathenau, *Von kommenden Dingen* (Berlin, 1918), pp. 129ff.

exacerbate to the extreme the nature of those forces extensively analysed by Marx, which operate 'behind men's backs' with the peremptory necessity of natural events. Still, however generous one tries to be, in the case of someone like Heidegger the basic theme always remains that of the critique of the intellect. The reified world is the physical-natural world. Estrangement is the separation of subject and object. What alienates and dehumanizes man is science.

Regarding all this critical literature on 'culture' and 'society', the main virtue of the books which came later, like Horkheimer and Adorno's *Dialectic of Enlightenment*, is that – since they lacked any real analysis, even of a purely philosophic kind, and reduced the relevant categories to mere empty sophistry or personal *bavardage* – they give us a sort of *Summa* of all the 'horrors' and idiosyncrasies which lie at the basis of philosophical production over many decades, without the effort of decipherment required to read Heidegger, or even Husserl's *Krisis*.

The very title of Horkheimer and Adorno's work deserves some praise. The target of the two authors' polemical impulse is Enlightenment itself. This is so even if it is not taken to mean a particular historical period (which would demand precise arguments), but an age which is dominated in Hegelian fashion by 'ordinary human understanding' and its fatal distinction between subject and object, and which therefore extends not only to Homer's *Odyssey* but to all historical eras. Even confining ourselves to the first eighty pages of the work, its value as a *Summa* appears to be confirmed. Horror of the scientific mind here takes on forms which (did we not fear the strictures of youth) we would even be tempted to call grotesque. For Horkheimer and Adorno, 'the very deductive form of science reflects hierarchy and coercion'.[48] Common sense is 'reactionary', science 'positivistic'.[49] The Enlightenment, then, i.e. that period of clarity which prompted Kant to say, 'Enlightenment is man's emergence from his self-incurred immaturity... *Sapere Aude!* Have courage to use your *own* intelligence! is therefore the motto of the

48. M. Horkheimer and Th. Adorno, *Dialektik der Aufklärung* (Frankfurt, 1969) p. 27.

49. ibid., pp. 47 and 22.

enlightenment'[50] – this Enlightenment is for our authors little more than a concentration camp. It 'proclaims, in a matter-of-fact fashion, authority as a dichotomy (*Entzweiung*), . . . the rift between subject and object . . .'.[51] 'Enlightenment is totalitarian in a way that no previous system has been.' As far as reification is concerned, it is clearly attributable to mathematics. With 'the Galilean mathematization of nature', thought 'reifies itself into an . . . automatic process'. And since this is what science is, one can imagine that our authors do not hold a view of *industry* that is any more favourable – an industry examined (of course) without specifying any particular social relationships, i.e. in its neutral aspect as pure technology, irrespective of whether it is *capitalist* industry or any other kind. Here too we now know what to expect: 'industry reifies the souls of men';[52] 'today machinery mutilates men, even as it nourishes them', for the machine is 'estranged reason', thought in its 'solidified form as a material and intellectual apparatus'.[53]

But Horkheimer and Adorno show an equal revulsion for society; and again, not in so far as it is organized in *this* way or *that* (as one might expect from professors of social science) but simply in so far as it is *organized* at all. 'Radical socialization means radical estrangement.' Whether before the 'bourgeois "night-watchman" State', which transforms itself 'into the violence of the monopolistic collectivity', or before 'state socialism. . . , which was the undoing of Robespierre and Saint-Just in its initial form',[54] our historians tremble with equal indignation. They simply will not stand for discipline.

We shall avert our eyes from their harsh judgment of Bacon, guilty of having opened the era of 'man's domination over nature'; as from their reference to 'the gloomy writers of the early bourgeoisie, such as Machiavelli, Hobbes, and Mandeville'.[55] Even at the heavy price of going beyond the first eighty pages it must be said that the will of these 'beautiful souls' to the destruction and *nihilistic*

50. *Kant's Political Writings*, ed. Reiss (Cambridge, 1970), 'What is Enlightenment?', p. 54.

51. Horkheimer-Adorno, op. cit., p. 46.

52. ibid., pp. 31 and 34.

53. ibid., p. 44.

54. ibid., pp. 69 and 125.

55. ibid., p. 97.

negation of the highest achievements of human thought comes out fully only in their judgment of Kant. 'Kant intuitively anticipated what only Hollywood was to consciously achieve.' 'With the affirmation of the scientific system as the form that truth takes – a conclusion arrived at by Kant –, thought seals its own fate as trivia, since science is simply a technical exercise. . . .' 'Science itself has no consciousness of itself; it is a mere instrument. Enlightenment, however, is the philosophy which identifies truth with the scientific system.'[56]

It is evident that within the line of thought which we are dealing with here, Horkheimer and Adorno represent a limiting case. Together with Marcuse, they are the most conspicuous example of the extreme confusion that can be reached by mistaking the romantic critique of intellect and science for a socio-historical critique of capitalism. Nevertheless, the focal point of their arguments – that is, the thesis that science is an *institution of the bourgeois world* – would perhaps have never taken shape without a book of decisive importance in contemporary thought: Lukács's *History and Class Consciousness*. In this book for the first time two lines of thought were linked together which were not only antithetical, but which had until then been devoid of any internal connection. These two lines of thought are, on the one hand, the critique of the intellect and of materialism, and, on the other hand, the analysis of reification (or estrangement, or fetishism) developed by Marx in *Capital* with reference to the socio-historical conditions of modern capitalist commodity production.

As Lukács's self-criticism has made clear on a number of occasions in the last few years, the connection and confusing of these two theories (in reference to which it is important to note, however, that Lukács never speaks of a 'critique of the intellect', but only of materialism) was carried out by him within the framework of a still unclear vision of the relationship (and especially of the *difference*) between Hegel and Marx. The work had been written in the light and on the basis of the Hegelian theory of the *identity of subject and object*. And that did not fail to show itself in the 'crucial problem of

56. ibid., pp. 91 and 92.

the book, the problem of reification, in the sense that throughout the basic line of argument reification (alienation, estrangement)' – *Verdinglichung* (*Entäusserung, Entfremdung*) – was 'identified, as in Hegel, with objectivity'.[57]

In his introduction to the recent edition of the book Lukács has returned to this argument in even clearer terms: 'it is in Hegel that we first encounter alienation as the fundamental problem of the place of man in the world and *vis-à-vis* the world. However, in the term alienation he includes every type of objectification. Thus "alienation" when taken to its logical conclusion is identical with objectification. Therefore, when the identical subject-object transcends alienation it must also transcend objectification at the same time. But since, according to Hegel, the object, the thing exists only as an alienation from self-consciousness, to take it back into the subject would mean the end of objective reality and thus of any reality at all. *History and Class Consciousness* follows Hegel in that it too equates alienation with objectification (*Vergegenständlichung*) (to use the term employed by Marx in the *Economic-Philosophical Manuscripts*). This fundamental and crude error has certainly contributed greatly to the success enjoyed by *History and Class Consciousness*.'[58]

The error of the book consisted, therefore, in confusing two ideas: Hegel's conception in which alienation is identified with the objectivity of *nature* and thus with the externality or heterogeneity of being in relation to thought (the materialist, or 'dogmatic', point of view of common sense and of 'ordinary human understanding', whose alienation is to be suppressed with the realization of the principle of idealism); and Marx's conception where by contrast the object is *estranged*, not in that it is 'external', but in that it takes on the (socio-historical) character of a *commodity* and *capital*, i.e. the character of a product of wage-labour. That is, it is an 'alienated' product precisely in the sense that it not only does not belong to the producer, but is used in the further utilization of the producer himself as labour-force sold by the day.

57. Cf. Lukács's statement of September 1962, in I. Fetscher, *Der Marxismus*, Vol. I (Munich, 1962).

58. G. Lukács, *History and Class Consciousness*, op. cit., pp. xxiii–xxiv.

This difference between his own conception and that of Hegel is clarified by Marx himself quite unequivocally in the *Manuscripts*. With Hegel, he writes, 'It is not the fact that the human being *objectifies* himself *inhumanly*, in opposition to himself, but that he *objectifies* himself by *distinction* from and in *opposition* to abstract thought, which constitutes alienation as it exists and as it has to be transcended'; therefore, 'the appropriation of alienated objective being, or the supersession of objectivity in the form of *alienation* ... signifies for Hegel also, or primarily, the supersession of *objectivity*, since it is not the determinate character of the object but its *objective* character which is the scandal of alienation for self-consciousness'.[59]

Lukács himself has brought out the importance which these pages of the *Manuscripts* – he was able to read them in 1930, even before they were published – had in helping him understand the error which was the basis of his own book of 1923. Nor does he fail to add, and rightly so, that the benefit which he drew from it was his alone, and not shared with others, since 'even the publication of Marx's early work has unfortunately not been of much help' – as it has been 'predominately interpreted in Hegelian terms, rather than as a fundamental critique of this conception of Hegel's'.[60] '... I can still remember even today the overwhelming effect produced in me by Marx's statement that objectivity was the primary material attribute of all things and relations.' What derived therefrom was an understanding of the fact that 'objectification is a natural means by which man masters the world. ... By contrast, alienation is a special variant of that activity that becomes operative in definite social conditions'. And with that were 'completely shattered the theoretical foundations of what had been the particular achievement of *History and Class Consciousness*'.[61]

Of course, today this self-criticism may appear even too strong. Whatever may be its shortcomings, *History and Class Consciousness* remains an important book which cannot and must not be confused with anything that has come after it – from Karl Mannheim's

59. K. Marx, *Early Writings*, op. cit., pp. 201 and 209.
60. Cf. I. Fetscher, op. cit.
61. G. Lukács, *History and Class Consciousness*, op. cit., p. xxxvi.

Ideology and Utopia up to the writings of Horkheimer and Marcuse. To speak seriously and disregard false modesty, *History and Class Consciousness* is the first Marxist book after Marx (Labriola was too isolated a phenomenon) which deals with Hegel and German classical philosophy at a European level and with a thorough knowledge of the subject; it is the first book in which philosophical Marxism ceases to be a cosmological romance and, thus, a surrogate 'religion' for the 'lower' classes. Furthermore, in order to evaluate properly the significance of this work and the turning-point which it represented in the history of the interpretation of Marx, it is, certainly, revealing to compare it with the unrefined farrago of the positivist and evolutionist Marxism of the Second International. But more important still is one simple fact: its rediscovery (even with all the limitations and equivocations mentioned above) of an entire area of Marx's thought, in every sense essential to an understanding of *Capital*; i.e., the theory of estrangement or reification. This theory, which had been entirely buried in the interpretative work of Engels, Plekhanov, and Lenin (not, of course, out of bad faith, but as a consequence of a radical inadequacy of their theoretical tools), was again buried, immediately afterwards, in all of 'dialectical materialism' till our day.

Nevertheless, having made this acknowledgment, I too – even though I belong to the (only too wide) circle of the admirers of *History and Class Consciousness* – believe that one should agree with the self-critical severity of Lukács's judgment. The 'fundamental and crude error' which was the basis of this work is also – as the author has clearly seen – what has been in large part responsible for its success; and not only at the beginning of the thirties, but also in the following decades up to today. One need only think of Sartre and – following another of Lukács's allusions – the 'mixture of Marxist and Existentialist ideas' produced 'after World War II, especially in France'.[62]

Goldmann's well-known thesis – implicitly confirmed by Lukács in his essay on *Heidegger 'redivivus'*, written on the occasion of the *Brief über den Humanismus* – argues that the roots of *History and Class Consciousness* lie in the Heidelberg School (Rickert and Lask)

62. ibid., p. xxiii.

and that it influenced *Sein und Zeit*. Heidegger's work is to be understood, according to Goldmann, as in large part a polemical response, 'perhaps even unconscious', to Lukács's book of 1923. The 'true' and 'false' consciousness discussed by Lukács became, presumably, the 'authentic' and 'inauthentic' existence of Heidegger; Lukács's distinction between 'essence' and 'phenomenon' became Heidegger's distinction between 'ontical' and 'ontological', etc.[63] And it is also significant – although it is not worth giving any particular emphasis to this fact – that, in tracing out the line of development that runs from classical philosophy through Fichte, Schelling, and Hegel to modern and contemporary philosophy, Goldmann does not fail to put at the head of the list in which he locates Lask, Lukács, Heidegger, and Sartre, the name of Bergson.[64]

However, leaving aside these problems of genealogy and 'influences' (in which one cannot rule out the possibility that Goldmann made some use of his *romanesque* imagination), and returning to our main argument, it remains a fact that the focal theme of *History and Class Consciousness* is in the identification of capitalist reification with the 'reification' engendered by science. Lukács's thought in this respect is, admittedly, not free of blurrings and oscillations. Frequently, for example, his polemic against science is only a polemic against the naturalistic and deterministic conception of 'social science' which was a feature of the Marxism of the Second International. 'When the ideal of scientific knowledge is applied to nature it simply furthers the progress of science. But when it is applied to society it turns out to be an ideological weapon of the bourgeoisie.'[65] Indeed, Lukács states that the method of the natural sciences 'rejects the idea of contradiction and antagonism in its subject matter'; whereas, 'in the case of social reality', the contradictions (which in the natural sciences are only an indication that 'our knowledge is as yet imperfect') '*belong to the nature of reality itself and to the nature of capitalism*'.[66]

63. Lucien Goldmann, *Mensch, Gemeinschaft und Welt in der Philosophie Immanuel Kants* (Zurich, 1945), pp. 13 and 245–6. English translation by R. Black, *Immanuel Kant* (London, 1971), pp. 25–6 and 127–8.

64. Goldmann, op. cit., pp. 26–7.

65. G. Lukács, op. cit., p. 10.

66. ibid., p. 10.

At other times – as also in Korsch's *Marxism and Philosophy* – the problem at the focus of attention is the even more complex one (scarcely ever seen by the entire interpretative tradition either before or after *History and Class Consciousness*) of the nature and actual position occupied by 'law' and 'economy' in Marx's conception. The formation of these two spheres, with their mutual separation and 'purity' as objects of autonomous 'sciences' is traced back by Marx to the division into economic or 'civil' society and 'political' society or the State, a phenomenon specifically characteristic of modern capitalist society. Without attempting to enter here into the peculiar interpretative difficulties of this problem (in relation to which the questions raised at the end of this essay may perhaps be of some value), it is a fact that it brings two essential matters to the fore: the question of the withering away of Law and Politics, linked to the withering away of the State; and the question of the withering away of 'political economy', linked to the end of commodity production. This latter is a theme which emerges clearly from the way in which Marx entitles his work, which is the 'Critique of Political Economy', and not just of 'bourgeois' political economy (as a consequence of the explicit premiss that political economy as such must be understood not as a *science*, but rather as a metaphysics).

This perspective enables one to see the positive side to Lukács's polemic against the false 'scientificity' of the positivist Marxism of Cunow, Kautsky, Plekhanov, Conrad Schmidt, etc. It also – and I almost wrote it *even* – lets one see the value of his recourse to the category of 'totality', whenever this serves to underline the problem of the *unity* of the capitalist socio-economic formation. Totality, i.e., in the sense of a 'totality' of those spheres (economy, law, politics, etc.) awkwardly hypostatized and rendered autonomous by the scholasticism still reigning in the area of the so-called 'moral sciences' (in which it is as if whoever wakes up first, can found a new 'science' if he feels like it).

Nevertheless, if we wish to consider the whole picture without conceding anything to the 'anti-mathematical frenzy' still in vogue today (but tomorrow, who knows. . . ?), we must immediately add that the real focus of *History and Class Consciousness* is upon very different themes from those just indicated. At the basis of the work there lies the distinction between the method of the socio-historical sciences and that of the natural sciences, as elaborated by Rickert in his *Grenzen* – a distinction which already in Rickert is, of course (at least in the third and fourth editions which I have seen), a good deal more than a mere distinction of 'methods' or subjective points of view. It is an actual duality of 'objective' spheres or areas, the duality of 'nature' and 'history',[67] of *Natur* and *Kultur*, and extending to a contrast (the later 'applications' of which are only too well-known) between *Kulturvölker* and *Naturvölker*.[68] Not only is there this distinction at the basis of the work, but there is also, more important, that inevitable development of it which leads to a denial of nature as possessing true reality, and so to denying the possibility of real knowledge to the physical-natural sciences.

The point of view of *History and Class Consciousness* does not allow of any doubt on this score. The fact that the modern science of nature has developed in and with the development of modern capitalist society (one need only think of the 'industrial revolution') and that it constitutes the technological basis of large-scale industrial production means, according to Lukács, that the 'idea, formulated most lucidly by Kant but essentially unchanged since Kepler and Galileo, of nature as the "aggregate of systems of the laws" governing what happens', is a 'development out of the economic structures of capitalism'.[69] 'Nature,' he writes 'is a social category.'[70] The vision of reality revealed to us by the conceptual constructs of natural science are thus a projection into the world of capitalism's ideological point of view. Significantly, Lukács cites Tönnies here: 'scientific concepts which by their ordinary origin and their real properties are judgements by means of which complexes of feeling are given names, behave within science like commodities in society. They gather together within the system like commodities on the market. The supreme scientific concept which is no longer the name of anything real is like money. E.g. the concept of an atom, or of energy.'[71]

67. H. Rickert, op. cit., pp. 145 and 362–3. 68. ibid., pp. 394–5.
69. G. Lukács, op. cit., p. 136. 70. ibid., p. 130. 71. ibid., p. 131.

Fortunately, the radical antithesis between this argument of Tönnies and Lukács and Marx's own thought can be documented this time. In the *Manuscripts* of 1844, Marx links the absolute Notion or *Logos* of Hegel's *Science of Logic* (this is a point which we shall develop later) together with 'value' as it is produced in a commodity-producing society. The relationship in Hegel between the Notion and sense-reality is the same as the relation between the 'value' and the 'use-value' of commodities. The '*Logic*', Marx says, 'is the *money* of the mind, the speculative *thought-value* of man and of nature, their essence indifferent to any real determinate character and thus unreal; *thought* which is *alienated* and abstract and ignores real nature and man'.[72]

For Tönnies and Lukács it is not the hypostasis of the *speculative* Notion which is the reflection of (and also one aspect of) that process of hypostatization or substantification of the abstract found in the production of 'value' and capital; rather, it is the *scientific* concept (and the reification presumably linked to it) which are the cause and the birthplace of capitalist reification. Reification, in other words, is engendered by science. And since there is an absolute homogeneity and solidarity of nature between science and capitalism – to the point that science itself appears as an *institution of the bourgeois world*, destined to be swept away with it – what also gets swept away is that other cornerstone of Marx's entire analysis (upon which rests his whole appraisal of capitalism as a progressive historical phenomenon). That is, his thesis of the necessary contradiction between modern *productive forces* and the private *mode of appropriation*, or between the development of science and industry on the one hand, as the premisses and condition for the social emancipation of man, and the capitalist *involucrum* within which this development takes place.

Capitalist reification, in short, *is* the reification engendered by science itself. It is a fact, Lukács says, that 'capitalist society is predisposed to harmonize with scientific method'.[73] This predisposition finds expression already in Galileo's call for ' "scientific exactitude" ', which presupposes 'that the elements remain

72. K. Marx, *Early Writings*. op. cit., p. 200.

73. G. Lukács, op. cit., p. 7.

"constant" ',[74] i.e. that solidification of the world from which the 'so-called facts that are idolized' arise. In other words, 'the "pure" facts of the natural sciences', facts which exist in 'an environment where (their) laws can be inspected without outside interference', are always to be considered in relation to the recognition that 'capitalism tends to produce a social structure that in great measure encourages such views' and that 'it is in the nature of capitalism to process phenomena in this way'.[75]

In appearance, the argument focuses on capital; in reality, it is the 'intellect' which is being accused. The 'fetishistic forms of objectivity' – even before surplus value, profit, income, and interest – are represented by 'the determinants of reflection' of the intellect, – just that intellect which is referred to by Lukács as the 'reified mind'.[76] And since the origin of estrangement is found to reside primarily in the distinction between subject and object – and only secondarily in the separation between capital and labour – the overcoming of estrangement is entrusted to a process in which 'the duality of subject and object (the duality of thought and being is only a special case of this), is transcended, i.e. where subject and object coincide, where they are identical'.[77] In fact, the zenith of fetishism is . . . materialism, i.e., 'the dogmatic acceptance of a merely given reality – divorced from the subject'.[78]

Just as for Sartre–Roquentin, the scandal of alienation is that a natural world should *exist*. And since this is the enslavement from which we must free ourselves (one thinks of Hegel on ancient scepticism here), the enslavement imposed on us by the *things* and the 'facts' (*le* cose *e i 'fatti'*), human emancipation comes again to coincide with that *sceptical* destruction of the intellect and of natural objectivity – which can be attained, as is well-known, by merely understanding (guided by Bergson perhaps) that 'what we are wont to call "facts" consists of processes', and that 'the facts are nothing but the parts, the *aspects* of the total process that have been broken off, artificially isolated and ossified'. Understanding, in short, that facts are only the 'highest fetish in both theory and practice (of) the

74. ibid., p. 25.
75. ibid., pp. 5–6.
76. ibid., pp. 14 and 105.
77. ibid., p. 123.
78. ibid., p. 200.

reified thought of the bourgeoisie'. Liberation, in other words, lies in the apprehension of the 'total process, which is uncontaminated by any trace of reification and which allows the process-like essence to prevail *in all its purity*', and 'represents the authentic, higher reality'.[79]

Bergsonian spiritualism, as one can see, is hot upon our Marxist's heels. And since every position has its logic, Lukács, who goes into a factory not with *Capital* but with *Essai sur les données immédiates de la conscience*, finds that the supreme affront to Man on the assembly line is that it has eliminated . . . *durée*. The factory 'reduces space and time to a common denominator', 'degrades time to the dimension of space'. 'Thus time sheds its qualitative, variable, flowing nature; it freezes into an exactly delimited, quantifiable continuum filled with quantifiable "things" '; 'time is transformed into abstract, exactly measurable, physical space' in an environment in which *la durée vécue* no longer exists.[80]

The evil of the factory is thus that it is above all an objective system, a system of machines in which the overall process is regarded *objectively* – as something in itself and for itself – and is analysed into its constituent parts, and in which the problem of performing each partial process and then linking them all together is settled through a technical use of mechanics, chemistry, etc. This then is the evil: *mechanization*, i.e. that the system of machines presents itself as a totally *objective* organism of production, which the worker finds before him as a pre-existing material condition of production. The evil, in other words, is not the *capitalist use* of machines, but the very fact of using *machines* at all. The problem is not that the physical sciences, incorporated into the productive process, appear as *powers of capital over labour*, but that the system of machines has everywhere as its basis the conscious application of the sciences and therefore also the 'mathematization' or 'quantification' of nature. Like Marx's *bête noire*, Dr Ure, Lukács is unable at times to distinguish between what is true for any and all use of machinery on a large scale, and what characterizes its use under capitalism.[81]

79. ibid., p. 184.

80. ibid., pp. 89–90.

81. K. Marx, *Capital*, translated by Eden and Cedar Paul, Vol. I, Part Four, Chapter 13.

Of course, since *History and Class Consciousness* is a serious book, this error is often corrected. As in few other writings, Lukács has here taken account of *Capital* and *Theories of Surplus Value*. Nevertheless, glimmers of the romantic critique often appear; and precisely in those places (if one looks closely) where Lukács, in pursuing his polemic not against capital but against rationalization as such, has just put 'the growth of mechanization, dehumanization, and reification' on the same plane,[82] and feels the need to take his distance from Carlyle, Ruskin, etc. – in short, to disassociate his critique from the 'struggle against reification' waged by romanticism.

It would be a waste of time to point out here the extent to which Lukács, in these places where the analysis of capitalism is replaced by the critique of . . . materialist fetishism, becomes a disciple of Rickert. The polemic against experimental knowledge, to which Lukács ascribes a 'contemplative' (!) posture towards nature, is taken in large part from Rickert's *Grenzen*.[83] And the same is true for the whole improbable conception of the structure and methods of the 'natural sciences'[84] – as well as the critique of the *Abbildtheorie*, the materialist theory of 'reflection'.[85] The principal essay in *History and Class Consciousness* is on 'reification', and can be better understood if one bears in mind the chapter of the *Grenzen* where Rickert develops the distinction between *Dingbegriffe* and *Relationsbegriffe*.[86]

Leaving aside these and other secondary questions (like that of the influence exercised by Max Weber on *History and Class Consciousness*) it nevertheless appears opportune here to take a position concerning Lukács's assessment of Kant and classical philosophy in the chapter of his book entitled 'The Antinomies of Bourgeois Thought'. The importance of this chapter, in which Lukács's entire argument on reification reaches its culmination, lies in the fact that in it he brings to light a fundamental problematic parallel to the one which we have been attempting to define – even if, as we shall see, he does so only to arrive at a solution that is the opposite of our own.

The problem is perceived by Lukács as being at the centre of the

82. G. Lukács, op. cit., p. 136.
83. H. Rickert, op. cit., pp. 279 and 306.
84. ibid., pp. 164–5ff.
85. ibid., pp. 51ff.
86. G. Lukács, op. cit., p. 115.

Critique of Pure Reason and indeed of Kant's entire work. Kant is the philosopher in whom 'the paradox and the tragedy of classical German philosophy', no less than what Lukács calls the surrender to the fetishism and reification of bourgeois society, find their highest expression and this problem derives from the assumption that the real is *ir-rational*, i.e. that it is something external to and heterogeneous from thought, something which cannot be derived from thought – and then, from the repercussions which this assumption has on the way in which the principle of *totality* is viewed.

As Lukács makes clear, what is at issue is on the one hand the 'problem of the content of the forms' of knowledge; and on the other hand, the 'problem of the whole', or in other words, 'of those "ultimate" objects of knowledge which are needed to round off the partial systems into a totality, a system of the perfectly understood world'.[87] These objects – which Kant of course expresses with the idea of 'God', the 'soul', etc., and regards as questions which, from the point of view of knowledge, have been improperly posed – are also rejected by Lukács. But they are rejected by him only formally (as what he considers 'mythological expressions to denote the unified subject or, alternatively, the unified object of the totality, *qua* the totality 'of the objects of knowledge'); not, however, in terms of their content or their substance, in which Lukács sees, on the contrary, an irrevocable necessity evaded by the *Critique* precisely because, as he says, 'Kant is the culmination of the philosophy of the eighteenth century', and both the development of English empiricism 'and also the tradition of French materialism move in this direction'.[88]

Kant regards content or 'matter' in terms of the *givenness* of facts, or of a basic 'irrationality' (where, it should be noted, the term 'irrationality' serves to indicate the extralogical nature of sense-phenomena and therefore their irreducibility to thought, with the consequent negation of the identity of subject and object, thought and being). This entails – and here is Lukács's thesis – a crisis in the principle of *totality* at the level of concepts or categories. In the sense that since 'empirical facts . . . are to be taken as "given" in their

87. ibid., note 6 on p. 115, the text of which is found on p. 211. 88. ibid., p. 116.

facticity' (in which 'the existence and the mode of being of sensuous contents remain absolutely irreducible') and since, therefore, 'the problem of irrationality resolves itself into the impossibility of penetrating any datum with the aid of rational concepts or of deriving them from such concepts',[89] or of deducing them from thought (and in fact, for Kant, as one knows, 'matter' or existence is not extracted from the mind), the consequence, Lukács says, is that the *totality*, i.e. the possibility of the concepts to form a 'system', comes to be irreparably compromised. In other words – and in simpler terms – the fact that Kant establishes a difference between the individual concept and its particular contents, between *concept* and *object*, produces also, Lukács says, a difference among *concepts themselves*, preventing the various fragments of knowledge from becoming integrated into a totality or 'a system of the perfectly understood world'; so that 'the irrationality of the contents of the individual concepts' generates 'the impossibility of apprehending the whole with the aid of the conceptual framework of the rational partial systems'.[90] Here, says Lukács, 'we are forced to concede that actuality, content, matter, reaches right into the form, the structures of the forms and their interrelations and thus *into the structure of the system itself*'. And the consequence is that 'the system must be abandoned as a system', or that 'it will be no more than a register, an account, as well ordered as possible, of facts which are no longer linked rationally and so can no longer be made systematic even though the forms of their components are themselves rational'.[91]

The argument obviously strikes to the heart of the matter. The 'tragic quality' of Kant's philosophy, i.e. the impossibility of its overcoming the 'crisis' of 'bourgeois estrangement' (a crisis which, for Lukács, is here of course identified with the materialist distinction between subject and object, thought and being), can be traced back to the assumption that existence is an extralogical reality. *History and Class Consciousness* cites those pages in which the *Critique* demonstrates 'the impossibility of an ontological proof for the existence of God'.[92] Kant says: ' "*Being*" is obviously not a real

89. loc. cit.
90. ibid., p. 120.
91. ibid., p. 118.
92. loc. cit.

predicate; that is, it is not a concept of something which could be added to the concept of a thing.' *From the point of view of logic*, therefore, 'A hundred real thalers do not contain the least coin more than a hundred possible thalers.' 'For as the latter signify the concept, and the former the object and the positing of the object, should the former contain more than the latter, my concept would not therefore be an adequate concept of it. As concerns my financial position, however, there undoubtedly exists more (*ist mehr*) in one hundred real dollars, than in the mere concept of them (that is, of their possibility). For the object, as it actually exists, is not analytically contained in my concept, but is added to my concept . . . synthetically; and yet the conceived hundred thalers are not themselves in the least increased through thus acquiring existence outside my concept.'[93]

Here, with this thesis that existence is not a predicate, i.e. a concept, but is something 'more' in relation to thought (as also in the pages devoted to the critique of Leibniz), Kant rejects any and every acritical identification of 'logical possibility' with 'real possibility' – or of the process of development 'according to nature' with the process of development 'according to the concept'. Just as the relationship between thought and reality cannot be reduced to a simple relationship of concepts within thought – since existence is not a predicate – similarly all transposing of logic into ontology is illegitimate. Just as a comparison of things among themselves and of thought with things is not the same as a comparison made solely within thought, similarly the internal coherence of thought cannot be directly equivalent to the congruence of thought with reality.

It remains a fact – which we shall shortly have occasion to refer to again – that this argument, at the same time as it signals the culmination of Kant's critical consciousness, is on the other hand also the place where (perhaps more clearly than anywhere else) one perceives his inability to fuse in an organic fashion the 'logical process of development' and the 'process of development in reality', ideal causes and effective causes, finalism and causality. This

93. I. Kant, *Critique of Pure Reason* (Kemp Smith translation), pp. 504–5 (translation modified).

accounts for Kant's final failure to proceed beyond the straits and narrows of pure epistemology to a genuine understanding of the world of *work* and real *historical* action, to the production of things and man's real self-reproduction. It is true that this exclusion by Kant of the world of history certainly explains the lack of interest and comprehension always shown by Marxism in regard to Kant's thought.[94] However, it remains also true – and the chapter dedicated to it in *History and Class Consciousness* confirms this – that what has impeded a genuine understanding of Kant's thought has been the prejudicial 'critique of the intellect' (and together with the intellect, the principle of non-contradiction and, therefore, science as well) which Marxism acritically borrowed from Hegel, whether in the form of so-called 'Western Marxism' or in its Soviet form as 'dialectical materialism'.

Lukács's experience can be taken, in this case, as exemplary. During the period of *History and Class Consciousness*, i.e. during that phase in which he mistook 'estrangement' for 'materialism' and confused 'alienation' with the 'intellect', Kant's thesis concerning the extralogical nature of existence made him view the *Critique of Pure Reason* as the high point of bourgeois 'reified' consciousness. Then in the following period, when he had given up his anti-materialist bias and passed over into the camp of 'dialectical materialism', what was to make him view the *Critique* as the high point not of 'fetishism', but of 'metaphysical dualism', was Engels's identification of the 'intellect' with 'dogmatism', and of metaphysics with the principle of non-contradiction.

Nothing in this regard could be more significant than the self-critique in which Lukács explained his renunciation of the positions of 1923 and his adherence to the principles of 'dialectical materialism'. Although the question of materialism has always been indicated by him as the principal watershed between the two periods, there is not a single word which ever alludes to a need for a re-examination of Hegel's critique of *Verstand*. Hegel's identification of objectivity

94. This assessment is not invalidated, in my view, either by the 'ethical' socialism of Bernstein and C. Schmidt, or by the reading in a Fichtian key of the *Critique of Pure Reason* given by Max Adler in *Kausalität und Teleologie* and in *Marxistische Probleme*.

with alienation is rejected; however, the theoretical presuppositions from which that identification derived – i.e. the critique of the intellect, the critique of the principle of non-contradiction – are calmly adopted and allowed to persist.

It is clear that this deep-seated logical inconsistency on Lukács's part has its explanation in reasons going far beyond his person. He in fact believed that a revival, against Hegel, of the materialist point of view did not necessarily entail a revision of the critique of the understanding (and thus also a revival of the principle of non-contradiction). And this depended essentially on the fact that when he went over to 'dialectical materialism', among all the matters on which Lukács felt constrained to change his opinion there was at least one – this one – in which no effort was required of him.

What he had learned to criticize and combat from his old positions of 1923 – the 'distinctions' and 'divisions' introduced by the intellect – he went on to criticize and combat, no less vehemently, from the standpoint of 'dialectical materialism'. What changed was, at the most, only the name; in the sense that what Lukács had opposed as 'reification' during the period of *History and Class Consciousness*, could now be opposed by him as 'metaphysics'. In both cases, however, the substance was the same, whatever the name was under which it was promulgated. It was always understood that the objective was to eliminate 'determinate' concepts, the notorious 'empirical' concepts (whether those of common sense or of 'traditional' science) and, in short, all knowledge grounded on non-contradiction, i.e. knowledge having as its *substratum* determinate objects.

Thus, in his arduous passage from one bank to the other, in his painful transmigration from the refined 'nuances' of Western Marxism to the rough-hewn truths of Russian 'dialectical materialism', Lukács found some basic comfort in the fact that, beneath apparent differences, he continued to move within the same tradition. The 'finite mode of knowledge' which had had its 'dogmatic scabs' (in his own words) 'scratched' by Hegel with the dialectical acids of ancient Pyrrhonism; knowledge in terms of concepts that are *figés et distincts*, against which Bergson had objected that *things* do not exist, but only *processes* and that 'facts' are nothing other than parts, 'moments' which the intellect has artificially isolated from the uninterrupted continuity of 'spiritual becoming'; all the things, in short, which he had learned to loathe from the example of Rickert and Simmel, etc., and which are re-echoed today in the platitudes of Kojève and Marcuse – Lukács found them all again, proscribed and excluded once more by the very essence of 'dialectical materialism'. There are no things, but only processes. Nothing is, everything passes away. Everything subsists in the twilight of Heraclitian becoming. The light of scientific and intellectual knowledge is but the glare and illusion of metaphysics. Metaphysics, as the *Dialectics of Nature* says, is 'the science of *things* – not of movements'.[95] And in *Ludwig Feuerbach*: 'The world is not to be comprehended as a complex of ready-made *things*, but as a complex of *processes*, in which the things apparently stable no less than their mind-images in our head, the concepts, go through an uninterrupted change of coming into being and passing away. . . .'[96]

Materialism, then, plus the dialectic of matter. *Widerspiegelungstheorie* plus the 'dialectic of the finite'. Such was the new shore towards which Lukács was moving after 1930: the 'dialectical materialism' of Engels. And since, in order to have the first thing – materialism – it was indispensable to break away from the Hegelian critique of the understanding and of non-contradiction, whereas, in order to have the second, what was indispensable was precisely that critique itself (i.e. the *Annihilation des Verstandes* and the destruction of the finite) one can well understand the profoundly contradictory nature of Lukács's self-criticism.

His statement of 1962 traces back all of the shortcomings of *History and Class Consciousness* to two essential points: the failure to recognize the 'fundamental principle of the Marxist theory of knowledge – an objective reality existing independently of consciousness'; and the denial of the dialectic of matter.[97] A literature at times brilliant, but more often weak in analysis, has always agreed

95. F. Engels, *Dialectics of Nature*, op. cit., p. 155.
96. F. Engels, *Ludwig Feuerbach*, op. cit., p. 44.
97. Cf. the statement of 1962 in I. Fetscher, op. cit.

with Lukács in recognizing that these were (as is indeed true) precisely the two main distinguishing features between 'Western Marxism' and 'dialectical materialism': the *Widerspiegelungstheorie* and the 'dialectic of matter'. But also that *both* conceptions contributed to define the fundamentally *materialist* nature of Russian Marxism, in contradistinction to the 'Western' version (one need only think of Merleau-Ponty's *Les aventures de la dialectique*).

In point of fact, both the Lukács who passed over to 'dialectical materialism', and so-called 'Western Marxism', have always remained trapped within the same theoretical limits. Neither has ever arrived at an understanding of how the 'critique of the intellect' compelled both theories to share fate, above and beyond all of their other differences.

Abbildtheorie plus the 'dialectic of matter'. Even the slightest degree of critical consciousness should be enough to understand the degree of dilettantism that is implicit in any claim to couple these two things together. Materialism, in fact, is inconceivable without the principle of non-contradiction; the 'dialectic of matter', contrariwise, is the negation of this principle. For the former, the particular object is the *substratum* of judgment: the particular is *external* or irreducible (one need only think of Kant) to the logical universal. For the latter, however, just the opposite is true: in the sense that, if the finite has as its essence and foundation the 'other' than itself, it *is* 'truly' itself only when it is *not* itself but is the ideal finite or the finite *within* thought.

A page from *History and Class Consciousness* confirms the syncretism that lies at the basis of Engels's naïve combination of *Abbildtheorie* and 'dialectic of matter'. Lukács cites two passages from *Ludwig Feuerbach*, the first of which he rejects and the other he accepts. Engels writes: 'We comprehend the concepts in our heads once more materialistically – as reflections of real things instead of regarding the real things as reflections of this or that stage of the absolute concept.' Now, Lukács comments, 'this leaves a question to be asked and Engels not only asks it but also answers it on the following page quite in agreement with us. There he says: "that the world is not to be comprehended as a complex of ready-made *things*, but as a complex of *processes*".' 'But then,' Lukács concludes, 'if there are no things, what is "reflected" in thought?'[98]

In this remark, which may appear little more than a joke, the difference between Western Marxism and dialectical materialism finds – even if only implicitly – its proper dimension. The transformation of 'things' into 'processes' presupposes the overcoming not only of the distinction between one thing and another, but also of that between subject and object. Reality as process is, in fact, the fluidity, the uninterrupted continuity which is established whenever the 'material' and the 'immaterial', the subjective and the objective, the finite and the infinite, are *taken together* – i.e. taken up as 'moments' of a single unity. As we know, this is an essential point of Hegel's thought. Reason, he says, is not the subjective as against the objective: it is the unity of the one and the other; it is not the infinite of the understanding, but the unity of the finite and infinite. Now, to take up this dialectical view of reality as process and, at the same time, to claim to continue to be talking about thought that 'reflects' things, as if there still existed a mutual *externality* between the two things, is patently absurd (precisely Lukács's objection).

In my opinion it is undeniable that in this regard, i.e. in its rejection of syncretism or eclecticism, Western Marxism demonstrates its superiority over 'dialectical materialism'. Western Marxism recognizes, at least in the case of its principal exponent, that the adoption of the dialectical principle as the principle (not only of reason but also) of *reality* leaves no room for materialism of any kind. And the extent to which this position, with all its limitations, is more correct than the other one is demonstrated by simply calling to mind the decadence of Lukács's thought after *History and Class Consciousness*, as he tried to discover in Hegel himself what in 1923 he had rightly denounced as an eclectic contamination of Engels's: that is to say, the adoption of the dialectic as the principle of reality and, together with it, the possibility of introducing a 'theory of reflection'.

The common element in these two positions, underlying their significant differences, is their character as epigonous and 'corrupted'

98. G. Lukács, *History and Class Consciousness*, op. cit., pp. 199–200.

manifestations of Hegel's original thought. In the case of 'dialectical materialism' this 'corruption' has been amply discussed: here, philosophy mistakes the 'dialectic of matter' with which Hegel realizes absolute idealism for a form of materialism. In the case of 'Western Marxism', this corruption is expressed in the tendency – today quite widespread – to view Hegel's unity of the 'material' and the 'immaterial', the subjective and the objective, as something neutral (i.e. as something encompassing both of them, without however being either one of them) – and, therefore, as something which can be taken for granted henceforth as going beyond the 'archaic' stage of mere epistemological inquiry. Take as an example the 'praxis' of all the philosophical works that draw their title therefrom!

That we are dealing with a kind of epigonism that is altogether too casual about the actual meaning ascribed by Hegel to his unity of the subjective and the objective, may be demonstrated with reference to any number of texts. For example the second *Zusatz* to subheading 24 of the *Encyclopedia* where it is stated that 'God alone is the thorough harmony of Notion and reality';[99] or the note to subheading 389 of the same work, in which – after having called to mind that 'in the philosophies of Descartes, Malebranche, and Spinoza, a return was made to such unity of thought and being, of spirit and matter, and this unity was placed in God' – Hegel observes that by 'placing the unity of the material and the immaterial in God, who is to be grasped essentially as spirit, these philosophers wished to make it known that this unity must not be taken as something neutral (*ein Neutrales*) in which two extremes of equal significance and independence are united', but rather as that unity which can encompass within itself both thought and being only in so far as it itself is spirit or thought.[100]

If this is true, then the difference between 'dialectical materialism' and 'Western Marxism' shows itself in a novel light; i.e. not so much as a difference between Marxism of a materialist cast and Marxism *qua* 'philosophy of praxis', but rather as the difference between two

99. *En.L.*, p. 52.
100. G. W. F. Hegel, *Philosophy of Mind*, being Part Three of the *Encyclopaedia of the Philosophical Sciences*, translated by William Wallace (London, 1971), p. 33.

opposing and greatly adulterated offshoots of the same Hegelian tradition. In Western Marxism this tradition was filtered through the 'medium' of so-called 'contemporary German Historicism' and its particular problems (notably that of the distinction between the natural sciences and the socio-historical sciences); and also through the entire anti-objectivist orientation peculiar to Neo-Hegelianism, including Croce and Gentile. This accounts for the repudiation on the part of that Marxism of the 'dialectic of matter' and, in general, of Hegel's entire philosophy of nature.

In dialectical materialism, on the other hand, the same tradition is taken up precisely and especially in this latter version. This is true both as regards the belief that the 'dialectic of matter' is itself a form of materialism – and indeed the most refined and rigorous form thereof – and as regards the possibility that it offered – thanks to this misinterpretation and to the nature of the period when 'dialectical materialism' was elaborated – of being placed in relationship to and in osmosis with the great cosmogonic 'syntheses' of evolutionist positivism.

The extent to which both of these lines of interpretation appear aberrant in relation to the core of Marx's thought can be seen in the fate of what, in my view, is the unifying theme at the basis of his entire work: the theme of 'reification' or 'estrangement' or – what is really the same thing – the theme of the hypostatization or substantification of the abstract.[101] This theme of Marx's is the basis of his critique of both Hegel's speculative logic and of political economy in general, as well as of his critique of the hypostatization *in reality* of the State and capital. The former is hypostatized as the reification (or particularization) of the general or *universal* interest which posits itself as a self-contained entity, the State, divorced from the body of all those concerned; and the latter as the reification of a *social* productive power which, in its separation from the body of workers, becomes 'the power of a part of society, (which) preserves itself and multiplies by exchange with direct, living labour-power'.[102]

101. The perception of this unifying motif in Marx's work appears in its general outline – even if perhaps never in fully conscious terms – in Karl Korsch's well-balanced *Karl Marx* (London, 1936).

102. K. Marx, *Wage-Labour and Capital*, op. cit., p. 30.

Now, the fate that has befallen this essential theme of Marx's entire work finds expression, significantly enough, in Lukács's own experience. *History and Class Consciousness* – as the author has correctly recalled – is that work in which the 'question of alienation, . . . for the first time since Marx, is treated as central to the revolutionary critique of capitalism'.[103] After Marx and up until 1923 the problem had never been examined. An entire area central to Marx's thought – developed in hundreds of pages of *Capital, Theories of Surplus Value*, and the *Grundrisse*, etc. – had totally escaped the horizon of his interpreters' knowledge. Engels, Kautsky, Plekhanov, Lenin did not devote even a single line to it. They did not manage to see the point of it. In their reconstructions of Marx's thought there was no room for this theme.

Lukács's book breaks for the first time with this tradition, and discovers this unexplored ground in the *corpus* of Marx's writings. Since, however, the problem of capitalist reification is then confused by Lukács with that of materialism and science, an explanation for this basic *impasse* in the entire preceding tradition of interpretation posed no great difficulty for him: he thought that the Engels–Lenin tradition excluded the theme of reification as a consequence of its materialist nature.

When his bias against materialism had disappeared after 1930, and he was in a position to re-examine the problem right from its roots, the continuity existing between his old positions and his new ones (as far as concerns the 'critique of the intellect') kept him from arriving at a new appraisal of the question. Although much more learned and expert than countless others, he had now become a 'dialectical materialist' with all the trimmings. And the theme of reification gradually loses importance and significance in his work, reappearing only (when it does reappear) in the same manner as in 1923. The critique of reification is the same as the critique of 'positivity' developed by the young Hegel.[104] Metaphysics resides in the understanding, in the principle of non-contradiction.

103. G. Lukács, op. cit., p. xxii.

104. Here one should carefully examine Chapters II and VI of *Der junge Hegel* concerning Hegel's critique of 'positivity' and, in particular, concerning the critique of

'positive religion'. In general, one must note that although Lukács points out on a number of occasions that Hegel's critique of positive religion is 'the philosophic expression of the ultra-idealist dissolution (*Aufhebung*) of any and all objectivity' (p. 124) and that Hegel 'does not reject and oppose religion in general, but rather counterposes a non-positive religion to positive religion' (p. 130), his argument nonetheless tends to give greater emphasis to those features of Hegel's argument which represent 'intimations of those sorts of social objectivity (*Gegenständlichkeit*) which Marx subsequently designated with the term 'fetishism' (p. 124). The reason for the continual oscillations found in Lukács's argument is to be sought, in my view, in his failure to carry out a thorough analysis of Hegel's critique of the intellect. That prevented him from seeing that Hegel's critique is a critique of positivity and not of religion; or, better stated, that this critique is indeed a critique of religion, but only in so far as it is characteristic of religion – as opposed to philosophy – to conceive of God, who is spirituality, in terms that are still naturalistic. The critique of positive religion is in Hegel above all the critique of *Catholicism*. The critique hinges on the theme of naturalistic and pagan objectivism, which calls into question positive religion *par excellence*. The long *Anmerkung* to sub-heading 552 of the *Encyclopedia* (Hegel's *Philosophy of Mind*, translated by W. Wallace, London, 1871) states that with Catholicism 'God is in the "host" presented to religious adoration as an *external thing*. [In the Lutheran Church, on the contrary, the host as such is not at first consecrated, but in the moment of enjoyment, i.e. in the annihilation of its externality, and in the act of faith, i.e. in the free self-certain spirit: only then is it consecrated and exalted to be present God' (pp. 284–5).] The critique opposes, in short, the representation of the Spirit as a *thing*, re-establishing in this way a link with Hegel's critique of pre-Kantian metaphysics. This position, which is from his period of full maturity, is analogous – as Karl Rosenkranz saw clearly in his life of Hegel (*Georg Wilhelm Friedrich Hegels Leben*, Berlin, 1844) – to that adopted during his early period. What is confirmed in both periods is that 'Hegel's philosophy, as far as concerns religion, is essentially *Protestant*'. And Rosenkranz adds: 'I term Protestantism that form of religion which bases the conciliation between God and man on the recognition that the essence of human self-consciousness has as its contents divine self-consciousness and thus freedom as its form.' Rosenkranz rightly makes a connection between the critique of positive religion and Hegel's critique of the 'understanding', and in particular the former's connection with the critique developed by Hegel of the relationship that the intellectual understanding establishes between the finite and the infinite when it represents the finite as the 'here and now', or 'worldly existence', and the infinite as the empty 'beyond'. Lukács, on the contrary, tends to see in Hegel's critique 'the theoretical unmasking and annihilation of the transcendental objectivity of positivity' (p. 118), as if the meaning of Hegel's argument were the negation of transcendence, rather than the attempt to establish transcendence as the absolute and the *sole* true reality by shifting God from the beyond to the here and now. Here again one comes across the dialectical-materialist limitation of Lukács. In fact, the dialectic of the finite and the infinite is conceived by him as if it were a means by which Hegel negated the suprasensible or God – rather than a means to negate the finite. As Lukács says (p. 302): 'Already at Jena he begins to find a correct dialectical formulation of this problem, and precisely by means of this dialectic of the infinite and the finite which he has discovered he begins to eliminate all transcendental and supranatural (*jede Jenseitigkeit*) traces from the infinite').

Lukács was not only incapable of understanding the reason why the old dialectical materialism was not able to interpret and elaborate on Marx's analysis of reification; he in turn became a prisoner of the limitations of that tradition. Metaphysics is for him the differentiation of subject and object, the particular viewed to the exclusion of *everything* that it *is not*; in short, it is the particular outside the logical universal. Now, precisely this argument is what excludes Lukács from the mainstream of Marx's thought, just as previously it had excluded Engels and Lenin. For Marx, in fact, metaphysics is the *realism of universals*; it is a logical totality which posits itself as self-subsisting, transforms itself into the subject, and which (since it must be self-subsisting) identifies and confuses itself acritically with the particular, turning the latter – i.e. the actual subject of reality – into its own predicate or manifestation.

What we have attempted to show is how this idea of metaphysics refers back to an entire tradition which has as its modern cornerstone Kant's *Critique of Pure Reason*. Marx brought a fundamental and decisive innovation to this tradition. Just as for Hegel a fully realized metaphysics is the *realization* of idealism, i.e. the Idea or Logos that becomes reality, so for Marx metaphysics is no longer only a particular form of knowledge, but a process that concerns the very core of *reality* itself. In other words it is no longer only the (metaphysical) representation of reality, but reality itself, which is upside down or 'stood on its head'; hence the world itself has to be undermined and then set 'right way up'. The hypostatization of the universal, its substantification or reification, does not concern only (or even primarily) Hegel's Logic; it concerns reality itself. In short, what the hypostasis of Hegel's Notion refers back to is the hypostasis of capital and of the State.

As the reader can see, Lukács is here mistaking the immanentization of transcendence for its elimination. As far as concerns the persistence in Lukács of the old conception that identifies alienation and fetishism with the 'intellect's' distinction between subject and object, one need only point to the use he has made of Schiller's Letters, particularly the sixth one, in *Ueber die ästhetische Erziehung des Menschen* (in *Schillers Werke*, edited by E. Jenny, Vol. X (Basel, 1946), particularly pp. 92ff.). Schiller's critique of the distinction between the 'sense-world' and the 'understanding' is read by Lukács in the light of Marx's critique of fetishism; cf. G. Lukács, *Goethe and His Age* (London, 1968), pp. 101ff.

XI. The Concept of the 'Social Relations of Production'

Marxism is not an epistemology, at least in any fundamental sense – in Marx's work *Widerspiegelungstheorie* as such has little importance. Nonetheless, it is important to take epistemology as one's point of departure, in order to understand how a concept like the 'social relations of production', so original and also so foreign to the entire speculative tradition, could be born out of the development and transformation of the very problems of classical philosophy. The point which must be clearly understood is that the difficulties of epistemology are the same difficulties that exist in the relationship between 'intellect' and 'reason'. Since epistemology has to explain the genesis of knowledge, the formation of concepts, it cannot take knowledge as already given, but must go back to the *conditions* from which knowledge itself is produced (sensation *and* intellect, thought *and* being). All of which means that epistemology cannot help but present itself as an *Elementarlehre*, i.e. as a 'theory of elements', where thought is not only 'one of the two', but is conditioned by the 'other' external to it. Yet on the other hand, inasmuch as the stipulation of the conditions in which knowledge is produced is itself a cognitive act, that which at first appears to place limiting conditions on thought from the outside can subsequently reveal itself to be a limiting condition which thought has *posited* for itself. Far from being just 'one of two', thought then shows itself to be the 'totality' of the relationship. In the first case, when epistemology purports to be an inquiry into the genesis or formation of knowledge, it has to view concepts as a resultant, a point of arrival that depends on extra-logical conditions. In the second case, just the reverse: since the very attempt to explain the cognitive process implies a cognitive act, concepts are seen in terms of an *original organic unity* that is essential to them, and epistemology is reduced to logic.

These difficulties in the theory of knowledge are the pivotal point from which Hegel's and Kant's thought develop. The first paragraphs of the *Encyclopedia* demonstrate with exceptional clarity how Hegel had mastered all aspects of the problem. Unless it is to be a form of immediate knowledge or a faith, knowledge must be able to manifest itself at the end of a process that proceeds from empirical reality (*non-sapere*) to knowledge, from being to thought; the Notion must, therefore, show itself to be something that is mediated and conditioned; hence the statement at the beginning of subheading 12 that 'the *rise* of philosophy (has) its point of departure (in) *Experience*'. On the other hand the need for inquiry into the rise of philosophy or knowledge clashes with the fact that such research itself cannot come about except in the light of and on the basis of what should be its outcome. 'A main line of argument in the Critical Philosophy (of Kant) is that before proceeding to inquire into God or into the true being of things, one must first of all examine the *faculty of cognition*.... Unless we wish to be deceived by words, it is easy to see ... that the examination of knowledge can only be carried out by an *act of knowledge*. To examine this so-called instrument is the same thing as to know it. But to seek to know *before* we know is as absurd as the resolution of Scholasticus, not to *venture into* the water until he had learned to *swim*.'[1] On the one hand, then, there is the need for mediation in the passage *from* experience *to* philosophy, from being to the Notion; for were this mediation and this conditioning either impossible or illusory, then Jacobi's intuitionism would be correct (and along with Jacobi, the Indian who worships the cow and and monkey). On the other hand, however, inasmuch as the Notion is a *prius* it is impossible for the Notion to be the resultant of external conditions. 'The rise of philosophy (has) its point of departure (in) Experience'; but, Hegel immediately adds, 'If mediation is represented as a state of conditionedness (*Bedingtheit*), and this is brought out in a one-sided fashion, it may be said – not that the remark would mean much – that philosophy owes its *origin* to experience (the *a posteriori*).'[2]

1. *En.L.*, p. 17 (translation modified).
2. ibid., p. 20 (translation modified).

In other words, the difficulties of epistemology derive from the clash of two opposing principles. The first holds that since all explanation is a *scire per causas* (one need only think of Jacobi), any theory that proposes to explain knowledge cannot do other than stipulate the *limiting conditions* on thought, i.e. apply to thought the principle of causality. This accounts for the tendency towards materialism present in every epistemology. (Hegel, who in opposition to Jacobi calls attention to the need for mediation, can only uphold the sort of mediation that 'sublates' itself, i.e. that eliminates the limiting conditions placed on thought.) The second principle holds that since thought is 'subjectivity' and therefore spontaneous 'activity', it is irreducible to any causal explanation (thought, as Hegel says, is ungrateful like eating which 'devours that to which it owes itself'). This means that in so far as the theory which represents it as an effect is itself an act of thinking, it is evident that what epistemology presents to us is not, despite itself, the priority of real conditions but rather the priority of the thought that articulates them; and therefore, the limiting conditions are not really external, but only the limiting conditions conceived by thought, conditions that are a product and consequence of thought itself.

Here we have the roots of Hegel's thesis, already referred to a number of times, that philosophy is always and inevitably idealism. Materialism is, in this view, inconceivable because a philosophy that affirms the priority of being or matter over thought and therefore the dependence of the latter on the former, does not realize that it is overturning the very order which it proposes – in the very act by which it arrives at this declaration. Matter, which was to have been primary, actually manifests itself only as an ideal content, i.e. as a product of thought; thought, contrariwise, which was to have been secondary, turns out to be primary. Hegel writes: 'The principles of ancient or modern philosophies, water, or matter, or atoms are *thoughts*, universals, ideal entities, not things as they immediately present themselves to us, that is, in their sensuous individuality – not even the water of Thales. For although this is also empirical water, it is at the same time also the *in-itself* or *essence* of all other things, too, and these other things are not self-subsistent or grounded in themselves, but are *posited* by, are *derived* from, an *other*, ... that is they are ideal entities.'[3]

On the other hand, even if concepts represent that original unity beyond which it is impossible to go and which it would be absurd to overlook – even hypothetically – it remains true nonetheless that Hegel himself must constantly call attention to the need for mediation. The concept cannot be just 'first'; it must also appear as 'last', not only as a point of departure but also as a point of arrival. For otherwise the concept would become an unmediated presupposition (a blind faith or an instinct), and the knowledge which is to be built up would turn out to be already *given*.

The same difficulty was also experienced by Kant, although he was proceeding in a direction very different from that of Hegel. The *Critique of Pure Reason* is in a sense the only great work of modern thought which attempts to construct epistemology as a science. The distinction between thought and being, which for Hegel is a regrettable necessity that must be circumvented and avoided, is with Kant a source of strength. For him, it is not epistemology that tends to lapse into logic, but vice versa. It is not the relationship 'being-thought' that tends to circumscribe itself to a mere relationship of thought with itself – if anything, the opposite is true. In its basic construction the *Critique of Pure Reason* is a 'theory of elements', i.e. a theory of the distinction between the *sense* element and the *logical* element (in which thought is not only the second element, but is conditioned by the first). On the basis of this formulation, Kant constantly remarks that if one wants to have knowledge, one must refer thought back to that which is *other* than itself; an 'other' – *nota bene* – whose heterogeneity is qualitative and not formal, 'transcendental' and not merely logical. 'Without sensibility no object would be given to us, without understanding no object would be thought. . . . These two powers or capacities (receptivity and spontaneity) cannot exchange their functions. The understanding can intuit nothing, the senses can think nothing. Only through their union can knowledge arise. But that is no reason for confounding the contribution of either with that of the other;

3. *L.*, p. 170.

rather is it a strong reason for carefully separating and distinguishing the one from the other. We therefore distinguish the science of the rules of sensibility in general, that is, aesthetic, from the science of the rules of the understanding in general, that is, logic.'[4]

It is symptomatic, however, that it is precisely from the heart of this 'theory of elements' that the difficulty described above in the case of Hegel should arise also for Kant. Inasmuch as there can be no knowledge unless there is already *given* something to be thought, thought is clearly only 'one of the two': it is conditioned by the 'other' that lies outside itself. On the other hand, since for something to be given to me, I must take *cognizance* of it as such (for the problems and things of which I am not conscious do not exist for me), the relationship is reversed; whereas in the first case in order for me to *think* something had to present or represent itself to me, now – vice versa – in order for me to *have representations*, they must appear from the very start as *mine*, i.e. as linked to and belonging already to my consciousness. As Kant says: 'For the manifold representations, which are given in an intuition, would not be one and all *my* representations, if they did not all belong to one self-consciousness'; i.e. 'only in so far as I can grasp the manifold of the representations in one consciousness, do I call them one and all *mine*'.[5]

In the first case, thought is only 'one of two', and 'that representation, which can be given before all thought', and which, as Kant writes, may be termed 'intuition' (*Anschauung*), is the *thing* as it manifests itself to me. In the second case, however, just as thought is a 'totality', i.e. the 'original synthetic unity of apperception', so representation is only 'an act of spontaneity', a creation of thought, i.e. an act by which thought objectifies itself. In the first case, there can be no thought unless an object to be thought is already *given*; in the second, there can be no consciousness of the *object* except by means of and in dependence on the *self-consciousness* of the subject. The 'theory of elements', with its distinction between the sense element and the logical element, aims to go back to the conditions

4. I. Kant, *Critique of Pure Reason* (Kemp Smith translation), op. cit., p. 93.
5. ibid., pp. 153–4.

antecedent to thought; but it reveals itself also to be, on the other hand, a mere subcategory of *theory*, i.e. a distinction within logic itself, in which thought – far from appearing as the second or conditioned element – shows itself to be that original activity which determines (one need only think of the 'transcendental schematism') the entire area of the sense world.

It is not hard to recognize in these epistemological difficulties the same problems which we have already encountered. Thought as 'one of two' and thought as the 'totality' of the relationship, or – to use the terms that emerged above – thought as consciousness of the *object* and thought as consciousness of self or *self-consciousness*, are all figures of speech analogous to those which were previously termed induction and deduction, process of development 'according to nature' and process of development 'according to the Notion', process in reality and logical process. In both instances, it is a question of two causal processes. The first one is an instance of efficient or material causality, where it is empirical or sense data which condition and thought which is conditioned. The second one is an instance of the inverse process, or ideal causality, where the Notion, instead of appearing as a resultant, is *prius*, an *a priori* condition. In short, causality versus finalism, causality versus teleology: 'The purpose,' as Kant writes, 'is the object of a concept, in so far as the concept is regarded as the cause of the object (the real ground of its possibility); and the causality of a *concept* in respect of its *object* is its purposiveness (*forma finalis*).'[6]

It would be senseless to waste time on those who think these alternatives are mere metaphysical 'archaisms' from Kant and Hegel. Myrdal has recently clearly shown that these alternatives represent, rather, 'the logical crux of all science';[7] a problem which follows from the fact that whereas the idea or theory must be, on the one hand, always a *prius* in scientific inquiry, on the other hand they must also appear as a *posterius*, i.e. as a theoretical 'nucleus . . .

6. I. Kant, *Critique of Judgement*, translated by J. H. Bernard (London, 1914), p. 67.

7. Cf. Gunnar Myrdal, *Economic Theory and Under-Developed Regions* (London, 1957), whose chapter XII is entitled 'The logical crux of all science' (cf. also G. Myrdal, *Value in Social Theory* [London, 1958]).

which . . . can only be constructed on (empirical research) as a basis'.[8] The same may be said for the connection, referred to just above, between deduction and finalism, hypothesis and ideology. In every scientific analysis, Myrdal writes, there is an *a priori* element which is inescapable. 'Questions must be asked before answers can be given. The questions are an expression of our interest in the world, they are at bottom valuations. Valuations are thus necessarily involved already at the stage when we observe facts and carry on theoretical analysis, and not only at the stage when we draw political inferences from facts and valuations.'[9] Joan Robinson also expresses herself in like terms: Ideological (or as she inappropriately calls them, 'metaphysical') propositions, 'provide a quarry from which hypotheses can be drawn', i.e. objectives or projects without which we would not know what to investigate. 'They do not belong to the realm of science and yet they are necessary to it' (which means that, in actual fact, they really do belong to it); for 'without them we would not know what it is that we want to know'.[10] This *a priori* element – whether ideological or anthropomorphic – contained in the ideal 'anticipation' or in the 'question', is certainly eliminated by the 'answer', i.e. through experimental control; but, as Robinson concludes, '. . . the point is that without ideology we would never have thought of the question'.[11]

Let us return to Kant and Hegel. It is now a question of seeing not only how they resolve the difficulties of epistemology, but also of bringing to light the *conception of man* which underlies their arguments.

Hegel: his solution is already known to us. Epistemology is

8. G. Myrdal, *Economic Theory and Under-Developed Regions*, op. cit., p. 163.

9. G. Myrdal, *The Political Element in the Development of Economic Theory* (London, 1953), p. vii. The remarks that precede the text cited above are the following: 'This implicit belief in the existence of a body of scientific knowledge acquired independently of all valuations is, as I now see it, naïve empiricism. Facts do not organize themselves into concepts and theories just by being looked at; indeed, except within the framework of concepts and theories, there are no scientific facts but only chaos.' And one need only think of Marx's statement in the *Introduction* of 1857 [cf. above, chapter VIII]: 'If we start out . . . with population, we do so with a chaotic conception of the whole.'

10. Joan Robinson, *Economic Philosophy* (London, 1962), p. 3.

11. ibid., p. 4.

evaded and resolved into logic. Real mediation, i.e. the relationship being-thought (the former the conditioning element, the latter the conditioned) lapses into and is absorbed within the relationship of thought to itself. The distinction between empirical data and the intellectual understanding is only 'apparent', since it exists within that unity or original totality that is 'reason'. The Notion was never born: it is the unconditional. The particular or the finite upon which it *appears* to depend as its limiting condition, is in reality its resultant and effect. Consequently, that *from which* the Notion appears to come forth, is in actual fact that *into which* the Notion itself passes over in order to make itself real. What appears to be induction is deduction, i.e. the passage from the beyond into the here and now. The positive is not autonomous, it is not grounded in itself, but is only the 'positive exposition of the absolute'. The logical process is the process of reality itself; the process of development 'according to nature' is only the manifestation of the process of development 'according to the Notion'. Finally, in so far as the process of the formation of knowledge is a merely apparent one (and mediation dissolves itself), the Idea that results therefrom – since it was not actually derived from anything – is only a presupposition, i.e. *immediate* knowledge (or mediated only formally). This accounts for the unavoidable point of contact between Hegel and Jacobi, and between idealism and spiritualism in general.

As concerns the conception of man that derives from this, what must be brought out immediately is that Hegel understands the traditional definition – *homo animal rationale* – in the sense that the predicate (reason) is the substance while the real subject (i.e. man as a natural or finite being) is only a predicate of his predicate. In other words, for Hegel finite man represents no problem. The real essence of man is spirituality, i.e. the divine *Logos* that dwells within him. Setting himself off from the philosophy of the Enlightenment's 'understanding' (intellect), which represents reason as a property *of* man, Hegel emphasizes that it is the spirit which alone 'makes man man'. This phrase, which is found on the first page of the *Philosophy of Religion*, shows – as Löwith has correctly observed – that 'Hegel's notion of the spirit is not intended anthropologically, but theologically, as the Christian Logos. It is thus superhuman.'[12] Or as Hegel states in the *Encyclopedia*, subheading 377: '*Know thyself* – whether we look at it in itself or under the historical circumstances of its first utterance – is not to promote *mere self-knowledge* in respect of the *particular* capacities, character, propensities, and foibles of the single self. The knowledge it commands means that of man's genuine reality – of what is essentially and ultimately true and real – of spirit as the true and *essential being*.'[13]

The addendum to this subheading goes on to say that, just as the point of reference with regard to man's essence (that is, with regard to that which makes him 'man' strictly speaking) is 'the relation of the human spirit to the Divine' (since the essence of man is God), similarly, 'it was Christianity, by its doctrine of the Incarnation and of the presence of the Holy Spirit in the community of believers, that first gave to human consciousness a perfectly free relationship to the infinite and thereby made possible the comprehensive (*begreifende*) knowledge of spirit in its absolute infinitude'.[14] And since 'thought, (besides being) the constitutive substance of external things, . . . is also the universal substance of what is spiritual', thus man's humanity, his divine spirituality, corresponds – as is made clear in *Zusatz* 1 to subheading 24 – to man's being the organ and vehicle of speculative Logic. The correct statement, therefore, is not that man thinks or that thought is a property of man, but that man is a property of thought, an organ or vehicle of the *Logos*. As Hegel makes clear: when, in fact, 'it is presented in this light, thought has a different part to play from what it has if we speak of a faculty of thought, one among a crowd of other faculties, such as perception, conception and will, with which it stands on the same level. When it is seen to be the true universal of all that nature and mind contain, it extends its scope far beyond all these and becomes the basis (*die Grundlage*) of everything.' We can then say: *Ich und Denken sind dasselbe*, or more exactly, *Ich ist das Denken als Denkendes* (the ego is Thinking as something that thinks). And Hegel concludes thus:

12. Karl Löwith, *From Hegel to Nietzsche*, translated by David E. Green (New York, Chicago, San Francisco, 1964), p. 308.

13. G. W. H. Hegel, *Philosophy of Mind*, op. cit., p. 1.

14. ibid., p. 2.

'What I have in my consciousness, is for me. "I" is the vacuum or receptacle for anything and everything: for which everything is and which stores up everything in itself.'[15]

In substance, it is not man who thinks about reality, but the Spirit or the *Logos* which, by means of man, establishes a relationship to that which it itself has *posited* as reality, and thereby redeems itself from alienation and attains to a full consciousness of itself. As clearly indicated in the outline of the *Phenomenology*, the path by which man ascends to the comprehension of reality is only a screen behind which there unfolds the other process (profounder and more essential) by which the Spirit arrives at self-consciousness. This accounts for 'the paradoxical proposition of Hegel's: "Consciousness of God is God's self-consciousness" '; this proposition, as Feuerbach pointed out, 'means only this: that self-consciousness is an attribute of substance or God, that God is the ego (*Gott ist Ich*)'.[16] In other words, Hegel 'makes the ego an *attribute* or the *form* of *divine substance*'; even if it later turns out that 'for Hegel the essence of God is actually nothing other than the essence of thinking or the thinking (of man) *abstracted from the ego, from the thinking subject*' and 'represented as a being distinct from the latter'.[17]

Marx's assessment moves in this same direction. For Hegel, he writes, 'man is regarded as a *non-objective, spiritual* being'. '*Human life, man,* is equivalent to *self-consciousness.*' 'But it is entirely false to say on that account, "*Self-consciousness* has eyes, ears, faculties." Self-consciousness is rather a quality of human nature, of the human eye, etc.; human nature is not a quality of *self-consciousness.*'[18] Marx continues: 'A being which does not have its nature outside itself is not a *natural* being and does not share in the being of nature. A being which has no object outside itself is not an objective being. A being which is not itself an object for a third being has no being for

15. *En.L.*, pp. 47–8.
16. L. Feuerbach, *Vorläufige Thesen zur Reform der Philosophie*, in *Kleine Schriften*, op. cit., p. 125.
17. L. Feuerbach, *Grundsätze der Philosophie der Zukunft*, in *Kleine Schriften*, op. cit., p. 179.
18. K. Marx, *Early Writings*, op. cit., p. 204.

its *object*, i.e. it is not objectively related and its being is not objective.'[19]

And Marx goes on to say: 'Just as the *entity*, the *object*, appears as an entity of thought, so also the *subject* is always *consciousness* or *self-consciousness*'; which means that the outcome of the movement is only 'the identity of self-consciousness and consciousness – absolute knowledge – the movement of abstract thought not directed outwards but proceeding within itself; i.e. the dialectic of pure thought is the result'.[20] Marx concludes: 'This movement, in its abstract form as dialectic, is regarded therefore as *truly human life*, and since it is nevertheless an abstraction, an alienation of human life, it is regarded as a *divine process* and thus as the divine process of mankind.' In other words, the subject of the process is not man as a finite being but rather 'the subject (that) knows itself as absolute self-consciousness, (and) is therefore *God, absolute spirit, the self-knowing and self-manifesting idea*'. Whereas 'real man and real nature become mere predicates, symbols of this concealed unreal man and unreal nature'.[21]

For Hegel, therefore, Spirit is all: 'The *Absolute is Mind* (Spirit) – this is the supreme definition of the Absolute. . . . The word "Mind" (Spirit) – and some glimpse of its meaning – was found at an early period: and the spirituality of God is the lesson of Christianity'[22] – this Spirit is the true essence of man. As opposed to the Enlightenment, which refused to recognize 'God or the Absolute', and whose point of reference was rather 'man and humanity', Hegel maintains that the true understanding of man consists in conceiving his spirit as an image or copy of the eternal Idea (*den Geist als ein Abbild der ewigen Idee*).[23]

What is the result? It means that deduction or the teleological process, i.e. the objectification of the idea or man's externalization of his thoughts (whether in language or in real production) – and here one need only think of Marx's famous remark on the difference between the architect and the bee: the product of labour is the manifestation or *realization* of what was posited as an objective in

19. ibid., p. 207. 20. ibid., p. 202. 21. ibid., p. 214.
22. G. W. F. Hegel, *Philosophy of Mind*, op. cit., p. 18. 23. ibid., p. 5.

the worker's *idea* – this objectifying process appears to Hegel not as the manifestation or objectification of man's thought, i.e. not as the proof of his *Diesseitigkeit* or terrestriality (cf. the second *Theses on Feuerbach*); rather, it appears to him as the passage from the 'beyond' (*jenseits*) into the 'here and now' (*diesseits*), i.e. as a kind of epiphany, as the entry of God into the world. In other words, whereas, as Feuerbach says, 'the passage from the ideal to the real has a place only in practical philosophy',[24] i.e. in the study of the various forms of human praxis (included therein is also knowledge itself in that it too is an act of life); for Hegel, on the other hand, 'the Idea realises itself in just the same way that God externalises and reveals himself, secularises and actualises himself'.[25] So man's production of his own life, his historico-practical action, appears to Hegel – even if with an extraordinary richness of historico-empirical content and a high degree of rationality – as God's self-unfolding in the world; just as the events of the time always appeared to the Christian philosophy of history as *Gesta Dei per Francos*.

The process of development 'according to nature' becomes, in short, a mere moment within the process of development 'according to the Notion'. And since the Notion, lacking a substratum in reality (in relation to which it is rightly a predicate or function), hypostatizes and substantifies itself, it thereby transforms itself from a Notion that ought to be a property *of man* into the spiritual 'essence' of all of reality, i.e. into the divine *Logos*. Material or effective causality, in other words, becomes a moment within ideal causality, i.e. within finalism or teleology. This accounts for the fact that – since everything is governed by the goals and purposes of God – there is no causality which would also encompass teleology (and thus no materialism that could assume historical form: a *historical materialism* with its concepts of labour and production). Rather, all there can be is a contrived history – in short, a *philosophy of history*.

At this point it is easy to perceive the basic misunderstanding that dominates the famous chapter of *Der junge Hegel* on 'Work and the Problem of Teleology', on which hinges Lukács's entire analysis in

24. L. Feuerbach, *Vorläufige Thesen zur Reform der Philosophie*, op. cit., p. 132.
25. L. Feuerbach, *Grundsätze der Philosophie der Zukunft*, op. cit., p. 193.

this work. His plan to shift the origin not only of the critical analysis of capitalist society but even of historical materialism itself from Marx back to Hegel (for this is what is at stake), here comes out into the open, and enters into blatant collision with the texts. Lukács writes with reference to *Realphilosophie*: 'With Hegel the concrete analysis of the dialectic of human labour dissolves the dichotomous opposition between causality and teleology; i.e. it shows the concrete place occupied by human, conscious purpose *within* the overall causal inter-relationships.'[26] This means that for Hegel the foundation or real *base* is not finalism, but material causality itself, which, just as in Marx, contains within itself also teleology. Hegel conceives of work, Lukács writes, in the following way: that man 'can only use his tools or means of labour in a way that is consistent with the objective law intrinsic to these objects or to their combination, and that therefore the work process can never transcend the causal inter-relationships of things. . . . The specific character of purposive action (*Zwecksetzung*) consists, as Hegel and Marx rightly see, simply in the fact that the image of the objective exists prior to the *mise en marche* (*In-Bewegung-Setzen*) of the work process and that the work process exists in order to translate this objective into reality with the aid of the causal inter-relationships – ever more thoroughly known – of objective reality.'[27]

Lukács continues thus: 'In the *Logic* Hegel elaborates on these thoughts, stating that teleology, human labour, and human praxis point to the truth of chemico-mechanical causation. This formulation goes beyond the Jena observations in its systematic clarity; but here too the objective contents of its foundation are already contained in those Jena observations. What must be particularly emphasized here is that Hegel treats the relationship between teleology and chemico-mechanical causation in the same way that chemico-mechanical technique is related to the objective reality of nature. He therefore sees in the economic process of production that element (*Moment*) by virtue of which teleology becomes the truth of chemico-mechanical causation.'[28]

26. G. Lukács, *Der junge Hegel*, op. cit., p. 428.

27. ibid., pp. 428–9.

28. ibid., pp. 433–4.

In comparison with these pages, Marx's well-known remark that 'labour as Hegel understands and recognizes it is *abstract* mental labour' must seem (even if Lukács does not openly say so) a mere aberration of superficial youth. In actual fact, the boot is on the other foot altogether. In fact one need only open the *Logic* (which Lukács cites, moreover), in which all of the reflections of the Jena period come (as Lukács admits) to a culmination, in order to read that 'for the practical Idea, on the contrary, this actuality, which at the same time confronts it as an insuperable limitation, ranks as something *intrinsically worthless* that must first receive its true determination and sole worth through the ends of the good'.[29] Equally, all one need do is scan the table of contents of Volume II, Section 2 of the *Logic* in order to see that the relationship established by Hegel between mechanism and chemism on the one hand, and teleology on the other, is the exact opposite of what Lukács ascribes to him.

Mechanism and chemism come *before* teleology, which (as Lukács recalls) is regarded by Hegel as the 'truth' of the former two. Except that, since the *Logic* is designed so that what comes first is the *abstract* and what one arrives at by proceeding from the latter is the *concrete*, this order does *not* mean that teleology has been encompassed within causality (as would be the case with historical materialism) but that mechanism and chemism are, on the contrary, 'moments' within finalism, and that only teleology, in short, is the really concrete!

Furthermore, consider Lukács's statement that 'Hegel included the dialectic of man's "active side" within his conception of objective reality', i.e. finalism within material causality, to the point that 'the relationship between theory and praxis acquires thereby a higher degree of clarity than it had ever attained in the entire history of philosophy' – 'a high point with which Marx could directly establish a connexion and from which he could elevate the relationship of theory and praxis to definitive heights of philosophic clarity'.[30] That this statement by Lukács is to be understood less as a fruit of methodical analysis than as an impulse of generosity on his part is

29. *L.*, p. 821 (Colletti's emphasis).

30. G. Lukács, op. cit., p. 437.

proved by what he himself admits a few pages later, concluding his chapter on 'Work and the Problem of Teleology'. 'Since the totality of the developmental process of nature and history is for the objective idealist Hegel – as well as for Schelling – the work of a "Spirit" ', it is evident, Lukács writes, that 'here the old teleological concept, previously overcome by Hegel with regard to all historical and social details, must again return'; 'for if the historical process has a single subject as its representative (*Träger*), if the former is the consequence of the latter's activity', it then becomes inevitable 'for the objective idealist Hegel to see in the historical process itself the realization of that objective which this "Spirit" had set for itself at the beginning of the process.' Thus, Lukács concludes, 'the totality of the process is transformed in Hegel (just as in Schelling) into an illusory movement (*Scheinbewegung*): it is the return back to the beginning, the realization of something that had existed *a priori* from the very beginning'. Consequently, 'Hegel is not aware that in the process of carrying out his teleological principle in an abstract and logically consistent fashion he falls back into the old theological teleology'.[31]

Let us leave Hegel now and return to Kant, to his epistemology and the conception of man that underlies it. Here the argument is altogether different. Epistemology includes logic, instead of being resolved into it. And this insistence on epistemology, i.e. on the search for the *limiting conditions* placed on thought, just as it discloses the inevitable materialist bent that is a part of this point of view, so it also reveals how it is precisely epistemology – and this accounts for our own insistence on it – which opens the path to the *science of man* as a natural, finite being. Although with Kant this science is, of course, still only an *anthropology*, and therefore an uncompleted project.

The 'Conclusion' of the *Transcendental Aesthetic*, in which Kant draws the distinction between *intuitus originarius* and *intuitus derivatus*, expresses in very clear terms (as Heidegger saw clearly in his *Kant und das Problem der Metaphysik*) the real foundation of his *Elementarlehre* – i.e. the theory of the elements of knowledge – and is

31. ibid., pp. 450–1.

therefore the place in which epistemology as such reaches its culmination. Knowledge has 'two' sources, and the theory of the 'sense-world' cannot coincide with the theory of 'thought', since the subject of knowledge – man – is a natural, finite being: 'a dependent being, dependent in its existence as well as in its intuition, and which through that intuition determines its existence solely in relation to given objects'.[32] If man were like God, rather than the 'finite, thinking being' that he is, the distinction between the sense-world and the understanding receptivity and spontaneity, would no longer exist. There would be an 'intellectual intuition' (which is exactly what there is for Hegel); thinking and perceiving would coincide; the representation of an object and its *creation* would be one and the same act.

This argument, though barely outlined by Kant, contains *in nuce* an essential turning-point. Human thought has nothing to do with divine thought. It is not identical with the latter, nor different from it only as a matter of degree or limitedness. It is not an *Abbild der ewigen Idee*, as in Hegel (for whom, in logically consistent fashion, anthropology must be part of theology). The fact that man *thinks* implies, on the contrary, that the manifold of the sense-world, or matter, is not a product of his making, but something that is *given* to him. Thought, in other words, is the quality, the attribute of a finite being that receives impressions from objects existing outside itself (and which therefore is also the object of other objects). It is, in short, the quality, the specific prerogative *of man*. If thinking and creating coincided, i.e. if man did not receive external impressions, all knowledge would be, as Kant says, intuition 'and not *thought*, which always involves limitations' and presupposes the existence of given objects.

At first sight, there is nothing very 'transcendental' about all this. It appears that the discovery is little more – just imagine! – than that man is born and dies. However, the meaning of Kant's observation is not that man is *also* a natural, finite being, but that it is *precisely in this naturality* that man's highest attribute – thought, intelligence – finds its *raison d'être*. Man's highest attribute of course,

32. I. Kant, *Critique of Pure Reason* (Kemp Smith translation), op. cit., p. 90.

among those which are the object of study in the *Critique of Pure Reason* (since in *Practical Reason* the argument, as is well-known, is quite different). Precisely because man is a natural being, man thinks: this is the sense of Kant's reasoning. If, therefore, thought is truly a 'miracle' (as spiritualist rhetoric would have it), it is a miracle in which God or the Spirit have no part. In more technical terms, Kant holds fast to the 'understanding', the 'intellect', rejecting any claim that it should be absorbed within 'reason'. For him the distinction between empirical data and thought is not an illusory one, but corresponds to the 'naturality' of the human cognitive subject. As far as the other subject is concerned, the one with the capital 'S', and the way in which it is supposed to perceive and think, *represent* and *create*, *all at once*, what is left to that Subject and its earthly representatives is only the '*logic of illusion*': 'a sophistical art of giving to ignorance, and indeed to intentional sophistries, the appearance of truth, by the device of imitating the methodical thoroughness (*Grundlichkeit*) which logic prescribes, and of using its "topic" to conceal the emptiness of its pretensions'.[33]

This position appears to be nothing but actually means a great deal. It represents a judgment derived from the better part of the Enlightenment tradition: that man is a thinking being because he is a natural being; and that, if thought is what distinguishes man from all the other animals, that does not mean that man himself is not an animal (or that he has within himself the divine 'spark'), but merely that this is his natural, *specific* trait.

Here one can directly see the difference between Kant and Hegel – but also the difference between Kant and Jacobi and the entire spiritualist tradition. He focuses his interest precisely on that which the other two leave out as unimportant: the naturalness of man, his intellectual 'understanding'. He takes *science* as the only true form of knowledge, that science which for the other two is only illusory or 'finite knowledge' (Croce's 'pseudo-concepts', Bergson's 'labels', Lukács's 'reified' thought of 1923, etc.). He represents as the only valid theoretical *modus operandi* (one need only look at the argument on Galilei and Torricelli at the beginning of the *Critique*) precisely

33. ibid., p. 99.

that intellectual-experimental knowledge which Jacobi rejects because it is linked to the naturality of man, i.e. to that side of man which, for a certain philosophy, it is a point of honour to overlook. As Jacobi writes in his *Briefe über die Lehre von Spinoza*: 'If by reason one means man's soul *only* in that it has clear notions, and that it is with these that it judges, reasons, and forms anew other notions; then reason is a capacity of man which he acquires little by little, a tool which he makes use of – it belongs to him. If, however, one means by reason the principle of knowledge in general, then it is the spirit of which the entire living nature of man is made. It is through this that man exists; the latter is a form which reason has assumed.'[34]

And again, as stated in the *Introduction* of 1815 to his *Werke* (when Jacobi had already clarified the distinction between 'intellect' and 'reason'): 'Animals grasp only that which is sensible. Man, furnished with reason, grasps also that which is suprasensible, and he calls reason precisely that which enables him to grasp the suprasensible. . . . Animals lack the faculty necessary for apprehending the suprasensible, and as a consequence of this deficiency it is not possible to form a notion of a reason belonging exclusively to animals. Man does, however, possess such a faculty, and it is precisely and only with this faculty that he is a rational being.'[35] On the other hand, 'the intellect, to a certain extent, is also possessed by animals; and it must be possessed by all living beings because they cannot be regarded as living entities unless they have an associative consciousness, which is at the root of all intelligence'.[36]

Scientific understanding, in short, is common to both man and beast. Man's thought is that characteristic by virtue of which man is a part of nature. Speculative reason, contrariwise, belongs only to man in that only the latter is a spiritual 'creature'. And since the 'critique of the intellect' like everything else has a price, 'dialectical materialism' – which also specialized in this critique – cannot stop short of the most obscurantist conclusions. 'Intellect and Reason' (this is how Engels entitles a subheading of the *Dialectics of Nature*):

34. F. H. Jacobi, *Lettere sulla dottrina di Spinoza*, op. cit., p. 223.

35. F. H. Jacobi, *Idealismo e realismo*, op. cit., p. 9.

36. ibid., p. 35.

'This Hegelian distinction, according to which only dialectical thinking is rational, has a definite meaning. All activity of the intelligence we have in common with animals: *induction, deduction*, and hence also *abstraction* (Dido's – Engels's dog – generic concepts: quadrupeds and bipeds), *analysis* of unknown objects (even the cracking of a nut is a beginning of analysis), *synthesis* (in animal tricks), and, as the union of both, *experiment* (in the case of new obstacles and unfamiliar situations). In their nature all these modes of procedure – hence all means of scientific investigation that ordinary logic recognizes – are absolutely the same in men and the higher animals. They differ only in degree (of development of the method in each case). The basic features of the method are the same and lead to the same results in man and animals, so long as both operate or make shift merely with these elementary methods. On the other hand, dialectical thought – precisely because it presupposes investigation of the nature of concepts – is only possible for man, and for him only at a comparatively high stage of development (Buddhists and Greeks), and it attains its full development much later still through modern philosophy – and yet we have the colossal results already among the Greeks (!) which go far in anticipating investigation.'[37]

Thoughts which, as one can see, are not only very dubious but which as usual leave one nonplussed by the off-hand manner of their expression: 'ordinary' logic and . . . extraordinary logic, 'elementary' concepts and . . . sublime concepts. Behind these thoughts, of course, there lies the old metaphysical baggage over which some Italian Marxists still keep watch (although no longer with the arrogance of years gone by). 'For philosophy, which has been expelled from nature and history, there remains only the realm of pure thought (so far as it is left): the theory of the laws of the thought process itself, logic and dialectics.'[38] This is another famous 'heirloom' in the patrimony of 'dialectical materialism', cited a thousand times: 'pure thought' and the 'theory of the laws of thought'; as if there could be 'pure' thought in place of *man* who

37. F. Engels, *Dialectics of Nature*, op. cit., pp. 203–4 (translation modified).
38. F. Engels, *Ludwig Feuerbach*, op. cit., p. 59.

thinks, and as if the argument on thought need not be changed into the argument on the *sociality* or historicity of man (for this is precisely his nature: 'man's process of genesis', Marx says, is '*history*'.[39]) As if thought could instead have as its object thought 'in itself' – thought as a sphere or autonomous object endowed with *its own laws*.

In short, knowledge does not appear to Engels as a function and manifestation of *man's* life in his social relationship with nature. The meaning of Marx's argument in the *Theses on Feuerbach* is entirely lost. There exists a 'realm of pure thought', a movement of things (as stated in *Ludwig Feuerbach*: 'Thus dialectics reduced itself to the science of the general laws of motion – both of the external world and of human thought – two sets of laws which are identical in substance. . .'[40]). And since the subject of knowledge is no longer man himself but the identity or 'original unity' of thought and being, it is true what was observed by Lukács in *History and Class Consciousness*: that Engels 'does not even mention the most vital interaction, namely the *dialectical relation between subject and object in the historical process*, let alone give it the prominence it deserves'.[41]

As far as concerns the profoundest lesson to be drawn from Kant's *Critique* – i.e. the thesis that since thought is not a self-contained entity epistemology must necessarily complement the sciences of man as a natural being – what must be brought out next, of course, is that the radical limitation of this entire undertaking from start to finish, the thing which condemns it too to being another version of metaphysics, is the fact that the 'science of man' Kant refers to is nothing but an *anthropology*. Here all the fundamental deficiencies of the *Critique* re-emerge, beginning with its uncertain and contradictory conception of the 'sensible' (always half way between the real object and the subjective representation of it). According to this, sense-data as objects related to thought are not complete and true objectivity, but only 'phenomena' (with all the ambiguity that this term has in Kant's argument). Similarly, concepts do not manage to

39. K. Marx, *Early Writings*, op. cit., p. 208.
40. F. Engels, op. cit., p. 44.
41. G. Lukács, *History and Class Consciousness*, op. cit., p. 3.

make themselves really *sensible* by means of this *given* content, i.e. to acquire through it an actual *external* reality. In other words, that characteristic of man by virtue of which deduction implies finalism and knowledge itself is ideology or 'praxis' (i.e. a manifestation of the subject's life and therefore a realization or objectification of his ideas) finds no place within the framework of the *Critique of Pure Reason*. Hence, the concepts of *work* and productive activity remain entirely foreign to Kant – work and productive activity not only as man's adaptation to the world but also as the transformation and adaptation of the world to suit him. That is to say, Kant ignores that characteristic of man by virtue of which the object is not only something 'in itself' but is also the *objectification of the subject*; and by virtue of which the product of labour is, as Marx says, 'something which, when the process began, already existed in the *worker's imagination*, already existed in an *ideal form*'.[42]

This accounts for the dualistic separation of the *Critique of Pure Reason* from that of *Practical Reason*, of *Müssen* from *Sollen*, i.e. of nature's world of mechanism – in which man is basically only a link in the causal concatenation – from the 'realm of ends', understood not only as a sphere that is exclusively moral, but as the realm of a morality circumscribed to pure 'intent'. The theme of the objectification of the subject, i.e. of the *realization* of his ideas, of his goals, and therefore of man's self-production (in the work process, Marx says, man does not merely bring about 'a change of form in natural objects; at the same time, in the nature that exists apart from himself, he *realizes his own purpose*, the purpose which gives the law to his activities, the purpose to which he has to subordinate his own will'[43]), remains outside Kant's horizon here, and outside the horizon of the *Critique of Judgment* as well. Thus receptivity and spontaneity, causality and finalism never really manage to fuse with one another, neither at the level of the first two *Critiques* nor within the *Critique of Pure Reason* itself.

The sense element or *datum*, in those instances where it is actually an extra-logical existent, tends to present itself (here is the kernel of

42. K. Marx, *Capital* (Eden and Cedar Paul translation), op. cit., Vol. I, p. 170.
43. loc. cit.

truth in Lukács's 1923 critique) in the same way that *existence* was presented in the precritical period, e.g. in the *Beweisgrund* (where 'existence is the absolute position of a thing' which 'is distinct from all predicates' precisely due to the fact that whereas the latter 'are only posited in relation to another thing',[44] existence presents itself as non-relative, as *absolute*, i.e. as something that cannot be predicated nor taken up as the subject of judgment). Subjective spontaneity, on the other hand, incapable as it is of giving rise to a real self-objectification, tends to be confined to that purely formal or internal 'modus operandi' which is the synthesis of the *forms* of the sense-world – so that all that Kant manages to grasp of man's creativity and productivity is merely the act of . . . 'productive imagination'.

Work as the intermediary that socializes man, and then social relationships as the intermediary *to* man's mediation with nature through work: all of this, as stated above, remains totally outside Kant's horizon. Thus, what he presents to us as an alternative to the theological conception of man as a vehicle for God's unfolding in the world is, in the end, only a conception derived from the juxtaposition of anthropology and ethics, i.e. of man as a *natural* being and man as a *moral* subject. The former deals with the place which 'I occupy in the external world of sense, and it broadens the connection in which I stand into an unbounded magnitude of worlds beyond worlds and systems of systems'. A display 'of a countless multitude of worlds' is revealed to me; a display in which I appear as 'an *animal creature*, which must give back to the planet (a mere speck in the universe) the matter from which it came, the matter which is for a little time provided with vital force, we know not how'. The latter, however, 'infinitely raises my worth as that of an intelligence by my personality, in which the moral law reveals a life independent of all animality and even of the whole world of sense – at least so far as it may be inferred from the purposive destination assigned to my existence by this law, a destination which is not restricted to the conditions and limits of this life but reaches into the infinite'.[45]

44. I. Kant, *Scritti precritici* (Bari, 1953), p. 112.
45. I. Kant, *Critique of Practical Reason*, translated by Lewis W. Beck (Chicago, 1949), pp. 258–9.

The basic schema here is, certainly, that of the Christian dualism of soul and body; but with the additional element – not developed in the conclusion of *Practical Reason* but resounding distinctly throughout the *Pure Reason* – that that 'animal creature' which I am is meaningless ephemerality, but is also *intelligence* (even as it is, i.e. *as* an existence destined to waste away and die). It is an intellect that 'views itself, views and ponders the starred Heavens' and that, despite its transitory accidentality, can always say: '*I exist as an intellect* that is conscious of its unifying power.'[46]

This is perhaps the most significant model that has taken shape in the course of bourgeois humanism. The analysis of nature, the world of the physico-natural sciences, is already constituted as an autonomous world, henceforth emancipated from metaphysics, and within which man is included since he is himself a natural being. On the other hand, since this naturality of man's is still not grasped in terms of its intrinsic sociality and therefore as the force productive of history, the moral world continues to be a reserve of metaphysics. In other words, to the extent that the natural being 'man' appears only as a single individual whose relationship to the *species* represents an internal, unspoken – and therefore aprioristic – generality, the fashioning of man into a 'Person', i.e. into a moral subject, can be guaranteed only by means of a spiritualistic ethics. The natural world has already passed over to science, but the moral world still remains tied to metaphysics (liberal, bourgeois 'humanity' has never gone beyond this point). And since nature (even if it is not merely the 'negative') always remains nonetheless only a 'half' reality, the most exalted insight to which man can aspire, *qua* 'natural creature', is that of a well-tempered 'critical philosophy', i.e. a 'humanism of the intellect'.

One begins to perceive here the meaning of Hegel's thought and the place occupied in his philosophy by the problem of the 'actualization' of idealism, of the realization of the Idea. Even though he hypostatizes Reason and finalism, and therefore suffers from the limitation of still conceiving of man's historical process only in the

46. Luigi Scaravelli, *Saggio sulla categoria kantiana della realtà* (Florence, 1947), pp. 176–8.

form of a 'divine process', Hegel is the first to understand thoroughly how man's development passes through his self-objectification and how this process of making himself 'other' than himself is carried out, essentially, by means of work. As Marx remarks: 'The outstanding achievement of Hegel's *Phenomenology* . . . is, first, that Hegel grasps the self-creation of man as a process, objectification as loss of the object, as alienation and transcendence of this alienation, and that he, therefore, grasps the nature of *labour*, and conceives objective man (true, because real man) as the result of his *own labour*. The *real*, active orientation of man to himself as a generic being, or the affirmation of himself as a real generic being (i.e. as a human being) is only possible so far as he really brings forth all his *generic powers* (which is only possible through the co-operative endeavours of mankind and as an outcome of history) and treats these powers as objects, which can only be done at first in the form of alienation.'[47]

The 'one-sidedness' and 'limit' of Hegel consist rather in the fact that his 'standpoint is that of modern political economy', and that while viewing '*labour* as the *essence*, the self-confirming essence of man', 'he observes only the positive side of labour, not its negative side'; and that, in short, for him 'labour is *man's coming to be for himself* within *alienation*, or as an *alienated* man', for 'labour as Hegel understands and recognizes it is *abstract mental* labour'.[48]

It is the same argument, if one looks closely, as that stated by Marx in the first of his *Theses on Feuerbach*: 'The chief defect of all materialism up to now (including Feuerbach's) is, that the object, reality, what we apprehend through our senses (*Sinnlichkeit*), is understood only in the form of the *object* or *contemplation*; but not as *sensuous human activity*, as *practice*; not subjectively. Hence in opposition to materialism the *active* side was developed abstractly by idealism – which of course does not know real sensuous activity as such. Feuerbach wants sensuous objects, really distinguished from the objects of thought: but he does not understand human activity itself as *objective* activity.'[49]

47. K. Marx. *Early Writings*, cit., pp. 202–3 (translation modified).
48. ibid., p. 203.
49. K. Marx, *Theses on Feuerbach*, in *The German Ideology* (New York, 1947), p. 197.

Hegel forcefully grasped that the object is the objectification of the subject; but for him this subject is only spirit, self-consciousness, and not a natural, finite being that has objects outside itself and which is therefore itself an object for others. With materialism, by contrast, in which man's naturality is acknowledged and thought is no longer a subject unto itself, the world of history remains forbidden territory since there is no perception of how man, in the process of relating to the external, sensible objects by means of thought, at the same time objectifies himself – i.e. externalizes and realizes his own ideas in language as well as production, entering thereby into a relationship with other men. In the first case, material causality is evaded or transcended to the advantage of teleology; in the second, since causality does not manage to include within itself the subjective moment of praxis, finalism is degraded to an illusory or merely 'apparent' process, or else is dualistically counterpoised to the world of nature without ever managing to mediate itself through the latter.

Typical in this sense is what happens with Feuerbach. In his essay of 1839, *Zur Kritik der Hegelschen Philosophie*, he perceives the connection between logic and language. In so far as thought is not a subject unto itself but a function of man's being, it is inevitable that 'already in the process of thinking itself we express our thoughts, i.e. we speak'.[50] The logico-deductive process or 'proof' is therefore at the same time an exposition or objectification of my thought for the other. In point of fact, 'the meaning of the proof cannot be grasped without reference to the meaning of language'; and since 'language is nothing other than the *realization of the species*, the mediation of the ego with the other that reveals the unity of the species, overcoming the separation between one individual and another' – 'the proof is then based only on the mediatory role of thought *in relation to others*'.[51] Every proof, therefore, 'is not a mediation of thought in and for thought itself, but rather a mediation of *my* thought and that of the *other*, by means of language'.[52] Which

50. L. Feuerbach, 'Zur Kritik der Hegelschen Philosophie', in *Kleine Schriften*, op. cit., p. 92.

51. ibid., p. 89.

52. ibid., p. 90.

means that 'the forms of proof and syllogism are not therefore *forms of reason* in themselves, nor forms of the internal process of thinking and knowing', but are only *forms of communication*, modes of expression, expositions and representations, manifestations of thought'.[53]

This is the basis of Feuerbach's critique of the way in which Hegel confuses the 'for us' – which is the logico-deductive process – with the 'in itself–for itself', i.e. the process of reality. Hegel, he writes, 'transformed form into substance, the being of thought for others into being in itself'.[54] And since with Hegel 'the Idea does not engender nor bear witness to itself through the agency of a *real other*, . . . but engenders itself out of a *formal*, illusory contradiction',[55] the consequence is that having replaced causality with finalism and the process of development 'according to nature' with the process of development 'according to the Notion', 'absolute philosophy . . . turns subjective, psychological processes . . . into processes of the Absolute'; so that 'Hegel actually grasped representations which express only subjective needs as objective truth, due to the fact that he did not go back to the source of or *need* for these representations'.[56]

The importance that these formulations of Feuerbach's had in the formation of historical materialism needs no underlining here. In Hegel the unity of thought and Language is developed in the sense that – since the 'here' and the 'now' of speech are always universals – my relationship to things invariably resolves itself into a relationship within thought. With Feuerbach, on the contrary, it is the logico-deductive process which is resolved into intersubjective communication. One need only open *The German Ideology* in order to understand what that means. Consciousness, Marx says, is never 'pure' consciousness. 'From the start the "spirit" is afflicted with the curse of being "burdened" with matter, which here makes its appearance in the form of agitated layers of air, sounds, in short of language. Language is as old as consciousness, language *is* practical consciousness, as it exists for other men, and for that reason is really beginning

53. ibid., pp. 91–2.
54. ibid., p. 94.
55. ibid., p. 102.
56. ibid., pp. 114–15.

to exist for me personally as well'.[57] Further on Marx adds, '*language* is the immediate actuality of thought'; which means that the old problem of philosophy – that 'of descending from the world of thoughts to the actual world' – 'is turned into the problem of descending from language to life'; since 'neither thoughts nor language in themselves form a realm of their own' – 'they are only *manifestations* of actual life'.[58]

After 1839, these insights of Feuerbach's, while always remaining isolated *aperçus*, reappear with a certain frequency. The *Essence of Christianity* contains propositions – one might almost say aphorisms – whose echo can be easily recognized in the *Economic and Philosophical Manuscripts* of 1844. Man's relationship to nature is, at the same time, a relationship of man to another man. 'The object to which a subject essentially, necessarily relates, is nothing else than this subject's own, but objective, nature. . . . In the object which he contemplates, therefore, man becomes conscious of himself; consciousness of the objective is the self-consciousness of man. We know man through the object, through his conception of what is external to himself; in it his nature becomes evident; this object is his manifested nature, his true objective *ego*. And this is true not merely of spiritual, but also of sensuous objects. Even the objects which are the most remote from man, *because* they are objects to him, and to the extent to which they are so, are revelations of human nature. . . . That he sees them, and so sees them, is an evidence of his own nature.'[59] And again: 'The *first* object of man is man.' 'My *fellow*-man is the bond between me and the world. I am, and I feel myself, dependent on the world, because I first feel myself dependent on other men. If I did not need man, I should not need the world.'[60] Finally, analogous propositions – perhaps even closer to those formulated by Marx in 1844 – are contained in the short essay of 1841, *Über den Anfang der Philosophie*.

However, once this has been said, there is nothing more to say:

57. K. Marx, *The German Ideology* (Moscow edition), p. 42.

58. K. Marx, *The German Ideology*, pp. 503–4.

59. L. Feuerbach, *The Essence of Christianity*, translated by George Eliot (New York, 1957), pp. 4–5.

60. ibid., p. 82.

in Feuerbach causality and finalism never succeed in uniting with one another; so that 'when occasionally we find such views with Feuerbach, they are never more than isolated surmises and have much too little influence on his general outlook to be considered here as anything else than embryos capable of development'.[61]

On the one hand, Feuerbach 'never manages to conceive the sensuous world as the total living sensuous activity of the individuals composing it'; 'he does not see how the sensuous world around him is, not a thing given direct from all eternity, ever the same, but the product of industry and of the state of society';[62] he does not grasp, in other words, that the object is also the objectification of man, intersubjective communication and therefore a *social* relationship (here Feuerbach never goes beyond language; that other 'language of real life' which is industry and 'material production' escapes him).

On the other hand, since he 'conceives of men not in their given social connection, . . . but stops at the abstraction "man" ', inter-human relationships appear to him to be an end in themselves, i.e. *ethical* relationships ('he knows no other "human relationships" "of man to man" than love and friendship, and even then idealized'), instead of appearing as relationships directed at the transformation of the objective world. Thus, as Marx rightly concludes, 'as far as Feuerbach is a materialist he does not deal with history, and as far as he considers history he is not a materialist. With him materialism and history diverge completely. . .'.[63]

We shall close this topic here. Our main aim is to arrive at an explanation of the concept of 'social relations of production' – a concept which Marxists have always taken for granted, when in point of fact it is the most difficult of all. Previously articulated in *The German Ideology*, this concept has its clearest and most fundamental formulation in Marx's essay (still an 'early writing') on *Wage-Labour and Capital*. 'In the process of production, human beings work not only upon nature, but also upon one another. They produce only by working together in a specified manner and reciprocally exchanging their activities. In order to produce, they

61. K. Marx, *The German Ideology*, op. cit., p. 57.
62. ibid., pp. 59 and 57. 63. ibid., pp. 59–60.

enter into definite connections and relations to one another, and only within these social connections and relations does their influence upon nature (*ihre Einwirkung auf die Natur*) operate, i.e., does production take place.'[64]

A paraphrasing of this concept gives us some of the formulae encountered above. (a) Man's relationship to nature is at the same time man's relationship to his fellow man; i.e. production is intersubjective communication, a *social relationship*. (b) The relationship of man to his fellow man, on the other hand, is established for the purpose *of producing*, i.e. in view of and as a function of man's action and effect on nature. Formulated more concisely, the concept means these two things: first, that in order for me to relate to an object, I must also relate to other men, since the object itself is actually a *human objectification* ('the sensuous world . . . is not a thing given direct from all eternity, . . . but the product of industry and of the state of society'); which then means that the relationship of the species 'man' with other species is actually a relationship within his own species, i.e. that the *generic* (or inter-species) relationship is actually a relationship *specific* to man. Second, that in order to relate to other men, I must relate to the natural *object* itself, taken precisely with regard to its otherness or heterogeneity of species – for man's being is *nature* (one need only remember Marx's remark that 'a being which does not have its nature outside itself is not a *natural* being'). In other words, man does not have a being of his own, but has as his own being that of others; thus the *specific* relation (man's relationship to other men) implies the *generic* relationship of man to the other natural beings different from him.

The reader who has some familiarity with Marx's writings knows that the propositions just mentioned are the same ones that are the focus of the *Economic and Philosophical Manuscripts*; and that it is precisely these concepts which make this text by far and away the most tortuous and obscure of Marx's works. There, work is defined as man's *self*-production, not only in the sense that the product of labour is an objectification of the worker (and therefore the result of

64. K. Marx, *Wage-Labour and Capital*, in Marx/Engels, *Selected Works*, London, 1968, p. 81.

a work of transformation by which nature has been adapted and made to conform to our needs and our aims); but also in the opposite sense that in the work process man *adapts himself* to nature, and his idea is the *means* which enables him to respect the specificity of the materials with which he is working – i.e. it enables him to deal with the *object* of labour in terms of that which it truly *is*. In both cases, work is man's self-reproduction (both as 'creativity' and as 'adaptation'), precisely for the reason stated above. In the first case, because man's relation to objective otherness is actually a manifestation (through objectivity) of his relationship to other men. In the second case, because man's relation to other men and therefore to his own species or to himself implies – since man is a being that has 'his' nature 'outside himself' – that, in order to relate to himself, he must relate to a *being* that is *other* than human.

All of historical materialism is here *in nuce*, if one looks closely. The impossibility of separating 'economics' from 'society', 'nature' from 'history', 'production' from 'social relationships', 'material' production from the production 'of ideas' – if the roots of the concept are not here, then where are they? In Marx's words: '... The identity of nature and man appears in such a way that the restricted relation of men to nature determines their restricted relation to one another, and their restricted relation to one another determines men's restricted relation to nature...'.[65] On the other hand, just as the expansion of the first relationship is also an expansion of the second, so the opposite is true. From that follows the consequence that 'a certain mode of production, or industrial stage, is always combined with a certain mode of co-operation, or social stage' and vice versa; to the point that 'this mode of co-operation is itself a "productive force" '.[66]

Historical materialism and the 'logic' of *Capital* itself are rooted here. Since man, in the process of producing, produces *himself* – both in the sense that he produces his relationship with other men, i.e. with his own species, and in the sense that he produces his relationship with natural objectivity and therefore with the tools and materials of his work – one can understand not only the inter-

65. K. Marx, *The German Ideology*, op. cit., p. 42. 66. ibid., p. 41.

relation that exists between all the categories of *Capital*, but also the 'cyclicity' or principle of self-movement which presides over the process of capitalist accumulation. 'Capitalist production, therefore, under its aspect of a continuous connected process, of a process of reproduction, produces not only commodities, not only surplus-value, but it also produces and reproduces the *capitalist relation*; on the one side the *capitalist*, on the other the *wage-labourer*.'[67]

This is precisely what Marx discovered for the first time and elaborated in the 1844 *Manuscripts*. The manuscript on 'alienated labour' – which is the veritable *rebus* of this entire work – develops the circularity and interdependence of the following relationships: (a) that 'the relationship of the worker to the *product of labour* as an alien object which dominates him' is at the same time 'the relationship of the worker to his own activity as something alien';[68] (b) that 'since alienated labour: (1) alienates nature from man; and (2) alienates man from himself, from his own active function, his life activity; so it alienates him from the *genus*'; (c) that this 'genus', i.e. the 'specific essence of man', is just as much external nature ('his own body, as well as external nature') as it is other men; for, as Marx says, 'what is true of man's relationship to his work, to the product of his work and to himself, is also true of his relationship to other men, to their labour and to the objects of their labour'.[69] Thus, he concludes, 'through alienated labour, therefore, man not only produces his relation to the object and to the process of production as to alien and hostile men; he also produces the relation of other men to his production and his product, and the relation between himself and other men'.[70]

Let us attempt to put this in more linear terms. In positive terms (i.e. apart from the question of alienation), the network of relationships referred to above is already present in the concept of *work* itself. Work is both causality and finalism, material causality and ideal causality; it is (if we invert the actual order) man's action and effect on nature and at the same time nature's action and effect on

67. K. Marx, *Capital* (Samuel Moore translation), op. cit., Vol. I., p. 578.
68. K. Marx, *Early Writings*, op. cit., pp. 125–6.
69. ibid., pp. 127 and 129.
70. ibid., pp. 130–1.

man. This accounts for a twofold characteristic of the product of labour (and of objectivity in general), which it may be useful to bring out again. (a) The product of labour is the objectification of my ideas, i.e. of my needs and my conscious objectives; (b) it is a simple changing of 'the forms of matter', so that 'in the process of production, man can only work as nature works',[71] i.e. the object can only be handled in accordance with its particular specificity and so with respect to and in conformity with its own particular nature (one commands nature, Bacon would say, only by obeying her). With reference to this twofold character of objectivity, the function of the *idea* is also twofold. It is both a subjective goal that man pursues, and therefore praxis or ideology; and it is a function of truth, i.e. a *means* for recognizing and dealing with the object in accordance with the yardstick best-suited to it – and therefore a means of escaping from anthropomorphism and giving an *objective* dimension to human practice. Marxism is not – one should be clear on this point – either pragmatism or a *Wissensoziologie* (sociology of knowledge); it is the first theory of 'situated thought', but it is also a theory of thought as *truth*.

This argument, which in Marx assumes various forms, is developed (e.g.) in the second section of his *Introduction* of 1857 in terms of the production–consumption relationship. (a) Consumption creates production. It creates production in that 'consumption produces production by creating the need for *new* production, i.e. by providing the ideal, inward, impelling cause which constitutes the prerequisite of production. Consumption furnishes the impulse for production as well as its object (ideal or interior), which plays in production the part of its guiding aim. It is clear that while production furnishes the material object of consumption, consumption posits the object of production in an *ideal* form, as its inner image, its need, its impulse and its purpose. It furnishes the object of production in its subjective form. No needs, no production. But consumption reproduces the need.' (b) 'In its turn, production furnishes: first, consumption with its material, its object. Consumption without an object is not consumption, hence production works in

71. K. Marx, *Capital* (Eden and Cedar Paul translation), op. cit., Vol. I, p. 12.

this direction by producing consumption; but second, it is not only the object that production creates for consumption. It gives consumption its determinacy, its character, its finish. For the object is not simply an object in general, but a determinate object, which is consumed in a determinate manner mediated in its turn by production. Hunger is hunger: but the hunger that is satisfied with cooked meat eaten with fork and knife is a different kind of hunger from the one that devours raw meat with the aid of hands, nails, and teeth. Not only the object of consumption, but also the manner of consumption is produced by production, and not just objectively but also subjectively. Production thus creates the consumers. Third, production not only supplies the need with material, but supplies the material with a need.' Consumption, in fact, 'as a moving spring is itself mediated by its object. The need for it which consumption experiences is created by its perception of the product. The object of art, as well as any other product, creates a public capable of artistic appreciation and aesthetic enjoyment. Production thus produces not only an object for the subject, but also a subject for the object'.[72]

On the one hand, then, the object is the idea itself objectified; what consumption 'posits in an ideal form', production posits *in re*. On the other hand, this 'ideal, interior cause' is mediated by the object previously consumed; i.e. the idea is determined by the perception of the object. In conclusion and once again: finalism and causality.

Here is still another variation on the same theme, before we go on to take the bull by its horns. 'Man's musical sense is only awakened by music. The most beautiful music has no meaning for the non-musical ear, is not an object for it, because my object can only be the confirmation of one of my own faculties. It can only be so for me in so far as my faculty exists for itself as a subjective capacity, because the meaning of an object for me extends only as far as the sense extends (only makes sense for an appropriate sense). For this reason, the *senses* of social man are *different* from those of non-social man.'[73]

72. K. Marx, *Introduction to the Critique of Political Economy*, op. cit., pp. 278–80.
73. K. Marx, *Early Writings*, op. cit., p. 161.

In other words, objective sensuous nature is, in reality, my own subjective sensitivity itself. *Esse est percipi.* There is no consciousness of the object that is not self-consciousness. What I see of the world is what my *ideas* predispose me to see. My relationship to nature is conditioned by the level of socio-historical development. '. . . Their restricted relation to one another determines men's restricted relation to nature' (here is the point of departure for moving in the direction of a historicization of the sciences of nature themselves).

On the other hand, if 'it is only when objective reality everywhere becomes for man in society the reality of human faculties, human reality, and thus the reality of his *own* faculties, that all *objects* become for him the *objectification of himself*, . . . objects (which) confirm and realize his individuality, . . . are *his own* objects, i.e. man *himself* becomes the object', just *how* it is that these objects 'become his own depends upon the *nature of the object*'.[74] As Marx explains it: 'When real, corporeal man' posits objects, 'the *positing* is not the subject of this act but the subjectivity of *objective* faculties whose action must also, therefore, be *objective*'; which means that man 'creates and establishes *only objects, because* (he) is established by objects, and because (he) is fundamentally *natural*'; and, in short, that 'in the act of establishing (he) does not descend from (his) "pure activity" to the *creation of objects*; (his) *objective* product simply confirms (his) *objective* activity, (his) activity as an objective, natural being'.[75]

The reader with a developed taste for the reasoning process will understand that the essential outlines of historical materialism are already here in embryo – that is under the heavy cover of this incredible language. The further developments of the analysis, i.e. its detailed articulation, must of course be sought in *Capital.* However, the essential role of the 1844 *Manuscripts* (that reef on which a whole generation of French existentialist 'Marxists' foundered) is that it is precisely in them that the original key to unlocking the meaning of the concept of 'social relations of production' can be found – the key to this real *summa* of Marx's theoretical revolution.

74. ibid., pp. 160–1. 75. ibid., p. 206.

Marx writes: '. . . The history of *industry* . . . is an *open* book of the *human faculties*, and a human *psychology* which can be sensuously apprehended. This history has not so far been conceived in relation to human *nature*, but only from a superficial utilitarian point of view, since in the condition of alienation it was only possible to conceive real human faculties and *the acts of man as a generic being* (*menschliche Gattungsakte*) in the form of general human existence, as religion, or as history in its abstract, general aspect as politics, art and literature, etc.'[76] On the other hand, this pyschology, i.e. the world of projects and *ideas* that lies behind industry is as little subjective and anthropomorphic as can be imagined – precisely because the knowledge that sustains that practice is not metaphysical, i.e. not the dreams of clairvoyants, but *science*, i.e. the recognition of the objective world. 'Of course, animals also produce. They construct nests, dwellings, as in the case of bees, beavers, ants, etc. But they only produce what is strictly necessary for themselves or their young. They produce only in a single direction, while man produces universally. They produce only under the compulsion of direct physical needs, while man produces when he is free from physical need and only truly produces in freedom from such need. Animals produce only themselves, while man reproduces the whole of nature. The products of animal production belong directly to their physical bodies, while man is free in face of his product. Animals construct only in accordance with the standards and needs of the species (Marx himself uses the term 'species') to which they belong, while man knows how to produce in accordance with the standards of every species and knows how to apply the appropriate standard to the object.'[77]

To conclude: Historical materialism reaches its point of culmination in the concept of 'social relations of production'. This concept, in turn, had its first and decisive elaboration in the 1844 *Manuscripts*,

76. ibid., pp. 162–3. The term *Gattungsakte* has been translated in this way rather than as 'species-action' (the term adopted by Bottomore) in order to take account of Colletti's subsequent argument based on the distinction between 'species' and 'genus'. Similar terms such as *Gattungsleben* and *Gattungswesen* have likewise been rendered so that the word 'genus' or 'generic' appears in the place of Bottomore's use of 'species' or 'specific' (Trans.).

77. ibid., p. 128.

in the form of the concept of man as a 'generic natural being'. What remains is the task of attempting the analysis of this concept.

That man is a generic natural being – a *generic* being, be it said, and not a specific one (in the sense of, 'of a species') – means essentially two things. First, that man is a '*natural* being', i.e. that he is a part of nature, and therefore that he is an objective being among other objective natural beings upon whom he depends and by whom he is conditioned; in short, he has his *raison d'être* (*causa essendi*) outside himself ('a being which does not have its nature outside itself is not a *natural* being'). Second, that man is a *thinking* being, i.e. that what differentiates him from all other natural beings and constitutes his *specific* characteristic, is *not* a *thing*, i.e. a species of nature itself, but is *thought*, i.e. the universal, what is *general* or *common* in all things. This explains why man's specificity is not that of being a species, but that of being the *genus of all empirical genera*, i.e. the unity or overall *totality* of all natural species.

This formulation of extraordinary importance that Marx gives to the problem of man as a 'generic natural being' makes his thought the point of convergence and resolution for two deep-seated and antithetical currents of cultural-historical tradition. That of materialist determinism, in which man *qua* 'natural being' appears as a mere link in the causal objective concatenation; and that – which we shall now briefly discuss – of the tradition of Renaissance spiritualist humanism.

In point of fact, the notion that man's specificity is that of being a generic being, i.e. not a natural species but the *genus of all empirical genera*, is not an invention of Marx's (in history nothing is created out of nothing, and least of all revolution). It is a theme with a distant and complex ancestry – a theme nurtured in the heart of a tradition that is at first sight completely foreign to Marxism and without which (nevertheless) the *materialist conception of history* itself would never have come into existence.

The works which we must now briefly look at (and, of course, only within the terms of the problem posed by our argument) are Pico della Mirandola's *De hominis Dignitate* (the first text, as Garin has written, that gives us 'the conscious image of man characteristic of the modern world'[78]) and Bovillus's *De Sapiente*, which in Cassirer's words was 'perhaps the most curious and in some respects the most characteristic creation of Renaissance philosophy'.[79]

The theme that we immediately encounter in both works is precisely that of man's *genericity*, i.e. his non-specificity. Man, who has no reality in that he is not a species, can nevertheless encompass the universe within himself because he is *thought*. As Bovillus says: 'Man is not a part of the world of things. . . . Man's nature is the very nature of a mirror. The nature of a mirror consists in being outside everything, in standing off against everything, in not embracing anything, any natural image within itself. . . . The place appropriate to man and the mirror is therefore in opposition to and in negation of all things, to be there where nothing is, where nothing is fully actualized (*actu*):'[80] Man is therefore *Nothing*: 'In man the substance is nothing.'[81]

This theme of the 'nothingness', i.e. of the non-substantiality or immateriality of man (in that he is thought), is expressed by Pico (and later picked up by Bovillus) in the highly significant terms of a myth that it is worthwhile calling attention to here. Once arrived at the end of creation, *summus Pater architectus Deus* felt the desire to shape a being that would be able to know the reason for His work and to love it for its beauty. 'But there was not among His archetypes that from which He could fashion a new offspring, nor was there in His treasure-houses anything which He might bestow on His new son as an inheritance, nor was there in the seats of all the world a place where the latter might sit to contemplate the universe. All was now complete: all things had been assigned to the higher, the middle, and the lower orders. . . . At last the Best of Artisans ordained that that creature to whom He had been able to give nothing proper to himself (*cui dare nihil proprium poterat*) should

78. Eugenio Garin, *Giovanni Pico della Mirandola*, a lecture given on Mirandola on February 24, 1963, on the occasion of the fifth centennial of the birth of Giovanni Pico (Parma, 1963), p. 55.

79. Ernst Cassirer, *The Individual and the Cosmos in Renaissance Philosophy*, translated by Mario Domandi (New York, 1964), p. 88.

80. Charles Bovillus (de Bouelles), *Il sapiente*, edited by E. Garin (Turin, 1943), pp. 92–3.

81. ibid., p. 75.

have joint possession of whatever had been peculiar to each of the different kinds of being (*commune esset quicquid privatum singulis fuerat*). He therefore took man as a creature of indeterminate nature (*indiscretae opus imaginis*) and, assigning him a place in the centre of the universe, addressed him thus: "Neither a fixed abode nor a form that is thine alone nor any function peculiar to thyself have we given thee, Adam, to the end that according to thy longing and according to thy judgment thou mayest have and possess what abode, what form, and what functions thou thyself shalt desire. The nature of all other beings is limited and constrained within the bounds of laws prescribed by Us. Thou, constrained by no limits, in accordance with thine own free will, in whose hand We have placed thee, shalt ordain for thyself the limits of thy nature. We have set thee at the world's center that thou mayest from thence more easily observe whatever is in the world. We have made thee neither of heaven nor of earth, neither mortal nor immortal, so that with freedom of choice and with honor, as though the maker and molder of thyself, though mayest fashion thyself in whatever shape thou shalt prefer (*in quam malueris, tu te formam effingas*). Thou shalt have the power to degenerate into the lower forms of life, which are brutish. Thou shalt have the power to be reborn into the higher forms, which are divine." . . . Beasts as soon as they are born . . . bring with them from their mother's womb all they will ever possess. Spiritual beings, either from the beginning or soon thereafter, become what they are to be for ever and ever. On man when he came into life the Father conferred the seeds of all kinds and the germs of every way of life (*omnifaria semina et omnigenae vitae germina indidit*). Whatever seeds each man cultivates will grow to maturity and bear in him their own fruit. If they be vegetative, he will be like a plant. If sensitive, he will become brutish. If rational, he will grow into a heavenly being. If intellectual, he will be an angel and the son of God.'[82]

The historico-cultural motifs which converge in this oration of Pico's

82. Giovanni Pico della Mirandola, *Oration on the Dignity of Man*, in *The Renaissance Philosophy of Man*, edited by Ernst Cassirer, Paul Kristeller, John H. Randall, Jr. (Chicago and London, 1956), pp. 224–5.

(and which afterwards were wide-spread in Renaissance thought) are extraordinarily rich and complex. Cassirer points out in it, 'one of the basic conceptions of Florentine Platonism' – a conception which, as he indicates, could never be completely overwhelmed or defeated by the drive towards 'transcendence' and asceticism, although the latter 'gradually became stronger and stronger'. In this sense, he also notes that 'to be sure, Pico and Ficinus are generally under the influence of Neo-Platonic themes; but in this case, the genuine Platonic sense of the concepts *chorismos* and *methexis* is recaptured'.[83] And one need hardly point out – for those already familiar with the structure of Cassirer's *Individual and Cosmos* – the importance and significance which is reserved to the thought of Nicholas Cusanus in his argument (and particularly to *De conjecturis*).

Exactly how complex are the motifs that converge here, and what historiographic balance must be maintained between them, has recently been shown by Garin in his rich historical sketch, 'Le interpretazioni del pensiero di Giovanni Pico' ('the connexion of Pico's thought with the milieu of Ficinus undeniable even if there existed significant differences in attitude; the reduction of works and thinkers that were quite different amongst themselves to an altogether too generic Platonism; the situation of every revitalisation of thought between the fifteenth and the sixteenth centuries under the sign of a Platonic revival: all of this,' Garin writes, 'has favoured till our day a significant strain in the interpretation of Pico's works – a strain which situated Pico almost totally within the confines of the Italian Platonists, or rather within the so-called "Platonic academy" of Florence', not to mention that 'other example of reductionism' which 'is the depiction of Pico as a cabalist').[84]

It is not difficult to mark out those basic themes of Pico's essay which most directly concern us. The theme of man as a *creatura comune* (a being that has something in common with all things),[85]

83. E. Cassirer, op. cit., pp. 86–7.

84. Cf. the Acts of the International Congress on '*L'opera e il pensiero di G. Pico della Mirandola nella storia dell'umanesimo* (Florence, 1965), Vol. I, pp. 9ff.

85. E. Garin, *Giovanni Pico della Mirandola (Vita e Dottrina)* (Florence, 1937), p. 197.

who reunites within himself *all* natural determinations; or that of the human spirit, which – having an *omnifaria* (omnifarious) nature – is 'the actuality that resolves and reunites within itself the infinite aspects of the real, incoporating all of them within its infinitude';[86] or again, the theme which portrays man 'not (as) one being among beings, but as the *oculus mundi*, divinity and creator, the bond and axis of the universe'.[87] All of these themes take us right back to the image, already emphasized a number of times, of man as the *genus of all empirical genera*, i.e. as that being which, in that he is provided with thought, is the universal, what is *general* or *common* in all things.

The same can be said for Bovillus's *De Sapiente*. Bovillus was a disciple of Faber Stapulensis, who 'grasped the focal inspiration of Pico, organized it, linked it and fused it together with the central themes familiar to him in Cusanus's thought'. In this work as well the basic theme is analogous to that of *De hominis Dignitate*. Here, as Garin writes, 'man is the centre of the world because it is in him that the world comes to consciousness of itself, as an object that becomes subject, as being that becomes knowledge. Man in his immediacy is a thing, nature. He is one being among other beings. But God', Bovillus states (following Pico), 'did not give man a nature; man is not; his being is the fruit of his self-creation. Man is to be a rock, a plant, an animal, an angel, or God according to his acts. And these acts are for Bovillus the process of acquiring knowledge. Human dignity consists in being the consciousness of the world, in making the world a great display for oneself.'[88]

Inasmuch as man is thought, he is both everything and nothing; everything in that he is what is *general and common* to all things, in all natural, living species; nothing in that this generality which is the universal, or thought, *is* none of the particular species contained within it. As Bovillus writes: 'Nothing is peculiar to man or is man's alone, but rather he shares in common all those things which distinguish the others'; 'he fulfils within himself the nature of everything'. 'Man is not this or that determinate being, nor is his nature this or that, but rather it is contemporaneously all things:

86. ibid., p. 198.
87. ibid., p. 200.
88. Cf. Garin's introduction to C. Bovillus, *Il sapiente*, op. cit., pp. x and xii.

a confluence and rational synthesis of everything.'[89] In short, man is Reason itself; that reason which, as we have seen, is both 'this just as much as that' and 'neither this nor that'. He is, in other words, that which is devoid of substance and that which is the receptacle for everything; for, as Hegel says, ' "I" is the vacuum or receptacle for anything and everything: for which everything is and which stores up everything in itself.' In short, as Pico states, man is a Proteus, a 'chameleon'.

On the other hand, since what is general and common, even if not identical with any particular species, represents nonetheless something that is present in all species – then 'in every substance of the world' (Bovillus goes on) 'there is something human, in every substance there is hidden some human atom proper to man'.[90] Just as it can be said that 'the world is like the human body', so it can be said that 'man is the *anima mundi*'.[91]

Two themes emerge here with great clarity. In the first place, that of Prometheus – the first anticipation of Faustian *Streben* (striving) (the myth of Prometheus, Cassirer notes, fuses with 'the Adam motif [which] undergoes an inner transformation that enables it to merge with the [former]').[92] In other words, what we have to do with is that current of thought which sees *man's being as a product of his self-creation*: 'Man is nothing,' Garin writes, 'but he can make himself into everything, in that with his infinite might he actualises all realities, moving from one to the next. Man is everything in that he knows everything; whereas in every other being "*operari sequitur esse*", with man "*esse sequitur operari*"; man is actually a great miracle, for he goes beyond the barriers of the natural world to become activity that always creates itself, a being that is a product of its self-creation.'[93]

The second theme which emerges is that of man as the point at which the Universe acquires consciousness of itself. Man, Bovillus writes, is the universe made 'transparent to itself'; and 'not', *nota bene*, 'because everything has a notion of everything, but because

89. C. Bovillus, *Il sapiente*, op. cit., p. 88.
90. ibid., p. 89.
91. ibid., p. 82.
92. E. Cassirer, op. cit., p. 95.
93. E. Garin, *G. Pico della Mirandola*, op. cit., pp. 201–2.

one part of the universe has reason, concepts and a science of its entire self'.[94]

Cassirer puts forward a strong argument in this regard. In relation above all to *De Sapiente*, Cassirer notes that this complex of thoughts is 'of such pure speculative content and of such peculiarly new stamp that they are immediately reminiscent of the great systems of modern philosophical idealism – of Leibniz or of Hegel. . . . Bovillus anticipates the Hegelian formula, according to which the meaning and aim of the mental process of development consists in the "substance" becoming "subject". Reason is the power in man by which "mother nature" returns to herself, i.e., by which she completes her cycle and is led back to herself'.[95]

In the light of these two great themes of Pico and Bovillus, we can now try to conclude our *excursus* and return to Marx's argument. The first element that stands out clearly is the notion that in man *esse sequitur operari*. As reason, man is everything and nothing; he is able to concretize himself into an infinite series of forms. His being is *becoming*. The *motif* of man's 'protean-form' ('*proteiforme*') nature, of his 'active side', of the *tätige Seite*, here strikes us with all the expressive force of myth. The universe is the theatre of man's *concretizations*. Naturalistic materialism has never been able to open itself up to this dimension. The only way in which it has been able to represent real movement, historical praxis, is through the immobile form of *anacyclosis* (the cyclical view of history).

In another respect, this nature of man *qua* becoming is sustained by the concept of man as Nothing; an idea not intended – obviously – to represent a disparaging conception of the 'human' or the spiritual, but on the contrary a *negative* conception of matter or the sensate. Indeed, man 'is not' precisely because he is *not* a *thing*, i.e. an objective, natural being — in short, because he is *Unding*. All of which means – here is the second great theme demanding examination – that the other characteristic of this conception is that man is depicted '*not as one being among other beings*', but only as the *oculus mundi* or as a spiritual mirror; and, in short, that whereas it grasps the character of man as the genus of all other empirical genera, it

94. C. Bovillus, op. cit., p. 82.

95. E. Cassirer, op. cit., p. 89.

dilutes (or rather, loses sight altogether of) that other characteristic by virtue of which man remains always a *natural being*.

In other words, to adopt a somewhat terse formulation: the obviousness of the fact that man's specificity is to be *generic* obscures its counterpart; i.e. that this genericity remains the *specific* characteristic of an objective being, *an attribute and not the subject itself*; and therefore that if this is the characteristic that distinguishes man from all other natural beings, it does not do away with his naturality but is, rather, rooted in it.

The proof of this lies in the way in which Pico and Bovillus develop the theme of man as the point where the Universe comes to consciousness of itself. Here the motif or idea is not that man knows and produces himself by knowing and producing the *other* things, i.e. by *reproducing* (both in theory and practice) the otherness of nature, and thereby ascribing to each object the yardstick appropriate to it. Rather it is just the opposite: that knowledge of all nature on man's part coincides – as Pico explicitly states – with *γνῶθι σεαυτόν* because he who 'knows himself in himself knows all things. . .';[96] or in other words – as Garin perceptively shows in the case of Bovillus – that the wise man is a '*publica creatura*' just in that moment in which he bends inwardly to 'espy the movement of his spirit', and that he is all the more *public*, i.e. turned towards the outside, 'the more he concentrates himself upon himself'.[97]

'We can also define Reason,' Bovillus writes, 'as that faculty by virtue of which nature returns to herself, is restored to herself, and by virtue of which the circle of nature as a whole is completed.'[98] But since 'in every substance of the world there is something human, in every substance there is hidden some human atom proper to man'[99] – and it is precisely 'this fraction (that) man is born to lay claim to for himself'[100] – the journey by which nature returns to herself by means of man comes to coincide with a *relationship of Reason to itself*; or more precisely, coincides with the relationship of Reason 'in itself'

96. G. Pico della Mirandola, op. cit., p. 235.
97. Cf. Garin's introduction to C. Bovillus, op. cit., p. xiii.
98. C. Bovillus, op. cit., p. 28.
99. ibid., p. 89.
100. loc. cit.

(or as it was immersed in the world) to Reason 'in itself and for itself', i.e. to a mediation within consciousness. In other words, the Substance that becomes a Subject is the very Subject which – having 'posited' itself antecedently as nature – now returns to itself. It is, as Bovillus says, the passage from 'man as substance' to 'man as reason';[101] and in fact to such a point that what should have been a relationship of man to nature resolves itself (as an actual prefigurement of what will happen with Hegel – Hegel had a deep knowledge of Cusanus) into a simple relationship of thought to itself – following the line of Cusanus's statement that '*non activae creationis humanitatis alius extat finis quam humanitas. Non enim pergit extra se dum creat neque quicquam novi efficit, sed cuncta, aquae explicando creat, in ipsa fuisse comperit*'.[102]

Man's genericity (i.e. the fact that his being is thought or reason) is not developed in the sense that consciousness is a specific *attribute* of man, i.e. a function of his relationship both to the otherness of nature and to other men, but is rather converted into a self-contained *subject*. Thus, the process of self-consciousness comes to coincide with *asceticism*, i.e. with the gradual emancipation on Reason's part from all those natural or sensuous elements – including those present in man's own naturality – by which Reason would otherwise be adulterated or circumscribed. To use other terms, for Pico – just as for Ficino, the interpreter of Plato's *Parmenides* – it is necessary that our soul gradually shake off its impurities by means of moral asceticism and the dialectic (*per moralem et dialecticam suas scordes excusserit*), until 'she (our soul) shall herself be made the house of God';[103] or until we – 'like burning Seraphim rapt from ourselves, full of divine power' – 'shall no longer be ourselves but shall become He Himself Who made us'.[104]

The culmination of self-consciousness is *epopteia*, 'that is to say, the observation of things divine by the light of theology'.[105] By

101. loc. cit.

102. Cf. E. Cassirer, op. cit., p. 87: 'The active creation of humanity has no other end than humanity itself. For humanity does not proceed outside itself while it is creating, nor does it produce anything new. Rather does it know that everything it creates by unfolding was already within it.'

103. G. Pico della Mirandola, op. cit., p. 232.

104. ibid., p. 234.

105. ibid., p. 233.

contrast, the discursive or 'intellectual' nature of thought, the fact that it is inherent in language (as Marx says, 'The element of thought itself, the element of the living manifestation of thought, language, is sensuous in character'),[106] means that it is relegated to the sphere of illusory or inferior knowledge. We can be freed from this sphere only by the 'expiatory sciences' of the dialectic and divine rapture, i.e. by those 'Socratic frenzies' which, as Pico says, 'drive . . . us into ecstasy [so] as to put our mind and ourselves in God'.[107]

Here the deep mystical-religious motifs in the neo-Platonic critique of the 'intellect' re-emerge (in this true birthplace of the modern '*destruction of the intellect*' or of the principle of non-contradiction). Hegel's loathing for propositions and the judgment, Heidegger's childish horror for the 'fatal categories of grammar', both appear to me to be already anticipated in the preface (as pointed out by Garin[108]) with which Lefèvre d'Étaples, or Faber Stanpulensis, introduced in 1501 the early work of his pupil Bovillus on *Ars oppositorum*: 'Aristotle represents life within knowledge, Pythagoras represents death, but a death higher than life. Thus, Aristotle taught with the word, Pythagoras with silence; but this silence is perfection, that word is imperfection. In Paul and Diogenes the silence is great; there is silence in Cusanus and Vittorino. In Aristotle, however, the silence is little and the words are many. But silence speaks and words remain silent.'

We shall now attempt to sum up our argument and draw our conclusions with regard to Marx. The point that links Marx to Hegel – and through Hegel, to Cusanus and the spiritualist humanism of the Renaissance – is clearly the concept of what is Reason, as we have had occasion to say a number of times. Reason is the *genus of all empirical genera*, it is the 'totality' and comprehension of everything. Reason is both everything and nothing: it is 'this as well as that' and also 'neither this nor that'; the 'receptacle' of everything and also what is 'devoid' of substance. It is what is *general* and *common* in all things, without being any of the particular things or

106. K. Marx, *Early Writings*, op. cit., p. 164.
107. G. Pico della Mirandola, op. cit., p. 234.
108. Introduction to C. Bovillus, op. cit., p. x.

natural species contained within Reason. This accounts for the *tätige Seite* and the possibility of understanding the world as the *actualization* of man and of his multiformed spirit. It also accounts for the conception that sees objects as the *objectification* of the subject himself.

The difference is, however – by now the argument is sufficiently evident and can be abbreviated – that Marx, instead of turning reason into the subject itself (thereby elevating it into the divine *Logos*) holds fast to man's naturality, i.e. to the nerve of the true materialist tradition. As Marx says in opposition to Hegel: 'Self-consciousness is . . . a quality of human nature. . . ; human nature is not a quality of *self-consciousness*.'

Thus we return to the concept of man as a *natural, generic being*. This concept means that man's specificity is to be generic, i.e. that man's *differentia* from all other natural entities – (N.B.) – consists in being the *indifferentia* of all the *differentiae* (the genus of all the species); in other words, that his particularity is the totality. The characteristic that distinguishes him from everything is just what unites him and links him to everything. What we here find once more is the concept of reason as a tauto-heterology or dialectical contradiction, as the 'identity of identity and non-identity'. On the other hand, in so far as being this *indifferentia* – or unity – of all the *differentiae* does not do away with the fact that man is after all still a determinate natural entity whose *specific* characteristic is just this *genericity*, what comes to the fore here is the anti-dialectical or materialist principle that contradiction does not eliminate *non*-contradiction (the principle of reason as a predicate rather than a subject) – in short, the principle of existence as an extra-logical element. Two principles which, if reconsidered in their organic connection, lead us back to the central theoretical postulate of this study: i.e. to tauto-heterological identity or 'determinate abstraction'.

It would be too easy to score further polemical successes against 'dialectical materialism' and its chronic inability to solve the enigma of the 1844 *Manuscripts*, i.e. to understand the concept of man as a 'natural, generic being'. But the step that we must take here is in an altogether different direction. The theory of 'determinate abstraction' is the theory of abstraction as a 'rational totality' (a totality of reason) and also as fact or 'material determination' (a determination of matter). In short, it is the theory which we came across (in Chapter VIII) when an analysis of the initial pages of section 3 of the 1857 *Introduction* showed that abstraction is discussed there in a twofold sense: as a mental *generalization* or totality and as *one* aspect or analytic characteristic of the *particular* and multi-dimensional object under consideration ('value', it will be remembered, as a concept that is logically more general than and therefore precedes that of 'population'; and, at the same time, 'value' as 'an abstract *one-sided* relation of a concrete and living whole that is already given').

Now, the concept of man as a 'natural, generic being', while presenting us with the same structure (tauto-heterological identity) as the 'abstraction', shows us at the same time why this logical-epistemological theory did not give rise to a special analysis on Marx's part – it was immediately absorbed by Marx into his theory of *social relations of production*. Man is a natural, generic being. He is the genus of all empirical genera, what is general and common in all things. In so far as what is common to all things is not *any one* of the things in particular, this genericity is the *specific* element of man; it is the idea, reason, the rational totality. On the other hand, in so far as man – being a natural entity – has 'his' nature 'outside himself', i.e. does not have a being of his own but has only that of other entities as his own, the generality expressed in his idea shows itself to be the 'abstract *one-sided* relation of a concrete that is already given'. That is, it shows itself to be the most superficial and *generic* characteristic manifested by an object or a natural determinate species, and as such it is a characteristic which the object has in *common* with countless other natural species. (It is here that the materialist overturning of Bovillus and Hegel's point of view comes to light: it is not that 'in every substance of the world there is something human' or that 'in every substance there is hidden some human atom proper to man', propositions implying that in the final analysis nature itself is *idea* and that therefore the *finite is ideal* – anthropomorphism and abstract finalism. Rather the opposite: i.e. the specific human element, logical generality or the idea, is none other than the most superficial and *generic* element of the object.)

The concept of the social relations of production shows itself, at this point, to be nothing but the development of the two relationships which we have just now mentioned. In so far as genericity is a specific prerequisite of man, man's relationship to every other species manifests itself as a relationship within his own species; i.e., the *generic* relationship (that is, a relationship of more than one species) appears as a *specific* interhuman relationship. This means that man's process of relating to objective otherness is also a process whereby man relates to himself; i.e. a way of communicating to other men his needs and aims by means of objectivity. So that just as man's relationship to nature turns out to be also an interhuman relationship, similarly production also inevitably shows itself to be a social relationship. On the other hand, in so far as man's relationship to himself or to his own species is also a relationship to other natural entities (for the latter are actually 'his' nature), the relationship is reversed. In the sense that it is no longer objectivity that is a *means* for the manifestation of the idea, i.e. of man's needs and conscious aims, but the idea – qua 'an abstract *one-sided* relation of the given object', or more exactly, its most superficial or *generic* characteristic – that now appears as the *means* by which this generic element itself is linked and related to the object from which it was abstracted. Hence the latter finally turns out to be just that characteristic or relationship which not only assists in defining the *specificity* of the object under consideration, but also the characteristic and relationship by means of which this specificity manifests and asserts itself.

Let us halt here, without complicating the analysis any further. The essentials of what had to be said have been said. Though only in the broadest outline, the argument has shown the difficult path that led to the concept of 'social relations of production'. This path seems to be marked by a profound contrast between two irrepressible requirements which can (however) be reconciled only with great difficulty: the requirement imposed by critical epistemology and that imposed by philosophic logic; the requirement that thought appear as 'one of the two' and that it be at the same time the 'totality' of the relationship; the principle of a science of man as a natural, finite being and the impossibility for this science of ever transcending the limits of anthropology without reinstating the characteristic of man as reason, i.e. as an ideal totality.

It would be superfluous here to insist further on the antecedents of the concept of 'social relations of production'. It may, however, be useful to elaborate slightly one other point implied in our argument. If, in order to understand the 'social relations of production', it is essential to have an idea of the difficulties through which philosophic logic and anthropology have passed, it remains no less true that those problems and difficulties in their turn found a solution in Marx precisely because they were transferred on to a radically new terrain, never previously explored by philosophic thought. The concept of 'social relations of production' undoubtedly has very complex antecedents; that does not detract, however, from the fact that what emerged at the end of this development (i.e. that concept itself) was something completely heterogeneous with respect to the entire speculative tradition. If, as one historian (E. H. Carr) has called to mind not long ago, 'the tension between the opposed principles of continuity and change is the groundwork of history,'[109] one must also see to it that this tension is not arbitrarily played down and that it is permitted to burst forth with all its force. Problems, in a certain sense, are always the same, and yet they are also always new. In order to understand Marx one must reconstruct in some way the entire antecedent tradition. And yet it remains true that one cannot understand Marx if one does not understand at the same time how it is that the problems which once were posed at the level of Hegel's *Science of Logic* or of the *Critique of Pure Reason* became so different in Marx's hands that they no longer gave rise to a treatise on logic but to the analysis of *Capital.*

It is also indepensable that we insist on this point in order to correct the orientation of one line of interpretation of Marx's thought already referred to in this study. Della Volpe's *Logica come scienza positiva* is in my opinion the most important work produced

109. E. H. Carr, *Socialism in One Country* (London, 1958), Vol. I, p. 3.

by European Marxism during this post-war era. Notwithstanding my great indebtedness to this work, it remains a fact (although a fact that has been greatly exaggerated by often inaccurate interpretation) that this work – and even more so later developments based on it – have signalled an unmistakable tendency towards the restoration of a logic and epistemology (the theory of 'determinate abstraction') to Marx's thought, *rather than* sustained the deeper meaning and movement of that thought. A meaning which (by contrast) we have attempted to show and represent here by the transposition and resolution of the problems that were once posed at the level of logic and epistemology (and therefore at the level of the theory of 'determinate abstraction' as well) into the historico-materialist theory of the concept of 'social relations of production'. This Della Volpean tendency accounts for the privileged position and excessive weight accorded to the so-called logico-methodological writings within the general economy of Marx's works – works like the first part of the *Critique of Hegel's Philosophy of Right* or the *Introduction* of 1857 (it will be obvious that this bias is still felt in part in the present work). And it also accounts for the underevaluation of the essential role that must be accorded to the 1844 *Manuscripts* as that work in which Marx succeeded for the first time in transposing the entire preceding philosophic problematic to the new terrain of the concept and analysis of the 'social relations of production'. This work, although it had originally attracted Della Volpe's attention, in the end seemed to him to be of 'philosophic interest only in the last part dedicated to the critique of Hegel's philosophy, which is incomprehensible, moreover, apart from the *Critique of Hegel's Philosophy of Right*, consisting as it does in a kind of economic-philosophic "hodgepodge" that is rich in places with glittering theoretical insights and modes of reasoning which only later are fully developed'.[110]

110. Galvano Della Volpe, *Rousseau e Marx* (Rome, 1964), p. 150.

XII. The Idea of 'Bourgeois-Christian' Society

Hegel's thesis that man has his foundation and essence in God means not only that man attains consciousness of self *indirectly* – i.e. it is through knowledge of God's nature that man arrives at knowledge of his own – but also that this knowledge of the divine essence is the meaning and purpose of the entire historical process. The motive force of world history consists, according to Hegel (see, e.g., sub-heading 384 of the *Encyclopedia*), in the gradual progression in the representation of God from the particular or naturalistic forms in which He is at first represented, to His representation as *Spirit*; i.e. that representation in which He is affirmed in His authentic universality and in His complete independence from all ethnic or national characteristics. In Hegel's words: 'The universal in its true and comprehensive meaning is a thought which, as we know, cost thousands of years to make it enter into the consciousness of men. The thought did not gain its full recognition till the days of Christianity. The Greeks, in other respects so advanced, knew neither God nor even man in their true universality. The gods of the Greeks were only particular powers of the mind; and the universal God, the God of all nations, was to the Athenians still a God concealed. They believed in the same way that an absolute gulf separated themselves from the barbarians. Man as man was not then recognized to be of infinite worth and to have infinite rights . . . Christianity (is) the religion of absolute freedom. Only in Christendom is man respected as man, in his infinitude and universality.'[1]

1. *En.L.*, p. 293. As confirmation of Hegel's thesis and also as proof of his influence on the historiography of the ancient world (just to mention one among countless other authors, starting with Wilamowitz), cf. Bruno Snell, *The Discovery of the Mind*, translated by T. G. Rosenmeyer (New York, 1960), pp. 246–7: 'It is sometimes averred that the Greeks in their art did not portray any one man with his accidental traits, but that they represented *man* himself, the idea of man, to use a Platonic expression, which is not

The statement that 'we are all men', the recognition of the *equality* and universality of human nature, was thus achieved with the advent of Christianity – when men recognized that they were all equally sons of God, or in other words, when they grasped the divinity (and therefore their own principle and essence) no longer as this or that particular 'force' but as Spirit, in all its unconditional infinitude and universality.

The recognition of this historic function of Christianity (which is present in Feuerbach and Marx as well) recurs in Hegel's work with such insistency as to represent one of its true leitmotifs. Not only the principle of equality, but also the very idea of freedom – that freedom which 'is the very essence of spirit, that is, its very actuality' has its foundation and origin, according to Hegel, in

---

infrequently used to support the argument. The truth is that such a statement is neither Platonic nor even Greek in spirit. No Greek ever seriously spoke of the idea of man. . . .' And in the same vein, cf. also Max Pohlenz, *Der hellenische Mensch* (Göttingen, 1946), p. 446: 'The Greeks never coined a special word for this idea of "humanitas" [nor] did they have occasion to do so, since in point of fact they only thought in terms of the closed circle of their fellow countrymen.' As regards the theme, developed later in our analysis, of the integration of Greek man within the *polis*, cf. ibid., pp. 106, 108, 125, 131ff. ('The polis formed a spiritual unity. . . . For this reason the entire political life as well was permeated by religion'). In relation to how the modern concept of the 'rights of man' was extraneous to the Greek world, cf. ibid., p. 109. And again on p. 404: 'For the Greeks the polis was not an external legal institution, but rather a natural form of life which the spirit of a people creates for itself.' As concerns the differences – which we shall discuss later in our analysis – between the ancient world and Christianity, one must always mention the classic work of Fustel de Coulanges, *The Ancient City*, translated by Willard Small (Garden City, New York, n.d.). Cf. p. 390, where it is pointed out that with Christianity 'the divine Being was placed outside and above physical nature. Whilst previously every man had made a god for himself, and there were as many of them as there were families and cities, God now appeared as a unique, immense, universal being, alone animating the worlds.' And p. 392: 'Christianity . . . presented to the adoration of all men a single God, a universal God, a God who belonged to all, who had no chosen people, and who made no distinction in races, families, or states.' And concerning the relationship between Christianity and subjective freedom, cf. pp. 394–5: 'Christianity taught that only a part of man belonged to society; that he was bound to it by his body and by his material interests; . . . this new principle was the source whence individual liberty flowed . . . Politics and war were no longer the whole of man; all the virtues were no longer comprised in patriotism, for the soul no longer had a country . . . Christianity distinguished the private from the public virtues. By giving less honor to the latter, it elevated the former; it placed God, the family, the human individual above country, the neighbor above the city.'

Christianity. 'Whole continents, Africa and the East, have never had this Idea, and are without it still. The Greeks and Romans, Plato and Aristotle, even the Stoics, did not have it. On the contrary, they saw that it is only by birth (as, for example, an Athenian or Spartan citizen), or by strength of character, education, or philosophy (the sage is free even as a slave and in chains) that the human being is actually free. It was through Christianity that this Idea came into the world. According to Christianity, the individual *as such* has an infinite value as the object and aim of divine love, destined as mind to live in absolute relationship with God himself, and have God's mind dwelling in him: i.e. man in himself is destined to supreme freedom.'[2]

This process of universalization by means of which God frees Himself from all naturalistic semblance in order to appear as Spirit and therefore as *transcendent* infinitude is apprehended by Hegel in connection with another and simultaneous process, which is that of the dissolution of the earthly community of which the individual was originally a part. Hegel writes: 'Religion is the consciousness that a people has of what it itself is and of the essence of supreme being.... The way in which a people represents God is also the way in which it represents its relationship to God or represents itself; (such that) religion is also the conception that a people has of itself. A people that takes nature for its God cannot be a free people; only when it regards God as a Spirit that transcends nature does it become free and Spirit itself.'[3]

When God is posited outside of nature and therefore also above and beyond the naturalistic ties of consanguinity which are the basis of the first ethnic-tribal communities, this means both that the inner unity of these communities is dissolved and that the immediate natural tie of a common descent is no longer recognized as a real one. In this case, God is situated above and beyond the earthly community because man no longer looks upon this community as God. He separates God from the community because he no longer

2. G. W. F. Hegel, *Philosophy of Mind*, op. cit., pp. 239–40 (translation modified).
3. G. W. F. Hegel, *Vorlesungen über die Philosophie der Weltgeschichte*, Part I of Vol. 8 in his *Sämtliche Werke*, edited by Georg Lasson (Leipzig, 1920), p. 105.

recognizes his essence in the community, or because the community itself – and therefore men's relationships amongst themselves – are already internally disintegrated.

The meaning of the argument, which is developed with admirable historical insight particularly in the *Philosophy of Right* and the *Philosophy of History*, hinges upon Hegel's well-known analysis of the differences that separate the Greek world from the Christian world.

In ancient Greece, God is the *polis* itself. Far from appearing as a transcendent entity, the Spirit is here, as Hegel says, still in the form of natural or 'substantive customary morality' (*Sittlichkeit*). The divinity is the personified totality of the ethico-political community; a community that is founded in its turn on natural ties of blood, i.e. on the natural commonality of descent. Not only is the rift between the terrestrial world and the extra-terrestrial still not present, but for the same reason neither does there exist any separation between individual and community, between State and society. Everything holds together as in a perfect cosmos. The divinity is the very content of the spiritual life of the people, the substance and *raison d'être* of its political existence. And since 'this spiritual content is something definite, firm, solid, completely exempt from caprice, the particularities, the whims of individuality, of chance', it 'then constitutes the essence of the individual as well as that of the people'. 'It is the holy bond that ties the men, the spirits together. It is one life in all, a grand object, a great purpose and content', upon which the individual entirely depends.[4]

The will of the individual and that of the community – subjective will and objective will – coincide here without any mediation to form a single unfettered whole; for in the *polis*, as Hegel states, '(the Idea) does not yet present itself one-sidedly and abstractly for itself but as in direct connexion with the real – just as in a beautiful work of art the sensuous bears the mark and is the expression of the

4. G. W. F. Hegel, *Reason in History*, translated by Robert S. Hartman (Indianapolis, 1953), p. 52. This translation of the *Introduction* to the *Lectures on the Philosophy of History* contains certain passages from Lasson's edition. Apart from these few insertions there exists no English translation of the version edited by Lasson. (Trans.)

spiritual'. 'It is still spontaneous customary morality; not yet reflective morality, but rather that morality in which the individual will of the subject adheres to the unmediated custom and habit of the laws and of what is just. Thus the individual is in spontaneous unity with the universal goal';[5] to such an extent that 'an Athenian citizen did what was required of him, as it were from instinct'.[6] In this 'purely substantive' freedom, 'the laws and precepts are something sturdy in and for themselves (*ein an und für sich Festes*) in relation to which the subjects' conduct is one of utter subordination. These laws need not then correspond at all to the subjects' own will; and the subjects find themselves in the same position as children, who obey their parents – but not however out of their own will and understanding.'[7]

This condition of complete subordination of the individual with respect to the ethnic-tribal community of which he is a part (a community that towers over him and dominates him to the point of taking on in his eyes the character of a divine 'natural force') is also analysed in Marx's work, in terms not dissimilar to Hegel's. *The German Ideology* deals at length a number of times with the description of what is called the *naturwüchsige Gesellschaft* or the *naturwüchsige Verhältnisse* in contrast to the conditions that arise with the *Geldverhältnisse*. 'Consciousness is at first, of course, merely consciousness concerning the *immediate* sensuous environment and consciousness of the limited connection with other persons and things outside the individual who is growing self-conscious. At the same time it is consciousness of nature, which first appears to men as a completely alien, all-powerful and unassailable force, with which men's relations are purely animal and by which they are overawed like beasts; it is thus a purely animal consciousness of nature (natural religion). We see here immediately: this natural religion or animal behaviour towards nature is determined by the form of society and *vice versa*. . . . This beginning is as animal as social life itself at this stage. It is mere herd-consciousness, and at this point

5. G. W. F. Hegel, *Philosophie der Weltgeschichte*, op. cit., p. 239.
6. G. W. F. Hegel, *Reason in History*, op. cit., p. 53.
7. G. W. F. Hegel, *Philosophie der Weltgeschichte*, op. cit., p. 233.

man is only distinguished from sheep by the fact that with him consciousness takes the place of instinct or that his instinct is a conscious one.'[8] In analogous terms, and again with the aim of signalling its difference with regard to the subsequent rise and spread of mercantile relationships, *Capital* refers on a number of occasions to that condition of 'immaturity of the individual human being (who had not yet severed the umbilical cord which, under primitive conditions, unites all the members of the human species one with another').[9]

It goes without saying that just as for Hegel the period of 'substantive customary morality' is not limited to Greece but is extended well beyond it to embrace much more primitive conditions of life, so with Marx as well his propositions refer to more remote ages. Nevertheless, allowing for necessary distinctions, that feature of his argument that is certainly moulded to fit the conditions of ancient Greece is the notion that here the individual is not regarded as an autonomous entity sufficient unto himself, but rather as something that, with respect to the *polis*, stands in the same relationship as the *part* to the *whole* – in a fashion not unlike the relationship of a given organ of the body to man's body as a whole.

This way of viewing things, which was still the essence of the Greek conception of man at the height of the classical age, emerges forcefully in Aristotle's *Politics*. Here one finds an explicit affirmation of the intrinsically social nature of man: 'man is a being meant for political association, in a higher degree than bees or other gregarious animals . . .', so that one can say that 'the polis belongs to the class of things that exist by nature, and that man is by nature an animal intended to live in a polis. He who is without a polis, by reason of his own nature and not of some accident, is either a poor sort of being, or a being higher than man.' But one also finds a no less explicit statement as to the hierarchical priority of the community with regard to the individual. '. . . The polis is prior in the order of nature to the family and the individual. The reason for this is that the whole is necessarily prior (in nature) to the part. If the whole

8. K. Marx, *The German Ideology*, op. cit., pp. 42–3.

9. K. Marx, *Capital* (Eden and Cedar Paul translation), op. cit., Vol. I, p. 53.

body be destroyed, there will not be a foot or a hand. . . . We thus see that the polis exists by nature and that it is prior to the individual. . . . Not being self-sufficient when they are isolated, all individuals are so many parts all equally depending on the whole. The man who is isolated – who is unable to share in the benefits of political association, or has no need to share because he is already self-sufficient – is no part of the polis, and must therefore be either a beast or a god.'[10]

Hegel's judgment is in similar terms. The Greek world knows nothing of the individual's independence from the community; it does not know this independence and still less can it imagine the anteriority and priority in value of the individual with respect to the social body as a whole. 'In the states of antiquity, the subjective end simply coincided with the state's will. In modern times, however, we make claims for private judgement, private willing, and private conscience. The ancients had none of these in the modern sense; the ultimate thing with them was the will of the state.'[11] Whereas the 'essence of the modern State', Hegel remarks, is not only 'that the universal be bound up with the complete freedom of its particular members', but that 'the universal end cannot be advanced without the personal knowledge and will of its particular members, whose own rights must be maintained' (hence the necessity that that universal end be 'proven' to the individual 'in actual fact'); in the states of classical antiquity, however, 'particularity had not then been released, given free scope, and brought back to universality'.[12] The typical example is the Platonic State, in which 'subjective freedom does not count, because people have their occupations assigned to them by the Guardians'.[13]

Under these conditions the development of individuality, i.e. man's self-creation as autonomous subjectivity by which 'man descends from external reality into his own spirit'.[14] could not help but act as the principle of the internal dissolution and ruin of those

10. Aristotle, *The Politics*, translated by Ernest Barker (New York, 1962), pp. 5–6.

11. G. W. F. Hegel, *Philosophy of Right*, translated by T. M. Knox (London, Oxford, New York, 1952), p. 280.

12. ibid., p. 260.

13. ibid., p. 280.

14. G. W. F. Hegel, *Philosophie der Weltgeschichte*, op. cit., p. 233.

States. Hegel states: 'The development of particularity to self-subsistence is the moment which appeared in the ancient world as an invasion of ethical corruption and as the ultimate cause of that world's downfall. Some of these ancient states were built on the patriarchal and religious principle, others on the principle of an ethical order which was more explicitly intellectual, though still comparatively simple; in either case they rested on *primitive* unsophisticated intuition. Hence they could not withstand the disruption of this state of mind when self-consciousness was infinitely reflected into itself. . . . In his *Republic*, Plato displays the substance of ethical life in its ideal *beauty* and *truth*; but he could only cope with the principle of self-subsistent particularity, which in his day had forced its way into Greek ethical life, by setting up in opposition to it his purely substantial state. He absolutely excluded from his state, even in its very beginnings in *private property* and the *family*, as well as in its more mature form as the subjective will, the choice of a social position, and so forth.'[15] This inability in the Greek world to interpret the new spirit that was rising signals its historical inferiority with respect to Christianity. In fact, 'the right of the subject's *particularity*, his right to be satisfied, or in other words the right of *subjective freedom*, is the pivot and centre of the difference between *antiquity* and *modern* times. This right in its infinity is given expression in Christianity and it has become the universal effective principle of a new form of civilization.'[16]

As the reader can see, the acuteness of Hegel's historical perception comes out most fully from these passages. The autonomous development of the individual in the ancient world is linked to the development of *private property* – that property which Plato banned from his State precisely as a consequence of the inability of the Greek world to reconcile the organicist principle of the *polis* with that of subjective freedom. And one certainly need not force Hegel's text in order to comprehend all of its implicit meanings. 'Private property' and its 'more mature form as the subjective will, the choice of a social position', refer in transparent terms to that great historical process (analysed subsequently by Marx on a number of occasions)

15. G. W. F. Hegel, *Philosophy of Right*, op. cit., pp. 123–4. 16. ibid., p. 84.

represented by the disintegration of the compact and homogeneous 'patriarchical communities' of the ancient world as a result of the corrosive effect of the development of *commodity production* and exchange (and hence money) relationships. 'Just as all the qualitative differences between commodities are effaced in money, so money on its side, a radical *leveller*, effaces all distinctions. But money is itself a commodity, an external object, capable of becoming the private property of any individual. Thus social power becomes a private power in the hands of a private person. That was why the ancients (and here Marx cites Sophocles) denounced money as *subversive* of the economic and moral order of things'; whereas 'modern society which, when still in its infancy, pulled Pluto by the hair of his head out of the bowels of earth, acclaims gold, its Holy Grail, as the glittering incarnation of its inmost vital principle'.[17]

This analysis by Hegel and Marx, whose positions thus far largely coincide, naturally had a prehistory of its own in the eighteenth century, particularly in Rousseau. The organicism of the ancient city, the integration which it achieves between individual and community, the coincidence of public life and private life – not to mention the corrosive effect of exchange, commerce, and the circulation of money on the solidarity and cohesiveness of the ancient 'republics' – these are all themes which can be found already developed in the work of the great Genevan. However, what is perhaps not so well-known is that Rousseau conceived one of the most original formulations of the complex problem of the relationship between Christianity and the ancient world – and also one of the most fertile as a precursor of future developments.

The theme that we find here has at first sight a form analogous to the observation which Hegel uses as his point of departure. Rousseau points out that it is precisely because man in the ancient world is integrated organically into the *particular* community of his city that he is excluded from that broader and *general society* which is the community of the entire human species. 'The patriotic spirit is an exclusive one, which makes us regard all men other than our co-citizens as strangers, and almost as enemies. Such was the spirit of

17. K. Marx, *Capital*, op. cit., p. 113.

Sparta and Rome. The spirit of Christianity, by contrast, makes us regard all men as our brothers, as children of God. Christian charity does not allow us to make odious distinctions between compatriots and strangers; . . . its ardent zeal embraces all the human race without distinction. It is true, then, that Christianity by its very sanctity is contrary to the particularist (selfish) social spirit.'[18]

The idea that emerges here is again that of the ancient world's inability to raise itself to a recognition of the *equality* and universality of human nature. And the manifestation of this principle in the world is linked by Rousseau as well to the advent and propagation of Christianity: '. . . Ideas of natural right and the common brotherhood of all men were spread rather late and have made such slow progress in the world that only Christianity has generalized them sufficiently.'[19]

However, what is characteristic of Rousseau's argument is that while interpreting the passage from ancient society to Christianity as the passage from the *particular* societies of the former to the *general* society of the latter, and therefore as a progressive universalization of man, he apprehends in this process a genuine subversion of the principle involved. In the ancient world, the bond that ties man to the community is *particular but real*; i.e., if the former does not link man to the entire species but only to a particular ethnic group, it nonetheless binds him to this group in a political community that is *terrestrial*, and *purely human*. It is just the opposite with Christianity: here the individual is linked to the entire human species, but the tie that binds together this 'société générale' turns out to be *elevated and projected outside the world* – i.e., it is not a human-terrestrial bond, but rather *God*. Thus the '*société humaine en général*', '*l'institution sociale universelle*' that derives therefrom is a purely *ideal, abstract* society – not a political, but a transcendental one. It is the society of all men qua 'souls' and 'sons of God'; a heavenly society which is counterpoised here on earth by the atomistic disintegration, the struggle between opposing egos, and the unbridled competition which Rousseau believes distinguish modern

18. J.-J. Rousseau, *The Political Writings*, edited by C. E. Vaughan (Oxford, 1962), Vol. II, p. 166.

19. ibid., Vol. I, p. 453.

conditions from the 'virtue' of ancient republics. 'Society at large, human society in general, is founded on humanity, on universal benevolence; and I say, and I always have said, that Christianity is favourable to that society. But particular societies, political and civil societies, have an entirely different principle. They are purely human institutions, from which Christianity consequently detaches us as it does from all that is merely of this earth.'[20]

In its essential outline the picture is analogous to Hegel's. Man's elevation to consciousness of the universality and equality of his nature passes through the dissolution of the natural-ethnic tie of the particularistic communities of the ancient world. Under the impact of money and commerce those original formations – cohesive yet confining – dissolve; the individuals which were enclosed therein are cast forth like free atoms; the localistic barriers fall away together with differences of blood and lineage. Man is no longer free as an Athenian or as a Spartan, i.e. as a member of a determinate community, but has worth *as such*, i.e. independent of race, religion, nationality, etc. In broad terms, we repeat, the picture is analogous in both Hegel and Rousseau. The new situation is identified by both of them as one in which each man is of infinite worth because each man – taken in his isolation and separation from the others and therefore before and independent of any relationship with society – stands in an unmediated and direct relationship with God as Spirit; not, of course, with the God of the Athenians or of the Hebrews, but with the universal God of all peoples. But Hegel sees in this disintegration of relationships on earth and their formation anew around the God of the heavens the decisive advance by which God frees Himself from all naturalistic semblance in order to posit Himself at last as Spirit, i.e. as free and transcendental universality ('A people that takes nature for its God cannot be a free people; only when it regards God as a Spirit that transcends nature does it become free and Spirit itself'). Whereas Rousseau, who in *this* respect is truly a son of the ancient republics (man outside the community is only an animal; the man who has no need to share because he is already self-sufficient is no part of the polis, and must therefore

20. ibid., Vol. II, pp. 166–7.

be either a beast or a god), apprehends in this new relationship a situation completely unnatural and alienated. Consequently, where Hegel sees the emergence of the principle of modern freedom, Rousseau sees the formation of the conditions for servitude and tyranny. 'Christianity is a wholly spiritual religion which detaches men from the things of this earth. The Christian's homeland is not of this world. He does his duty, true: but he does it with profound indifference to the success of the effort which he makes. It matters little to him whether all goes well or ill down here: if the state should fall, he blesses the hand of God for punishing his people. . . . Christianity preaches only servitude and dependence. The spirit of Christianity is too favourable to tyranny for the latter not to profit from it constantly. True Christians are formed for slavery. They know this, yet hardly care; for this short life means too little to them.'[21]

It is certain that no self-respecting Marxist could ever support these conclusions. In these later developments of his argument Rousseau is wrong and Hegel right. Christianity *is* the principle of subjective freedom (or better put, it was the way – even if alienated – in which this principle came to light for the first time). Rousseau's political thought here re-echoes the limits of the ancients' mentality: it shows itself incapable of understanding new and modern conditions properly.

It is also evident (on the other hand) that Hegel's position – as we shall soon see – is by no means identical with the Christian-liberal point of view pure and simple, i.e. with the standpoint of natural-law contractualism that culminates in the concept of the *Rechtsstaat*. He considers it an advance that the emergence of Christianity shattered the original 'beautiful unity' of the Greek *polis*, freeing on the one hand subjective consciousness as consciousness withdrawn into itself and on the other hand elevating the divine universal above and beyond nature, and thus also beyond the ethnic community. But if this 'antithesis, one extreme of which is represented by God and the divine and the other by the subject as the particular', appears as an advance, it is no less true that Hegel's problem is

21. ibid., Vol. I, pp. 503–4.

precisely that of proceeding towards the *reconciliation* of the two. 'World-history is nothing other than the attempt to bring out the relationship whereby both of these extremes stand in absolute unity and genuine reconciliation, a reconciliation in which the free subject is not submerged in the objective character of the Spirit, but attains to his own autonomous status – but also a reconciliation in which the absolute Spirit, true objective unity, has obtained its absolute status.'[22]

However, the force of Rousseau's argument and its irreplaceable historical role lie in the way Rousseau perceives as an unnatural and alienated condition this fact: that what in the ancient world is a *worldly bond*, with Christianity presents itself not only as an *other-worldly bond*, situated *above and beyond men*, but also as a cohesive bond 'in heaven' that has its basis in the atomistic disintegration of the individuals 'on earth'. By grasping the complementariness of these two processes, Rousseau opens up for us the way to understanding something without which the meaning of Marx's work would be forever hidden from us behind seven seals: i.e. the differing relationship between unity and multiplicity, community and individual that is implicit in the worldly solution of the ancient *polis* and in the otherworldly solution of Christianity.

In the ancient world, the community or 'social tie' (to use the term which, as we shall see, is a key one in Marx's argument) is simply the nexus that links individuals amongst themselves. The 'whole' of the community and its 'particular' individuals are in the same relationship amongst themselves as, so to speak, the hand to its fingers or the totality of the body with respect to its individual organs. Just as the individuals do not have an existence independent of the community, a private life severed from the public one, so too *the community does not have an existence separate* from theirs – i.e. the State is a real affair of all the citizens. The *worldliness* of the social tie which was emphasized above ('But particular societies, political and civil societies, have an entirely different principle. They are purely human institutions'), has just this meaning: that since the community is nothing other than the *relationship* of the individuals

22. G. W. F. Hegel, *Philosophie der Weltgeschichte*, op. cit., p. 234.

amongst themselves, this relationship (obviously) does *not* exist outside of the mutually related entities – i.e. here the unity resides in the very interlinking of the manifold elements.

Under modern conditions it is just the reverse: the social tie which binds men to one another has become an *otherworldly* one (men are united by means of their common descent from God), the tie itself or their *unity* comes to acquire a *separate* existence of its own (in fact, it is God) – since it is now posited *above and beyond* men. Thus one arrives at the paradox of a *relationship* which posits itself for itself, independent of the entities that are mutually related. The situation that derives therefrom is of extraordinary importance. Here in fact the social relationship (the relationship of men amongst themselves) appears to be preempted and replaced by the relationship which each individual, in his atomistic separation from the others, is destined to establish with God as his essence and foundation – and therefore as the spiritual principle dwelling in the depths of the human soul (in Christianity, Hegel reminds us, the individual is of infinite worth because 'as the object and aim of divine love, [man is] destined as mind to live in absolute relationship with God himself, and [to] have God's mind dwelling in him . . .'). And since the individual must enter into a relationship with God, even before he enters into a relationship with other men (for he can be the brother of his brothers only through the Father) in order to acquire worth as 'humanity' or spirituality, the 'city' in which man changes from beast to man presents itself as a *societas in interiore homine* (cf. G. Gentile's *Genesi e struttura della società* [*Genesis and Structure of Society*] in order to have an idea of how these themes have survived even in our own times) a *societas* that is established in the dialogue of the soul with God, just as this dialogue is conducted in the inwardness of the spirit.

What results from this – taking one back to the classical model of Christian-liberal ethics and politics – is the concept of natural-law contractualism. According to this conception, since each individual appears, as a consequence of his relationship to the transcendent, to be directly endowed with 'original' or natural-absolute rights ('natural' precisely because they are presocial, i.e. antecedent to the historical relationship of men to one another), the *earthly city*, i.e. the society established by men on the basis of contract, appears only as a *means*, an expedient, to which men recur in order to have the enjoyment of their original rights and freedoms guaranteed by the 'law' (and therefore by the State's 'forces of public safety').

'*Enter* (if you cannot avoid social life) into a society with others such that each can preserve in it what belongs to him' (*suum cuique tribue*).[23] This formula from the first pages of Kant's *Rechtslehre*, presents us in a transparent fashion with the meaning of the revolution carried out by Christianity in relation to the conceptions of the ancient world. Whereas for Aristotle man is destined to live in the polis and whoever lives outside it is only a beast or a god, for the Christian-liberal conception society (when it simply cannot be avoided) is a mere means of guaranteeing and reinforcing (qua State) those conditions of reciprocal separation and competition in which men live in the 'state of nature'. Again, whereas in the Greek conception 'the polis is prior . . . to the family and the individual' just as 'the whole is necessarily prior to the part', in the Christian-liberal conception the individual seems paradoxically greater and higher than the community, the part greater than the whole. For if his 'rights' do not proceed from society itself but directly from God, it is evident that their sphere may never be violated, whatever may be the reasons – not even when such a transgression is in the interest of the people as a whole. It is a paradox which confirms how those rights are not the expression of popular sovereignty but, on the contrary, the expression of the private individual over and against society – as in Benjamin Constant's statement that 'sovereignty exists only in a limited and relative way' and that 'at the point where individual existence and independence begin, there the jurisdiction of this sovereignty comes to a halt', so that 'should society go beyond this line, it is no less guilty than the despot'.[24]

Now we come to the essential point. In Chapter XVI of *The Essence of Christianity* Feuerbach also takes into consideration 'the Distinction between Christianity and Paganism'. '. . . The pagans

23. I. Kant, *Scritti politici e di filosofia della storia e del diritto* (Turin, 1956), p. 415.
24. Benjamin Constant, *Principes de politique* (Paris, 1815), p. 17.

considered man not only in connection with the universe'; but they also 'considered the individual man in connection with other men'. 'They rigorously distinguished the individual from the species, the individual as a part from the race as a whole, and they subordinated the part to the whole'; whereas 'Christianity, on the contrary, cared nothing for the species, and had only the individual in its eye and mind'. 'The ancients sacrificed the individual to the species; the Christians sacrificed the species to the individual. Or, paganism conceived the individual *only* as a part in distinction from the whole of the species; Christianity, on the contrary, conceived the individual only in immediate, indistinguishable unity with the species.' 'To Christianity the individual was the object of an immediate providence, that is, an immediate object of the Divine Being'; but that means that 'the Christians left out the intermediate process, and placed themselves in immediate connection with the prescient, all-embracing, universal Being; i.e. they identified the individual with the universal Being *without any mediation*'. The conclusion was that in order to realize his own being, the Christian need not enter into a relationship with other men, 'for he as an individual is at the same time *not* individual, but species, universal being – since he has "the full plenitude of his perfection in God", i.e. in himself'.[25]

If read closely, this page from Feuerbach shows us how similar he is to Hegel and at the same time how he already diverges from Hegel. For *The Essence of Christianity*, the historical development of religion represents a means by which man advances in consciousness of self. Like Hegel, Feuerbach contends that man arrives at his own self-consciousness *indirectly* – i.e. through the knowledge acquired of the divine essence. In terms analogous to those in Hegel's statement in the *Philosophy of History* that 'the way in which a people represents God is also the way in which it represents its relationship to God or represents itself', so that 'religion is also the conception that a people has of itself', Feuerbach writes that 'man in religion – in his relation to God – is in relation to his own nature',[26] so that 'the antithesis of divine and human ... is nothing else than the anti-

25. L. Feuerbach, *The Essence of Christianity*, op. cit., pp. 151–2 (translation modified).
26. ibid., p. 25.

thesis between human nature *in general* and the human *individual*'.[27] Similarly Feuerbach also regards Christianity as the religion *par excellence*, i.e. as that particular religion that realizes all at once the 'essence' of all religions in so far as it does not conceive of God in this or that *particular* form (i.e. in naturalistic terms), but conceives of Him as the *universal* Spirit. But there is a significant difference between the two: what Hegel presents in a positive light, for Feuerbach has a radically different meaning. It is not man's essence that is made up of God's, but on the contrary what man represents as God is nothing other than man's own *alienated* essence – i.e. man's essence transposed outside himself, separated from himself and hypostatized into a self-subsisting entity. In other words, whereas Hegel, who argues from the standpoint of Christianity, considers it natural that man should arrive at consciousness of the *equality* and universality of his own nature (and therefore at consciousness of his relationship to his genus) by means of knowledge of God as spirit, for Feuerbach this indirect path that man follows to self-knowledge is the sign of man's *estrangement* from self. In God as *Logos* he sees only 'the idea of community strangely regarded . . . as a particular personal being';[28] i.e. he sees the *social unity* posited apart from the multiplicity of the members that it ought to link together, and in short sees the paradox of a *relationship* which posits itself for itself independent of the entities that it ought to mediate and relate to one another. 'Participated life is alone true. . . . But religion expresses this truth, as it does every other, in an indirect manner, i.e. inversely, for it here makes a *universal* truth into a *particular* one, the true subject into a predicate, when it says: God is a participated life, a life of love and friendship.'[29]

Rousseau's insight begins to take shape here. In the ancient world the tie that joins men is particularistic but real – i.e. an earthly society; with Christianity, however, in which the 'general society' is an otherworldly one, there is no *real* extension of man's relationship to the human genus, i.e. there is no actual universalization or socialization of this relationship. What there is instead is a reversal of principles. Social unity, in that it is otherworldly (and therefore

27. ibid., pp. 13–14. 28. ibid., p. 67 (translation modified). 29. loc. cit.

transformed into God) turns out to be posited *above and beyond* men; i.e. it presupposes their atomistic disassociation. On the other hand, in so far as this unity or universal must acquire an existence of its own – having been posited for itself – the divine spirit ends by fusing itself directly with the particularity of the individual; the individual who, just as from one viewpoint he has his grounding in the divine spirit, so from another viewpoint he is also its earthly incarnation (whence the figure of Christ as a man-God and of the Christian as a God-man, i.e. as the earthly, natural body within which an otherworldly soul is enclosed). As Feuerbach says: 'The most unequivocal expression, the characteristic symbol of this immediate identity of the species and individuality in Christianity is Christ, the real God of the Christians. Christ is the ideal of humanity become existent, the compendium of all moral and divine perfections to the exclusion of all that is negative; pure, heavenly, sinless man, the universal man, . . . not regarded as the totality of the species, of mankind, but immediately as *one* individual, *one* person.'[30] Christian man, in his turn – and especially the Christian of Protestantism, which for Feuerbach just as for Hegel represents authentic Christianity i.e. as it is freed from the still partly pagan mythical-phantasmagoric involucrum in which Catholicism or medieval Christianity is enmeshed – this Christian man appears as the union of the divine and the worldly, i.e. as the man of bourgeois or 'civil society'. This can be seen in Feuerbach's remark that 'Protestant morality is and was a carnal mingling of the Christian with the man, the natural, political, civil (*bürgerlich*), social man, or whatever else he may be called in distinction from the Christian'.[31]

Consider this intuition of the connection between Christianity and bourgeois 'civil society', beyond which Feuerbach was never able to go. With him it is only a marginal notation; but it is the focal problem for Hegel and Marx. Their two great conceptions can best be compared here. Their relationship comes, indeed, to a climax in the comparison between Hegel's argument concerning the 'Germanic-Christian world' and Marx's analysis of Protestant-capitalist society.

30. ibid., p. 154. 31. ibid., p. 139.

Hegel's point of departure is already familiar to us. After the 'substantive customary morality' of the ancient world was divided and rent asunder, there arose the antithesis between subjectivity and objectivity and 'from this point on the *worldly* kingdom and the spiritual kingdom stand opposed to one another'. The task confronting world-history is that of overcoming this antithesis and of reuniting the extremes. The modern State, in other words, must be able to reconcile the principle of the *polis*, i.e. organicism or substantive universality, with the principle of individuality or subjective freedom brought into the world by Christianity. The standard for this reconciliation is to be sought in Christ, qua God become man – i.e. qua the infinite *Logos* that has also come down to the 'here and now'. 'This is what Christ reveals to us: his own truth, which is the truth of man's inwardness (*Gemütes*), is to be placed in connexion with the divinity. Here the reconciliation is accomplished in and for itself; but since it is accomplished only within itself, this phase – as a consequence of its immediacy – begins with an antithesis. It is true enough that the phase begins historically with the reconciliation brought about by Christianity. Since, however, this reconciliation is just beginning and is accomplished for consciousness only in theory (*an sich*), it manifests itself initially as the most monstrous antithesis of all, which then appears as something unjust that is to be overcome and superseded.'[32]

In other words, Christianity in itself is already the principle of reconciliation; except that in its immediacy Christianity is only this *principle*, and not yet the reconciliation itself actually realized. In order to bring that about the principle of Christianity must be *translated into reality*; the reconciliation of the two worlds, which with Christ has taken place only in a single point, must pervade reality as a whole.

It is easy to recognize here the theme which we initially took as our starting-point for the analysis of Hegel's philosophy. The problem of philosophy is the *realization* of idealism, the realization of the Idea or the infinite, the Christian *Logos*. Idealism is self-consistent in actualizing itself. But this actualization implies the

32. G. W. F. Hegel, *Philosophie der Weltgeschichte*, op. cit., p. 244.

negation or idealization of the finite and the realization of the infinite; i.e. the passage from the 'beyond' over into the 'here and now'.

This twofold transposition, in which Hegel sees a climax to the meaning of the 'Germanic-Christian world' as the 'absolute reconciliation of self-subsisting subjectivity with the divinity that is in itself and for itself, with the true and the substantive',[33] is precisely what he represents as the relationship between State and religion.[34] The *foundation* of the State lies in religion, in that religion is 'the divine will' itself; which means that *the foundation of the here and now lies in the beyond.* ('It is evident and apparent from what has preceded that moral life is the State retracted into its inner heart and substance, while the State is the organization and actualization of moral life; and that religion is the very substance of the moral life itself and of the State. At this rate, the State rests on the ethical sentiment, and that on the religious, (for) religion . . . is the consciousness of "*absolute*" *truth.*'[35]) On the other hand, the *beyond* (which is the divine will contained in religion) has its *here and now* in the State and in the institutions in which it articulates itself – i.e. its *existence* and earthly incarnation. Thus one can say that 'the State is the divine will, in the sense that it is spirit present on earth, *unfolding itself* to be the actual shape and *organization* of a world'.[36]

The meaning of this broad-ranging argument emerges in clear and simple terms, with all of its profound historical ramifications, in the long *Anmerkung* appended to subheading 552 of the *Encyclopedia.* Here Hegel sets off the 'sanctity' of Catholicism against Protestant 'morality' (*Sittlichkeit*) by pointing out the divergent conceptions of God's spirituality that each of them has. With Catholicism God is conceived in such a way that He figures (as also in pre-critical metaphysics) as an *external object* and at the same time as an infinitude relegated to the *beyond* (hence the meaning of Catholic 'sanctity' as flight and removal from the world). With Protestantism however (identified by Hegel with philosophy itself inasmuch as it is a rational

33. loc. cit.

34. This relationship can be seen clearly particularly in subheading 552 of the *Encyclopedia* and in subheading 270 of the *Philosophy of Right.*

35. G. W. F. Hegel, *Philosophy of Mind*, op. cit., p. 283.

36. G. W. F. Hegel, *Philosophy of Right*, op. cit., p. 166 (translation modified).

theology), the opposite takes place; i.e., not God's displacement outside the world but rather His infusion 'into actuality', not sanctity but morality. 'Instead of the vow of chastity, *marriage* now ranks as the ethical relation; and, therefore, as the highest on this side of humanity stands the family. Instead of the vow of poverty (muddled up into a contradiction of assigning merit to whosoever gives away goods to the poor, i.e. whosoever enriches them) is the precept of *action* to acquire goods through one's own intelligence and industry, – of *honesty* in commercial dealings, and in the use of property – in short moral life in the socio-economic sphere. And instead of the vow of obedience, true religion sanctions *obedience* to the *law* and the legal arrangements of the State – an obedience which is itself the true freedom, because the State is a self-possessed, self-realizing reason – in short, *moral life* in the *State*.' And Hegel continues thus: 'The divine spirit must interpenetrate the entire secular life: whereby wisdom is concrete within it, and it carries the terms of its own justification. But that concrete indwelling is only the aforesaid ethical organizations. It is the morality of marriage as against the sanctity of a celibate order; – the morality of economic and industrial action against the sanctity of poverty and its indolence; — the morality of an obedience dedicated to the law of the State as against the sanctity of an obedience from which law and duty are absent and where conscience is enslaved.'[37]

The meaning of the argument could not be clearer: God becomes real in the world. And this indwelling of God's in the world is represented by His presence in the civil and political institutions of modern bourgeois society: marriage, the family, commerce, 'action to acquire goods through one's own intelligence and industry' (i.e. entrepreneurial activities), and finally obedience to the laws of the State. These institutions, which to us seem to be historical institutions, institutions of a determinate society that was born at one time and is destined to pass away at another, to Hegel appear (like the 'bread' and 'wine' of the *Jugendschriften*) as the presence itself of God in the world – not profane realities but 'mystical objects', not historical institutions but sacraments.

37. G. W. F. Hegel, *Philosophy of Mind*, op. cit., pp. 286–7.

However strange it may seem, this is precisely the point where Marx's work and Hegel's coincide – going so far as to accord with one another as regards the entire *exterior* form of their arguments. Those institutions of the bourgeois world which Hegel regards as the realization of God and therefore as the sensuous incarnations of the suprasensible (the positive exposition of the absolute) appear to Marx in the same light. *Capital* discusses at length the 'mystical character of commodities' and 'all the mystery of the world of commodities, all the sorcery, all the fetishistic charm, which enwraps as with a fog the labour products of a system of commodity production'.[38] Furthermore, while defining the commodity as 'a thing that is suprasensate in a sensate manner' (*ein sinnlich übersinnliches Ding*) in *A Contribution to the Critique of Political Economy*, Marx goes on to specify in *Capital* that whereas 'at first glance, a commodity seems a commonplace sort of thing, one easily understood, analysis shows, however, that it is a very queer thing indeed, full of metaphysical subtleties and theological whimsies'.[39]

One must assume that Marx's interpreters – and this is perhaps a measure of Marxism's sorry state today – in passing over these pages and the hundreds of others in which Marx discusses the 'fetishistic' character of capital, are implying that such expressions were mere literary *hors d'oeuvres*, rhetorical figures of speech, or even mere stylistic flourishes. In actual fact, what is at issue is something so important that it is difficult to imagine what meaning Marx's thought would have without it.

Just as Hegel sees in the 'Germanic-Christian' world the realization of the *verkehrte Welt* previously presaged in the *Phenomenology*; so Marx sees in this world, which is after all bourgeois society itself, a world 'stood on its head', starting with its most elementary institution, the commodity – a world which, if it is to be put back on 'its feet', must therefore be overturned from its very foundations. The difference is only that whereas Hegel sees the actualization of God in the suprasensate's becoming sensate, Marx (who obviously reasons in a way that goes beyond the Christian horizon) sees a

38. K. Marx, *Capital* (Eden and Cedar Paul translation), op. cit., Vol. I, p. 50.
39. ibid., pp. 43–4.

process whereby *forces alienated and estranged* from mankind become present and real, beginning with capital and the State themselves.

'. . . Everything in this mode of production appears to be upside down. . .'.[40] '. . . Capitalist production . . . is as truly cosmopolitan as Christianity. This is why Christianity is likewise the special religion of capital. In both it is only man in the abstract who counts . . . In the one case, all depends on whether or not he has faith, in the other, on whether or not he has credit.'[41] 'The complete *reification, inversion* and *derangement* of capital as interest-bearing capital – in which, however, the inner nature of capitalist production, (its) derangement, merely appears in its most palpable form – is capital which yields "compound interest".'[42] 'Suppose a society made up of the producers of commodities, where the general relations of social production are such that (since products are *commodities*, i.e. *values*) the individual labours of the various producers are related one to another in the concrete commodity form as embodiments of *undifferentiated human labour*. For a society of this type, *Christianity*, with its cult of the abstract human being, is the most suitable *religion* – above all, Christianity in its bourgeois phases of development, such as Protestantism, Deism, and the like.'[43] 'In money itself the totality exists as the whole, in representational form, of the commodities. It is in gold and silver that for the first time wealth (exchange-value both as totality and as abstraction) exists in its own distinct form to the exclusion of other commodities, as an individual palpable object. Money is therefore the God of commodities. As an isolated object that can be grasped in the hand money can therefore be solicited, found, stolen, and discovered, and the general wealth can be tangibly possessed by a single individual. From the lowly status which money appears to have as a mere means of circulation, it suddenly becomes the Lord and God of the world of commodities. It represents the heavenly existence of the commodities.'[44]

40. K. Marx, *Theories of Surplus-Value*, translated by Jack Cohen and S. W. Ryazanskaya (Moscow, 1971), Part III, p. 476.

41. ibid., p. 448 (translation modified).

42. ibid., p. 456 (translation modified).

43. K. Marx, *Capital*, op. cit., p. 53.

44. K. Marx, *Grundrisse der Kritik der politischen Ökonomie* (Berlin, 1953), pp. 132–3.

Here is a series of brief passages, selected almost at random from many others, which may give some idea of the extent to which the link between capitalism and Christianity is a constant and reiterated theme in Marx's work – and also some idea of the emphasis given to the thesis that this is a world upside down, 'standing on its head', a world that must be overturned and put right side up if one wants to put it back 'on its feet'. The first elaboration of the concept of an 'equivalent', which comes to us in the 'excerpts' from James Mill and contains an embryonic formulation of the theory of value, develops the concept of money as a 'universal equivalent', parallel to that of Christ as representative of 'man before God', of 'God before man', and finally of 'man before man'.[45] The theme of the link between bourgeois society and Christianity is the leit-motif, moreover, of all his early writings. The *Jewish Question*, e.g., which contains Marx's first major analysis of the liberal-democratic constitutions that came out of the French Revolution, hinges on the proposition that the democracy of *purely* 'political' or 'abstract' 'equality' is essentially *Christian democracy*.

Clearly, the breadth that this basic theme takes on in Marx's work in relation to that of all his predecessors (Hegel not excluded), makes it difficult to deal with it in these few concluding pages. In fact, this theme is extended to and fused into all of the economic-political analysis developed in his mature work. However the essential problem which is constantly re-emerging is that of the differing relationship between community and individual, *unity and multiplicity*, which exists respectively in 'natural' or precapitalist societies and in modern bourgeois society.

'Where labour is communal, the relations of men in their social production do not manifest themselves as "values" of "things". Exchange of products as commodities is a method of exchanging labour, (it demonstrates) the dependence of the labour of each upon the labour of the others (and corresponds to) a certain mode of social labour or social production. In the first part of my book, I mentioned that it is characteristic of labour based on private exchange that the

45. K. Marx, *Marx-Engels Gesamtausgabe* (Moscow and Frankfurt, 1927ff.), Vol. I, Part III, pp. 530–47.

social character of labour "manifests" itself in a perverted form – as the "property" of things; that a social relation appears as a relation between things (between products, values in use, commodities).'[46]

This is, in every sense, the key to everything: whether labour is in *common* or whether labour is *not* in common. This is the basic problem. Where labour is in fact in common, *individual* labour is, *without any mediation*, an articulation and part of the overall *social labour*. The relationship is that of the fingers to the hand; neither do the individuals exist apart from society, nor does the 'social tie' (Marx says '*das gesellschaftliche Band*') have an existence independent of them. Just as unity is the *multiplicity* in its *interdependency*, similarly the individuals and their activities appear as functions and *articulations* of the common *social* activity. Contrariwise, where labour is not in common and individual labour is *private* labour, i.e. labour in which each individual decides for himself how much and what to produce independent of a 'plan' or programme of the community ('The only products which confront one another *as* commodities are those produced by reciprocally *independent enterprises*'[47]); in this case, corresponding to the reciprocal disassociation or atomization of the producers amongst themselves there is a separation of *social unity* from the individuals themselves – i.e. the paradox arises of a *relationship* that posits itself for itself independent of the entities that it ought to relate and mediate.

In the first case, 'it was the specific kind of labour performed by each individual in its natural form, the particular and not the universal aspect of labour, that constituted then the social tie'; i.e., 'it is clear that in this case labour does not acquire its social character from the fact that the labour of the individual takes on the abstract form of universal labour or that his product assumes the form of a universal equivalent'; for 'it is the community (which exists as a *presupposition of production*) that makes it impossible for the labour of the individual to be private labour and his product to be a private product; on the contrary, it makes individual labour appear

46. K. Marx, *Theories of Surplus-Value*, op. cit., Part III, pp. 129–30.
47. K. Marx, *Capital* (Eden and Cedar Paul translation), Vol. I, p. 11.

as the direct function of a member of a social organism'.[48] In short, in the first case individual labour is an integral part *without any mediation*, of the overall social labour – and it is such in its own natural form as 'concrete' or 'useful' labour (spinning, weaving, ploughing, etc.). That is to say, just as social labour is here the whole, the link between the various kinds of individual labour, so too the social or general product is nothing other than the sum of the *use-values* produced – meaning by this last term that what is produced are labour-products in their form as objective, physical or natural objects.[49]

In the second case, it is just the opposite, since there is lacking the presupposition of a community that would distribute the overall work that must be carried out among its individual members, and would assign to each of them what he must produce (i.e., there is lacking a 'plan'). Thus the labour of the individual, i.e. labour in its natural form as useful or *concrete* labour, 'becomes social labor only by taking on the form of its direct opposite, the form of abstract universal labour',[50] i.e. the form of *abstract* labour; just as its product, in its turn, becomes a social product by taking on the form of its opposite, i.e. *value* – within the body or form that it, qua *use-value*, has as a natural object. And one must bear in mind that the term 'value' is to be understood in the sense of a 'coagulation' or objectification of *undifferentiated human labour-power*, as 'crystals of this social substance common to them all',[51] and therefore as a non-sensuous, *non-material objectivity* – or as Marx refers to it, a 'ghost-

48. K. Marx, *A Contribution to the Critique of Political Economy*, op. cit., p. 29 (Colletti's emphasis) (translation modified).

49. For Marx, 'use-value' is the natural object itself, whether produced by human labour or otherwise. Cf. *Capital* (Eden and Cedar Paul translation), Vol. I, p. 4: 'The utility of a thing makes it a *use-value*. But this utility is not a thing apart. Being determined by the properties of the commodity, it does not exist without them. The (body of the) commodity itself, such as iron, wheat, a diamond, etc., is therefore a *use-value* or good.' Also cf. *A Contribution to the Critique of Political Economy*, p. 20: 'This property of commodities to serve as use-values coincides with their natural palpable existence.' It is useful to call to mind these simplicities because some (theoretical) Marxists are currently passing through a period of intense mental derangement concerning the concept of 'use-value'.

50. ibid., pp. 29–30.

51. K. Marx, *Capital*, op. cit., Vol. I, pp. 6–7.

like' objectivity ('not an atom of matter enters into the objectivity of value'[52]), which is nothing but the social unity itself in its hypostatized form.

In so far as individual human activities are not directly linked to one another, they can be related to one another as integral parts of the overall social labour only on condition that each of them is reduced to *abstract* 'undifferentiated human labour', i.e. to labour as it presents itself when it is considered *apart from* the concrete subjects who carry it out. This means that in order to count as *social* labour (given the fact that it is not so without mediation), individual labour must here negate itself and transform itself into its *opposite*, i.e. represent itself *not* as individual labour but as the 'labour of no single individual', as *abstract* labour. ('The labour-time represented by exchange value is the labour-time of an individual, but of an individual undistinguished from other individuals in so far as they perform the same labour. . . . It is the labour-time of an individual, *his* labour-time, but only as labour-time common to all, regardless as to *which* particular individual's labour-time it is.'[53]) And here it is obvious that the subject is now work *in the abstract*, and man is the predicate. For, as Marx states, 'labour, thus measured by time, does not appear in reality as the labour of different individuals, but on the contrary, the various working individuals rather appear as mere organs *of* labour; or, in so far as labour is represented by exchange values, it may be defined as *human* labour *in general*. This abstraction of human labour in general virtually *exists* in the average labour which the average individual of a given society can perform.'[54]

Since the products of individual labour are products of *private* labour, it happens that in order to acquire a social character they, in their turn, must negate themselves as use-values in order to become their opposite: i.e., exchange-values or *values, exchangeable* objects.

52. ibid., p. 17.

53. K. Marx, *Critique of Political Economy*, op. cit., p. 27.

54. ibid., pp. 24–5. Remarks on the theory of value which amplify those of this chapter can be found in sections 7 and 8 of my introduction to *Eduard Bernstein, Socialismo e socialdemocrazia* (Bari, 1968). See pp. 76–97 of 'Bernstein and the Marxism of the Second International', in L. Colletti, *From Rousseau to Lenin: Studies in Ideology and Society* (London, 1972).

In short, they must negate themselves as this or that determinate *sensible thing*, which they are, in order to figure instead as expressions of a *single, identical subjectivity*, as 'expressions of one and the same social unit' – in a word, as expended human *labour-power*. ('... The different use-values are the products of the work of different individuals, consequently the result of various kinds of labour differing individually from one another. But as exchange values, they represent the same homogeneous labour, i.e., labour from which the individuality of the workers is eliminated.')[55]

The reader who has had the perseverance to follow us thus far can now draw all the necessary conclusions himself. 'Undifferentiated' or 'abstract' human labour takes us back to the 'abstract man' of Christianity. 'Value', as the objectification of *social unity* ('Where labour is communal, the relations of men in their social production do not manifest themselves as "values" of "things".'), leads us back to the paradox (previously examined in the analysis of Rousseau and Feuerbach) of the *social relationship* as a relationship that posits itself for itself, independent of the individuals which it ought to relate and mediate. In other words, it is the paradox of the social relationship which, at the same time that it posits itself *outside* and beyond the individuals concerned, dominates them like a God on high, even though it is only their own alienated *social power*, i.e. social power estranged from themselves. The extent to which this estrangement of the 'relationship', this *reification* of it, i.e. the fact that it creates for itself an independent existence in a natural object or use-value (which represents itself as the 'body' of value), is at the core of Marx's analysis can be seen by the way in which he discusses money, and even more so from his account of the money-capital relationship. 'Money is the community of men itself, posited as an external and therefore adventitious thing (*ihr Gemeinwesen selbst als ein äusserliches und darum zufälliges Ding*).[56] '*Das Geld ist damit unmittelbar zugleich das reale* Gemeinwesen, *insofern es die allgemeine Substanz*

55. Ibid., pp. 22–3. Cf. also *Theories of Surplus-Value*, op. cit., Vol. III, p. 128: '... The *individual commodity* as *value*, as the *embodiment of this* (social) *substance*, is different from itself as use-value...'. And again, loc. cit.: '... The value of a commodity ... is a quality differentiating it from its own existence as a thing, a value in use.'

56. K. Marx, *Grundrisse*, op. cit., p. 909.

des Bestehns für alle ist, und zugleich das gemeinschaftliche Produkt aller. Im Geld ist aber, wie wir gesehen haben, das Gemeinwesen zugleich blosse Abstraktion, blosse äusserliche, zufällige Sache für den Einzelnen, und zugleich bloss Mittel seiner Befriedigung als eines isolierten Einzelnen.' And so on, for a thousand pages.[57]

Finally, the reader who noted carefully Feuerbach's statement that with Christianity the individual 'is at the same time *not* indiv-dual' because besides being an individual he is Universal Being or God, will not find it difficult to recognize the same process in Marx's statement that wherever private production reigns, individual labour 'becomes social labor only by taking on the form of its direct opposite, the form of abstract universal labor'. Just as he will not fail to recognize – we hope – that Christians and commodities are made in the same way. The 'body' and 'soul' of the former correspond to the 'use-value' and 'exchange-value' of the latter.

Let us track our chimera down to its last place of refuge. Marx writes: 'The objectivity (*Wertgegenständlichkeit*) of the value of commodities thus resembles Mistress Quickly, of whom Falstaff said: "A man knows not where to have her." This objectivity of the value of commodities contrasts with the gross sensate objectivity of these same commodities (the objectivity which is perceived by our bodily senses) in that not an atom of matter enters into the objectivity of value. We may twist and turn a commodity this way and that – as a thing of value it still remains unappreciable by our bodily senses. Let us recall, however, that commodities only possess the objectivity of value in so far as they are expressions of one and the same social

57. ibid., p. 137. 'Money is thus, without any mediation, both the real *community*, in that it represents the general substance of existence for everyone, and at the same time the social product of everyone. With money, however, the community, as we have seen, is both a mere abstraction, a mere external, adventitious thing for the individual, and at the same time a mere means for his personal gratification as an isolated individual.' Cf. also *A Contribution to the Critique of Political Economy*, op. cit., pp. 51–2: 'That a social relation of production takes the form of an object existing outside of individuals, and that the definite relations into which individuals enter in the process of production carried on in society, assume the form of specific properties of a thing, is a perversion and by no means imaginary, but prosaically real, mystification marking all social forms of labor which creates exchange value. In money this mystification appears only more strikingly than in commodities.'

unit, namely human labour, since the objectivity of their value is purely social. . .'.[58] Here Marx is saying again that the commodity is a 'suprasensate thing in a sensate manner', a natural body (or use-value) which harbours within itself a *non-material objectivity*: value. If this statement means anything, it means that the commodity, just like the Christian, is the unity of the finite and the infinite, the unity of opposites, *being* and *non-being* together. And in fact, Marx says that 'a commodity *is* a use-value, wheat, linen, a diamond, a machine, etc., but as a commodity it is, at the same time, *not* a use-value'.[59] It *is* and it *is not* – the emphasis is Marx's. The notorious 'dialectic of matter', with which the Russians intend to build communism, is here confirmed as the logic of the bourgeois-Christian world, the logic of this upside-down world – in accordance with Marx's remarkable insight of 1844 that 'Hegel's *Logic* is the *money* of the Spirit'. The old 'dialectical materialism', it seems to us, here stands judged. And judged together with it is also the concept of *reification* as developed by Lukács in 1923 – the concept that today Marcuse is busy trading in . . . on the left.

Let us make one last effort, this time directly in the field of economic theory. There exists an age-old objection to the 'theory of value' which is repeated by Joan Robinson, Schumpeter, Myrdal, Lionel Robbins, and by countless others; an objection to which Marxists have never known how to reply. This objection is the same one raised by Samuel Bailey against Ricardo (and through which he earned himself a place in the histories of economic thought). It is also the objection raised by Böhm-Bawerk ('the Marx of the bourgeoisie', as he is usually called) against *Capital* in his *Zum Abschluss des Marxschen Systems* (1896).[60] This is the objection which explains why Marx is still accused of indulging in theology and metaphysics. It is this: that in their treatment of 'exchange-value', which is a *relationship* between things exchanged, and therefore a 'relative' value, Ricardo and after him Marx committed the 'typically

58. K. Marx, *Capital*, op. cit., Vol. I, p. 17.

59. K. Marx, *Critique of Political Economy*, op. cit., p. 41.

60. Eugen von Böhm-Bawerk, 'Zum Abschluss des Marxschen Systems' in *Festschrift* for Karl Knies (Vienna, 1896), pp. 151–2, 157–8.

scholastic' error of assuming that behind the exchange-value there was a real (not relative but absolute) value, i.e. a value existing *in* the related things themselves. In other words, Ricardo and Marx forgot that exchange-value, being a relationship, could not have an existence of its own or be a *real value*, existing in distinction from use-values or the related 'utilities'. This accounts for the scholastic error that they committed of hypostatizing 'value'.

We are not here concerned to point out how the crux of Marx's entire criticism of Ricardo lies precisely in the argument that 'Ricardo is . . . to be reproached for very often losing sight of this "real" or "absolute value" and only retaining "relative" and "comparative values" ';[61] and that this is precisely the line of argument by means of which Schumpeter salvages Ricardo from the accusation of being a metaphysician, while leaving Marx as the sole accused.[62] Nor do we now wish to show how it is precisely in this same context that present-day economic 'revisionism' has its roots, the 'revisionism' used by Piero Sraffa in his attack on Marx's analysis. What, however, we are concerned to point out – apart from the fact, already well-known, that Marxists do not read Marx – is that Marx, *horribile dictu*, accepts the argument that *'value' is a metaphysical entity* and merely confines himself to noting that is the thing, i.e. the commodity itself or value, that is a scholastic entity, and not the concept which he, Marx, uses to describe how the commodity is made! '. . . The "verbal observer" understands as little of the value and the nature of money as Bailey, since both regard the independent existence (*Verselbständigung*) of value as a scholastic invention of economists. This independent existence becomes even more evident in capital, which, in one of its aspects, can be called *value in process* – and since value only exists independently in money, it can accordingly be called *money in process*, as it goes through a series of processes in which it preserves itself, departs from itself, and returns to itself increased in volume. It goes without saying that the paradox of reality (*nota bene*) is also reflected in paradoxes of speech which are at variance with common sense and with what

61. K. Marx, *Theories of Surplus-Value*, op. cit., Part II, p. 172.
62. Joseph Schumpeter, *History of Economic Analysis* (London, 1954).

vulgarians mean and believe they are talking of. The contradictions which arise from the fact that on the basis of commodity production the labour of the individual presents itself as general social labour, and the relations of people as relations between things and as things – these contradictions are innate in the subject-matter, not in its verbal expressions.'[63]

This society based on capital and commodities is therefore the metaphysics, the fetishism, the 'mystical world' – even more so than Hegel's *Logic* itself! One may raise the objection that such a statement has no meaning, for if indeed the objectivity of value is a *non-material objectivity*, then this objectivity does not exist, just as the immortal soul of the Christian does not exist. Let us concede as much (and all the more willingly since the author is one materialist 'who is not ashamed of being such'). 'When we speak of the commodity as a materialization of labour – in the sense of its exchange-value – this itself is only an imaginary, that is to say, a purely social mode of existence of the commodity which has nothing to do with its corporeal reality.'[64]

An imaginary, but nonetheless social, existence! Let us attempt to analyse this concept in a more forthright and simple manner. When we say that the king or even the president *represents* national unity or popular sovereignty, in a certain sense what we say is laughable. One knows very well that, from this standpoint, they do not represent anything. And yet how many persons know it? Those who know it are – let us admit it – just a handful of 'non-constitutional' communists. Yet their insight does not do away with the fact that everything functions *objectively* as if the aforementioned did indeed represent something. It escapes the senses, and yet millions of men act *as if* it were a real presence. This 'as if' – it needs to be said – is in this instance an objective and real *social* fact.

We can now bring to a close this apparently endless argument. The reader must realize, even from these few remarks, that the 'theory of value' or (more basically) the very analysis of the *commodity* – such as it is found at the very beginning of *Capital* – has not

63. K. Marx, *Theories of Surplus-Value*, op. cit., Part III, p. 137.

64. ibid., Vol. I, p. 171.

exactly met with great success among Marxists. One cannot exactly say that it has been understood. The proof is the silence in which the theory of fetishism or alienation has always been enshrouded from Engels onward. What is the reason for this? The commodity and, even more so of course, capital and the State, represent *processes of hypostatization in reality*. Now, our thesis is that, given realities of this nature, it is impossible to understand them fully unless one grasps the structure of the processes of hypostatization of Hegel's *Logic*. In other words, Marx's critique of Hegel's dialectic and his analysis of capital hold together. Failing to understand the former it is also impossible to understand the latter.

This is a matter of which we have always been persuaded, even though it has always been difficult to prove our point. Hence the thanks that I owe to Rancière for having brought to my notice a text which is the confirmation we sought: Marx's *Die Wertform* (even though his own interpretation of it is quite mistaken).[65]

Marx writes: 'Within the relationship between value and the expression of value contained therein, the abstract universal does not count as a property of the concrete in its sense-reality, but on the contrary the concrete-sensate counts merely as the phenomenal or determinate form of the abstract universal's realisation. The labour of the tailor which one finds, e.g., in the *equivalent coat*, does not incidentally have the *general property* of being human labour within its value-relation as cloth. On the contrary: *To be human labour* is *its very essence*; to be the labour of the tailor is only the *phenomenal* or *determinate form taken by this its essence* in its *realization*. This *quid pro quo* is inevitable, since the labour represented in the labour-product *creates value* only in that it is undifferentiated human labour; such that the labour objectified in the value of a product is *not at all distinguishable* from the labour objectified in the value of another product.' And Marx concludes thus: 'This total reversal and over-turning, which means that the concrete-sensate counts only as the phenomenal form of the abstract-universal, and not contrariwise the

65. Jacques Rancière, *Le concept de critique et la critique de l'économie politique des "Manuscrits" de 1844 au "Capital"*, in L. Althusser et. al., *Lire le Capital* (Paris, 1965), Vol. I, pp. 137–8.

abstract-universal as a property of the concrete, characterises the expression of value. This is what makes its understanding difficult. If I say that Roman law and German law are both forms of law, this is obvious. If, however, I say that *the* law, this abstraction, *translates itself into reality* in Roman law and German law – these concrete forms of laws – then what emerges is a mystical connexion.'[66]

Die Wertform was added by Marx to the first edition of *Capital* while the work was already in press. It is a fact that the page which we have taken from it reproduces to the letter the arguments with which Marx first criticized Hegel's dialectic in his early writing, the *Kritik des Hegelschen Staatsrechts.* The abstract-universal, which ought to be the predicate – i.e. a 'property of the concrete or the sensate' – becomes the subject, a self-subsisting entity; 'contrariwise the concrete-sensate counts merely as the phenomenal form of the abstract-universal' – i.e. as the predicate of its own substantified predicate. This overturning, this *quid pro quo*, this *Umkehrung*, which, according to Marx, rules Hegel's *Logic*, rules also, long before the *Logic*, the *objective* mechanisms of this society – beginning right from the relation of 'equivalence' and the exchange of commodites. This accounts for the impossibility of grasping the second critique without having penetrated the first one; and, in general, it also accounts for the impotence which Marxism till now has demonstrated when it came to 'deciphering' – not to mention the problem of the relationship between the first and the third books of *Capital* – even the simplest elements of the 'theory of value' as they are developed at the beginning of the work. 'This *acriticism* (*Unkritik*), this *mysticism* is both the riddle of modern constitutions as well as the mystery of Hegelian philosophy. . .'.[67] 'To be sure, this perspective is an abstract one, but it is the "abstraction" of the political State as Hegel himself develops it. It is also atomistic, but it is the atomism of the society itself. The "perspective" cannot be concrete when the *object* (Gegenstand) of the perspective is "abstract".'[68] Consequently, 'Hegel is not to be blamed because he describes the

66. K. Marx, *Scritti inediti di economia politica*, edited by M. Tronti (Rome, 1963), p. 144.

67. K. Marx, *Werke* (Berlin, 1964), Vol. I, p. 287.

68. ibid., p. 283.

essence of the modern State as it exists, but rather because he passes off what exists for the *essence of the State*'.[69]

This is clearly a new way of reasoning, a way that necessitates a radical emendation of the old 'philosophic' mentality. It is not a question of contraposing 'determinate' abstractions to 'indeterminate' abstractions, a 'correct' logic to an 'incorrect' logic – methodology is the science of those who have nothing. Rather, it is a question of trying to understand that just as the problems of critical epistemology, when fully reasoned out, place us in the totally new dimension of the 'social relations of production'; so too Marx's critique of the processes of hypostatization really takes place in his critique of the political-economic institutions of modern bourgeois society.

The real 'indeterminate abstractions' – if they may still be termed such – are capital, surplus value, profit, interest, etc. Unless one takes this step forward, it is inevitable that, as concerns the theory of 'value' and that of the State, one remains on the other side. That is, if not before and outside 'Marxism', certainly before and outside Marx.

69. ibid., p. 266.

Index

Printed in the United States
by Baker & Taylor Publisher Services